# MY COUSIN
# THE SAINT

✠

*To my friends at
Pennyloger —
Best always.*

*Justin Catanoso
2009*

# MY COUSIN
# THE SAINT

☩

*A Search for Faith,*
*Family, and Miracles*

Justin Catanoso

Pennybyrn at Maryfield
109 Penny Road
High Point, NC 27260
(336) 821-4000

*wm*

WILLIAM MORROW
*An Imprint of* HarperCollins*Publishers*

HarperCollins books may be purchased for educational, business, or sales promotional use. For information please write: Special Markets Department, HarperCollins Publishers, 10 East 53rd Street, New York, NY 10022.

FIRST EDITION

*Designed by Kris Tobiassen*
*Map of Calabria, Italy, by Jeffrey Ward*

Library of Congress Cataloging-in-Publication Data
Catanoso, Justin.
  My cousin the saint : a search for faith, family, and miracles / Justin Catanoso. — 1st ed.
    p.  cm.
  ISBN 978-0-06-123102-5
  1. Catanoso, Gaetano, Saint, 1879–1963. 2. Canonization. 3. Catholic Church—Rites and ceremonies. I. Title.

BX4700.C77C38 2008
282.092—dc22
[B]                                           2007040473

08  09  10  11  12  OV/RRD  10 9 8 7 6 5 3 2 1

*This book is dedicated to the Catanoso family,*
*in Italy and America*

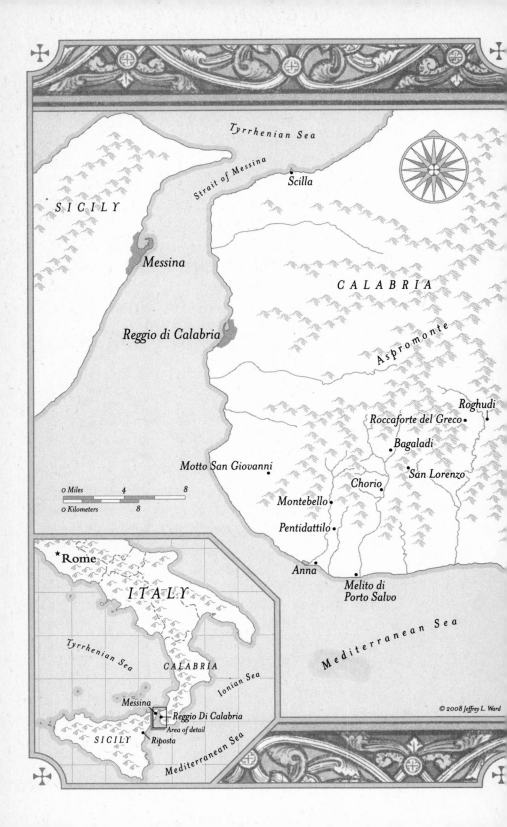

Tyrrhenian Sea

Strait of Messina

Scilla

SICILY

Messina

Reggio di Calabria

CALABRIA

Aspromonte

Roghudi

Roccaforte del Greco

Bagaladi

San Lorenzo

Chorio

Motto San Giovanni

Montebello

Pentidattilo

Anna

Melito di
Porto Salvo

Mediterranean Sea

0 Miles          4          8
0 Kilometers          8

Rome

ITALY

CALABRIA

Tyrrhenian Sea

Ionian Sea

Messina

Reggio Di Calabria

Area of detail

SICILY          Riposta

Mediterranean Sea

© 2008 Jeffrey L. Ward

# CONTENTS

✠

Cast of Characters ..................... ix

PART I  *Faith* ......................................... 1

Miracle Story—Patrizia............... 1

Prologue ....................................... 5

1. Cousins in Chorio..................... 11

2. A Saint's Mission...................... 23

3. *In Domino*............................... 42

4. Crown of Thorns...................... 58

5. Americans................................ 65

6. World War II............................ 74

PART II  *Family*................................... 97

Miracle Story—Sister Paolina .... 97

7. Going Back ............................. 101

8. A Family Baptism.................... 118

9. Alan ....................................... 125

10. Unanswered Prayers ................ 137

11. Soul Searching........................ 153

12. The Professor and Laurelyn ...... 163
13. A Pope's Blessing.................... 180

PART III   *Miracles* ........................... 193

Miracle Story—Daniela .......... 193
14. Our Saint............................. 197
15. Believe What You Can .......... 209
16. Making Saints........................ 222
17. Cousins............................... 243
18. The Real Gaetano.................. 251
19. Miracles and Medicine............. 261
20. Family Favors ........................ 278
21. One of Us ............................ 286
22. Piero.................................. 300
23. Gaetano's Love....................... 312
   Epilogue ............................. 323

   Selected Sources...................... 333
   Acknowledgments.................... 335

# CAST OF CHARACTERS

☩

CHORIO

Antonino Catanoso and Antonina Tripodi, parents of the saint

Padre Gaetano Catanoso (1879–1963), the saint

Antonino Catanoso and Elisabetta Mangiola, great-grandparents of the author

Maria Portzia Catanoso Priolo, great-aunt of the author


ARCHBISHOPS OF REGGIO CALABRIA (TIME OF SERVICE)

Cardinal Gennaro Portonova (1888–1908), ordained the saint a priest, 1902

Monsignor Camillo Rinaldo Rousset (1909–1926), called the saint to Reggio, 1921

Monsignor Carmelo Pujia (1927–1937), approved Veronican sisters founding, 1934

Monsignor Enrico Montalbetti (1938–1943), killed in WWII

Monsignor Antonio Lanza (1943–1950), ensured Vatican approval of the Veronican sisters, 1958

Monsignor Giovanni Ferro (1950–1977), administered Last Rites to the saint, 1963

## CAUSE FOR CANONIZATION

Monsignor Aurelio Sorrentino, archbishop of Reggio Calabria-Bova, initiated the cause, 1980

Monsignor Antonio Denisi, supervised the fact-finding process in Reggio, 1982–1987

Father Francesco Moccio, relator for the cause in Rome, 1987–1997

Monsignor Giuseppe D'Ascola, postulator for the cause in Rome, 1997–2005

Pope John Paul II, approved the cause at all levels; beatified Padre Gaetano, 1997

Pope Benedict XVI, canonized Padre Gaetano, 2005


## MIRACLES RECEIVED

Sister Paulina Ligato of Montebello, Italy, officially approved by the Vatican, 1997

Anna Pangallo of Roccaforte del Greco, Italy, officially approved by the Vatican, 2004


## AMERICA

Carmelo Catanoso (1887–1941), native of Chorio, cousin of the saint, grandfather of the author

Caterina Foti Catanoso (1891–1952), native of Riposta, Sicily, grandmother of the author

Their American children:

Elizabeth Catanoso Lamanna, 1914–1994

Bessie Catanoso LaRosa, 1915–1988

Anthony Catanoso, b. 1916

Leona Catanoso Betz, b. 1918

Leonard Catanoso, b. 1920, wife Connie, b. 1927, author's parents; children: Lenny, Marlene, Alan, and Justin

Mary Catanoso Nestor, b. 1923
Joseph Catanoso, b. 1925
Charles Catanoso, b. 1926; son: Anthony, cousin of the author
Peter Catanoso, b. 1931


ITALIAN RELATIVES

Piero Catanoso, family patriarch in Reggio, wife Adriana
Pina Catanoso, sister of Piero
Enza Catanoso Sartori, sister of Piero
Enzo Catanoso, brother of Piero
Giovanna Catanoso, cousin in Reggio
Daniela Catanoso, cousin in Reggio
Patrizia Catanoso, cousin in Reggio
Caterina Catanoso, husband Vincenzo Infortuna, cousins in Reggio
Daniela Catanoso, cousin in Rome


SPIRITUAL INFLUENCES

Father William Hodge, high school religion teacher
Manoel Cardozo, mentor
Father Louis Canino, mentor


AUTHOR'S FAMILY

Laurelyn Dossett, wife
Emilia, Rosalie, and Sophia, daughters

# PART I

---

# *Faith*

## MIRACLE STORY—PATRIZIA

Patrizia Catanoso knew she was in for a restless night. The thoughts she took with her to bed were too gruesome. Earlier that day, the son of a close friend had been struck by a car while riding a motorcycle on a country road just outside of Chorio, a rugged mountain village in southern Italy. The collision was head on, and the boy, just seventeen, landed in the road like a box of ceramic dishes. He now lay in intensive care in a hospital in the city of Reggio Calabria, cracked and broken, on life support. Patrizia worked as an administrative assistant at the hospital and had visited the boy's father there.

"The doctors tell me there is no hope," her friend sobbed. "They are just waiting to pull the plug."

Patrizia is a sensible woman, levelheaded, able to empathize easily with the suffering of strangers. But such pain rarely followed her home. Life is often short and cruel; hospital work teaches you that. But a young boy, a family friend, crushed by misfortune on a blind curve? She thought of her own two children, Salvatore and Michela, just a few years younger than her friend's son. She crossed herself and kissed her fingertips.

Understand now that Patrizia is no religious mystic. She is not one to burn candles before a statue of the Virgin Mary. Her eyes, dark and penetrating, suggest that she can spot nonsense a mile away, especially when she cocks an eyebrow. She favors long denim skirts and flat shoes. As for jewelry, she wears only a plain, gold wedding band. Her faith is the same: simple, honest, never showy.

Yet at home in bed that night, Patrizia felt compelled to pray—not to Jesus, not even to God—but rather to the only person she calls on in times such as these—her great-uncle, Gaetano Catanoso, a humble mission priest who died in 1963, the year after she was born. He was no ordinary priest. Her parents and grandparents believed Gaetano had lived the life of a saint during six decades of Christlike service to the poor of southern Calabria. The Vatican agreed to such an extent that Gaetano had been venerated by Pope John Paul II and was on track to become canonized. That rare Catholic honor confirmed to the faithful that the priest possessed divine powers to work miracles through God's grace. Patrizia never bothered her great-uncle with frivolous matters of lost keys or soccer victories. But she prayed hard for her friend's son.

Sometime before dawn, in that twilight zone between sleep and consciousness, Patrizia saw an image, a face, blurry around the edges but soon recognizable. It was Padre Gaetano, his soft eyes and sweet smile as real as if he were kneeling beside her bed.

"Don't worry," the image spoke to her. "He won't die. Ask the sisters for a handkerchief and tell them to pray."

Patrizia opened her eyes as the image disappeared. In all her years of prayers, she had never, ever, experienced anything like this. It was morning. She dressed and left her apartment in a hurry, driving quickly through Reggio's side streets to a small church in the hilltop neighborhood of Santo Spirito. She hustled past the courtyard statue of her great-uncle and spoke in a rush to the nuns inside the Mother House, nuns from an order Gaetano Catanoso had founded in 1934. They parted with a sacred handkerchief that belonged to the late priest and vowed to keep the dying boy in their prayers throughout the day.

At the hospital, Patrizia's friend was still there, still sobbing. "It's almost over," he said, slumped in a waiting room chair.

But Patrizia told her friend—pray, pray to Padre Gaetano.

She went to the boy's curtained bay in intensive care. He lay nearly lifeless, tubes sprouting from his arms and mouth. A nurse friend tried to shoo her away. Leave him alone, she implored, it's his time. Patrizia held her tongue, clutching the handkerchief, waiting for the woman to leave. Trembling, her heart racing, she unfolded the white cloth and gently passed it over the boy's face. *Am I doing this right?* She passed it over his body as well and tucked it under his pillow with a prayer card bearing the face of Gaetano, the same face that came to her in her sleep barely an hour earlier. She said another prayer and left.

That evening, with her husband, Orazio, she returned to the hospital. Again, she was greeted by her friend. Again he collapsed in their arms in tears. *My God*, Patrizia thought, *the boy's dead.* But through his choked cries and gasps for air, her friend was trying to tell them something different. My son. He is better. He is better.

Patrizia dashed to push back the curtain and there the boy was, sitting on the edge of the bed, his feet dangling. He looked a roughed-up mess, but he was alive. He managed a smile. Patrizia just stared, wordlessly, and then felt a shiver run down her back. The doctors can't explain it, her friend was saying just behind her. His injuries were so bad they were certain he would die. They don't know what happened.

Patrizia Catanoso doesn't believe in magic and never reads her horoscope. She can't be bothered. But she believes in her great-uncle to the very depths of her soul. In him she has no doubts, only faith.

I know what happened, she whispered to her friend, pulling him close, tears streaming down her own face. *"E stato miracolo."* It was a miracle.

# PROLOGUE

☩

How would you feel if, only recently, you had learned that you were descended from an ancient king? Would you feel more noble, more entitled to riches and power? What if you learned you were related to a historic explorer, a person of unimaginable courage and vision? Would you feel more bold, more inclined to blaze a new path for others to follow?

Now I wonder, how would you feel if you were related to a saint, a true member of the Catholic Church's communion of saints, an ethereal, holy being so virtuous that he is hailed as a miracle worker, sanctified by not one but two popes? Would it deepen your spirituality and make you believe you should receive blessings directly from God?

As far as I know, there are no kings or explorers on the long road leading through my past. But just a few years ago, I learned that there is a saint, newly named by the Vatican, with whom I share both a family name and family connection. He was a poor parish priest, born several years before my grandfather in the same remote Aspromonte village in southern Italy. He was a man of relentless faith and remarkable humility with a tireless desire to serve. He was, I realize, nothing like me.

If I ever bothered with confession, I shudder to imagine the number of Hail Marys and Our Fathers it would take to scrub my soul clean. I can't even think of anyone close to me whom I would consider saintly. Except for this cousin, Padre Gaetano Catanoso, who is, if you believe, close to God. Right there in heaven, a wing's length from our maker, capable of miraculous deeds. "Other cultural figures—the artist, the thinker, the explorer, the ruler, and the warrior—all excite the imagination," says the religion writer Kenneth Woodward. "But only in the saint do we encounter an 'otherness' that ignites a sense of mystery. Miracles are a part of that mystery." And if you believe, there's nothing else in your life like it.

My mother believes in Gaetano Catanoso and his miracles. My cousins in Italy, like Patrizia Catanoso, believe even more. They each have their own miracle stories, one more fantastic than the next. And me? I have come to believe that the mere knowledge of this sainted relative has moved me in ways gentle and powerful to look deep inside and ask the always thorny, often unanswerable questions of faith and belief, in ways that no cousin king or explorer ever could.

I had put such questions aside for years, but they were to come thundering back into my head as I watched my brother Alan battle cancer a few years ago, wearing a medal of Padre Gaetano around his neck. For months, my mother prayed for a miracle to save her son. Were we entitled to do so? Did we have a right to expect or even hope that our prayers to a remote and departed relative would be given special dispensation? I knew my mother was praying during Alan's ordeal, and the best I could do was hope that her prayers would be answered. Through it all, her faith was tested; mine lay dormant. But it began to stir, however faintly, several months later.

That's because having a saint in the family can be a powerful force, one that, if you think about it long enough, demands attention. It did for me, the very notion slowly working itself inside. For me now, the saint is always there, hovering somewhere above, sometimes tapping me lightly on the shoulder, reminding me of his virtuous life, urging me to be kinder, calmer, better. His link to me has been a call to grace, one I am able to hear more distinctively on some days than others. Sometimes I wonder if he will visit me in my sleep, as he did Patrizia, and deliver a message of startling truth. I wish he would.

I have been, I should note, a fairly typical American Catholic, mostly lapsed, mostly doubtful, often indifferent to the church's politics, and thoroughly disgusted by its many abuses of power. The troubles with the church have made it easy for me, as they have for millions like me, to take a certain satisfaction in my decision to live my life for so long outside the bounds of faith in general and Catholicism in particular. But I have had neither the heart nor the courage to entirely cast either aside.

Then came October 23, 2005. That's the day Pope Benedict XVI declared Padre Gaetano Catanoso a saint—the first priest ever to earn such recognition from the centuries-old region of Calabria, and more important to me, the only saint to ever bear the name Catanoso. The canonization took place in an exuberant, shoulder-to-shoulder scene in St. Peter's Square in a ceremony as rich and mystical as the church itself. Chants and incense and the sweet voices of the Vatican boys' choir reached to the heavens. Hundreds of gold-robed cardinals and bishops flanked the altar on the steps of the basilica as the Supreme Pontiff himself led a solemn drama, which played out over three hours. I was there with my wife and daughters and scores of close relatives who had crossed the Atlantic to join a cheering, dazzled throng of pilgrims from around the world.

A banner of Padre Gaetano hung between the tall, Corinthian columns of St. Peter's Basilica, along with those of four other Catholic heroes canonized that day. The smiling face of the saint bore an uncanny resemblance to my father. St. Gaetano Catanoso is, or had been, one of us. As I looked all around Bernini's arching colonnade, ringed as it is with so many ancient saints in marble, I realized that my cousin was now one of them, too. I got in a line to take Communion with hundreds of others. I felt strange at first, self-conscious, totally unpracticed. I had not been to Mass since Alan's funeral ten months earlier, and before then, who knows. But as the choir filled the square with its lush tones, as I shuffled along with the smiling Chileans and Sicilians and Ukrainians, I felt something I hadn't in a long time. I felt swept up in a piece of history, my own family history, the church's history, things I knew precious little about. I felt something stirring inside. I felt a part of something much larger than myself.

A saint, of all things, had brought me here to this place and this surprisingly welcome emotion. I turned and looked at his banner. It fluttered slightly in the breeze. Was he trying to tell me something?

Right there, right then, I got to thinking: As a second-generation Italian American, I had precious little knowledge of my grandfather Carmelo Catanoso, who fled his homeland for America as a teenager and never returned, dying long before I was born. I knew nothing of what drove him from Italy, separating his American children, and ultimately me, from our Italian relatives for generations. I knew less about Carmelo's cousin Gaetano, even though his heroic charity during desperate times in Calabria led two popes to utter his name and honor his memory. These men, these relatives, were fellow travelers on the long road that reached forward in time to deposit me in the middle of St. Peter's Square, my head spinning with questions. This is crazy, I thought. I had to know more. I am a journalist, a man who has been asking questions for a living for more than a quarter century. It was time for some answers. For starters, why did my father and his brothers and sisters come of age entirely oblivious to the life of a contemporary relative who would rise to such religious renown? Now that we knew he existed, what did it mean to have a saint in the family? And what, by the way, did I really believe?

I had other questions as well. Like most Americans, and most Catholics, I realized the saint-making process was a complete mystery to me. I wondered how one becomes a saint and why they are even necessary. Something else had been nagging at me ever since I first learned about this exalted relative. It became the proverbial elephant in the room, which, try as I might, even amid the canonization ceremony, I could not successfully ignore. George Orwell, in his essay "Reflections on Gandhi," wrote, "Saints should always be judged guilty until proven innocent." In other words, we should not assume that all saints are worthy of divine acclamation. After all, Pope John Paul II had canonized more saints than all the popes combined in the previous four centuries—482 during his twenty-six-year papacy. He was often accused of running a Vatican-based "saint-making factory." Critics argued that John Paul diminished the value of the true communion of saints by elevating some with suspect or meager spiritual credentials. That's where my professional skepticism clashed with my family pride. The elephant in the room refused to budge. Was my relative truly worthy of this still rare and sacred honor, or was he merely a good and prayerful guy who had been nudged onto John Paul's conveyor belt to sainthood? On a journey that spanned more than three years, I would venture out warily to learn as much as I could, the long road marked by both genealogical and spiritual mileposts. I would travel across town to return to church, and across the ocean to meet with church officials at the Vatican. I would spend hours with my parents and my aunts and uncles, hearing extraordinary stories of first-generation immigrant kids that I had never heard before. I would reconnect with long-lost Italian relatives whom I would quickly grow to love. I would watch my brother suffer and die.

There was a lot I was looking for. The roots of my Italian culture. The remnants of my Catholic faith. And the life of a cousin whose banner was hanging from the columns of St. Peter's Basilica. He was the thread pulling me along, connecting me to things seen and unseen.

# I

# Cousins in Chorio

Not everyone can become a saint. Aurelio Sorrentino and Giuseppe D'Ascola knew that. But the two priests, fellow seminary students and native sons of Calabria, believed they knew someone with the rare qualities to become one.

It was late fall 1978, and the priests were in a hurry, striding down Via della Conciliazione in Rome toward St. Peter's Square. They were on their way to an important meeting. All the bishops of Calabria, the southern-most region of the mainland of Italy, had been summoned to the Vatican. John Paul II, the newly elected pope, had called a series of such meetings to greet church leaders from Italy and share with them the priorities of his emerging pontificate.

Sorrentino, stocky and thickset with a round face and dark eyes, was the archbishop of Reggio Calabria-Bova, the largest diocese in Calabria. D'Ascola was not a bishop at all. He was a monsignor who lived in Rome and worked for the Vatican's Congregation for the Causes of Saints. Sorrentino had invited his friend D'Ascola to go along with him to meet the first non-Italian pope in centuries, Karol Wojtyla, a former Polish cardinal, young and vibrant at age fifty-eight.

The new pope, though, was not on their minds at the moment. Sorrentino began talking instead about a beloved fellow Calabrian, a humble parish priest who had left an indelible mark on both their lives and their shared vocation. His name was Padre Gaetano Catanoso. He had died in Reggio Calabria fifteen years earlier at age eighty-four. He had been their teacher during their seminary years in the 1940s, an enduring inspiration to them. He had been their confessor, as well, the priest they trusted most to hear their sins. Sorrentino had never forgotten Padre Catanoso's spiritual bearing and sweet, benevolent example. The archbishop had quietly organized a commission in Reggio earlier that spring to begin gathering information on the long life of his late mentor. He now divulged the reason.

"What do you think of a canonization cause for Padre Catanoso?" Sorrentino asked, knowing full well that the route to sainthood was long and laborious, never assured.

Monsignor D'Ascola, shorter and with a bit less girth than the archbishop, was a Vatican insider. He knew the long odds associated with attaining sainthood. He knew there had not been a saint declared from Calabria in more than four hundred and fifty years. He also knew that Padre Catanoso was different. He was special. D'Ascola embraced the idea as if it were his own. "Excellency," he said, "what are we waiting for?"

Arriving a few minutes later at the private offices of the pope near the basilica, the two priests joined their Calabrian peers for a small reception. Pope John Paul II, resplendent in his long white cassock and matching shoulder cape and skullcap, made sure to spend a few moments with all those attending. The pope was intrigued to hear that D'Ascola worked just across the square in the unheralded office of saint-making. He asked D'Ascola what aspect of his work with saints interested him the most.

"I am interested in all the saints of the world!" D'Ascola blurted, eager to demonstrate this enthusiasm to his new boss.

John Paul II gave him a peculiar look. Then raising a finger to accentuate his point, the pope offered some advice. It was the kind of advice he would later share with others of spiritual authority in Rome and around the world, advice that would lead to the most dramatic changes in the office of saint-making in hundreds of years, advice that in time would make the new pope the Catholic Church's busiest saint-maker in history.

"You must be interested in the saints of your land, your region," John Paul implored. *"That's* what *I* am interested in."

D'Ascola nodded solemnly, then looked to Sorrentino as the pope moved on to speak with others. The archbishop had heard the remarks and thought immediately of Padre Catanoso. The last saint named from Calabria had been St. Francis of Paola, a hermit known for strange miracles such as being able to levitate and sail across water using his cloak as his only means. He died in 1507, the year before Michelangelo began painting the Sistine Chapel ceiling. What a shame, Sorrentino thought, that the Church of Calabria, rich as it has been for ages with priests, monks, and nuns of extraordinary holiness, could not lay claim to a single native-born pastor from the region who had risen to sainthood. He and D'Ascola knew who should become the first.

If you are not familiar with the technical, Vatican-sanctioned definition of a miracle, you might be inclined to say that it was miraculous that a future saint could emerge from a remote and impoverished Calabrian mountain village such as Chorio, a place so small that it's usually excluded from Italian maps. Its history dates back to the fifth century and the Byzantine Empire following Roman rule. "Chorio," meaning "town" or "village," has its origins in Greek; indeed, Greek influences on the language and culture of the region ripple through the centuries.

Chorio sits in a swale of the lower Aspromonte, the mountain range that rises through the middle of Calabria. The Aspromonte, or "sour mountains," are so named because the steep, rugged terrain, prone to winter mudslides, made farming difficult for endless generations. The name fittingly describes the plight of the people there in the late 1800s and early 1900s when millions fled southern Italy for a chance at a better life in America. Chorio's western edge is tucked in against a mountainside that is brown and barren with gnarled fig and olive trees, and patches of prickly pear, which spread like cactus weeds. Its eastern edge is hugged by the bend of a small river, the Tuccio, which, like most rivers in southern Italy, rages in winter with heavy rains but is dusty-white and dry during the parched summers. The region's climate is typically Mediterranean. Winter's rough edges are smoothed over by Gulf Stream–warmed breezes off the sea, and summer's tropical heat is intensified by cruel, hot winds from the Sahara and Libyan deserts of northern Africa. Where the land flattens in places, closer to the coast, it yields olives and almonds in abundance. Much of Italy's citrus crop—oranges, lemons, limes, and bergamot, a lemony-looking fruit that grows only in southern Calabria and is used in perfumes, candies, and Earl Grey tea—is harvested there.

As the crow flies, Chorio, at 1,053 feet above sea level, sits less than ten miles from Italy's coastline and the Ionian Sea, gateways to civilizations north and south. But more than a century ago, it stood as remote and isolated as all the nearby mountain villages in the region. With few roads and transportation limited to the stamina of your donkey (if you were fortunate enough to own one), villages like Chorio were desolate, self-contained worlds where the lives of most were defined by subsistence farming, lawlessness, squalor, and misery.

Gaetano Catanoso was born on a narrow backstreet in a two-story, stone and stucco row house on February 14, 1879—St. Valentine's Day. He was the third of nine children in the family of Antonino Catanoso and Antonina Tripodi, one of several Catanoso families in the village of about three hundred people. The Catanosos there in Chorio—which included my grandfather, Carmelo Catanoso—traced their common ancestry back five generations to a pair of Spanish brothers, Gian Pietro and Pasquale Catanoso. A brief family history written by a relative in the 1950s notes that the Catanoso clan originated from the Spanish marquees of Cathanos, a lineage thought to have "very old and generous nobility in it, and that among the descendants are many illustrious men: soldiers, politicians, intellectuals and church men." For reasons unexplained, brothers Gian Pietro and Pasquale Catanoso migrated east across Spain and France and down the long stem of Italy before stopping in the Calabrian village of Motta San Giovanni in the mid-1700s. A knife fight involving a group of locals and an ox at a drinking fountain compelled the brothers to flee that town just ahead of an angry mob seeking revenge. They split up. Pasquale settled just a few miles away in the hillside village of Pentidattilo; Gian Pietro headed a little farther up into the Aspromonte to Chorio. They both had money to buy land and became farmers. Those two brothers, their progeny branching out over the generations, begat a family tree that grew to include, among many others, my grandfather, my father, me, and our cousin the saint.

My grandfather, Carmelo Catanoso, was born in Chorio eight years after Gaetano on November 13, 1887. He was the second of three children to Antonino Catanoso and Elisabetta Mangiola. The two Catanoso family homes—Carmelo's and Gaetano's—were similar in size and hearty stone construction, and they were less than half a mile apart, connected by a few winding streets whose midpoint in either direction was the village piazza where the church stood. The small church, little more than a chapel really, was built in 1725 and dedicated to St. Pasquale Baylon, a sixteenth-century Franciscan friar.

The Catanoso families in Chorio, including Gaetano's and my grandfather's, were remarkably prosperous by Calabrian village standards. The written family history is sparse, but it is filled with professional titles uncommon to most in the region at the time. Catanosos in Chorio and nearby villages were landowners, doctors, pharmacists, notaries, politicians, and clergy. A Catanoso, Don Francesco, was the parish priest in Chorio between 1858 and 1895 and probably baptized both the future saint and my grandfather. In 1861, a relative named Pasquale Catanoso was appointed mayor of Chorio, even though he placed seventh in the election for public office that spring. The elected mayor, Bruno Rossi, was promoted to a higher post in Melito di Porto Salvo down on the Ionian coast, so he selected the Catanoso relative as his mayoral replacement, instead of the runner-up. When the odd decision was questioned by regional political authorities, Rossi explained: "Signor Catanoso was chosen because he possesses the capacity, morality, and high patriotism such superior to the others that received more votes in the elections." The famous Italian penchant for ignoring rules and law was alive even then, perhaps especially then.

Meanwhile, Gaetano's father was a landowning farmer. He cultivated acres of wheat and corn as well as olive, almond, and fruit orchards in the fertile river valley just outside the village. He also leased a few acres to sharecroppers. Carmelo's father, my great-grandfather, had a small tailor and barber shop on the first floor of his home, next to the room that sheltered the livestock: sheep, a cow, and some goats. Unlike the peasants, the family lived on the second floor, above the animals, not with them.

This modest prosperity stood in stark contrast to the poverty of their neighbors in Chorio and throughout southern Italy. Census data taken in that part of the country in the 1880s indicates that only one out of ten southern Italians owned land or even worked it as share-croppers. The vast majority of people were landless peasants, doing whatever they could to survive. Mostly that meant working the fields as seasonal farmhands. Few ate meat regularly, using their animals instead for farm work and transportation. They subsisted on tomatoes and onions, along with bread and fava beans, rice and macaroni. Infant mortality rates were high, and peasants were often defenseless against annual scourges such as malaria and tuberculosis.

"I could not help thinking how many times I heard the words on the tongues of the peasants," writes Carlo Levi in *Christ Stopped at Eboli*, a classic telling of southern Italian suffering during World War II, illustrating how little things had changed since the turn of the nine-teenth century. "'What did you eat today?' '*Niente* (nothing).' 'What are your prospects for tomorrow?' '*Niente*.' 'What shall we do?' '*Niente*.' Always the same answer, and they roll their eyes back toward heaven in a gesture of negation."

The pitiful standard of living in the Italian south, also called the *Mezzogiorno* (Land of the Midday Sun), was exacerbated at the time by the socioeconomic climate. For ages, Italy was a peninsula of dis-parate, warring city-states ruled in grim succession by many of her invading neighbors. In the early 1800s, the Italian peninsula was di-vided into eight states, with only the Piedmont region in the north not lorded over by a foreign government or the papacy. A small band of revolutionaries, led by Giuseppe Garibaldi and a volunteer army, was determined to return Italy to the kind of core nation it had been during the ancient Roman Empire nearly two thousand years ear-lier. Claiming the battle cry *Risorgimento*, the resurrection of Italy, Garibaldi swept upward from Sicily and Calabria and liberated all the regions south of Rome from two hundred years of tyrannical French Bourbon rule. The village of San Lorenzo, not far from Chorio, was the first community in the south to raise the new tricolored flag of a united Italy in August 1860.

A year later, as the United States was threatening to split itself in two, Italy began uniting its northern and southern halves under a new ruler, Victor Emmanuel II, king of the Piedmont region. Let's be clear about the outcome. Just like the end of the American Civil War, Italy's bloody struggle for unification brought no actual unity between north and south, setting the stage for a massive wave of emigration that began to accelerate in the 1870s.

No wonder. Beneath the thin veneer of bucolic village life in places like Chorio festered a community with its share of despair and crime, prostitution and infidelity. Most people lived in shacks and shanties. Drinking water was in chronic short supply. Desperation among the poorest men often led to drunkenness, then violence, which meant knife fights in the alleys over pocket change, or worse, a whispered insult. It was, mostly, an unholy place.

Northern Italians often viewed the south as a paradise inhabited by the devil, a land blessed by nature with a warm climate and abundant crops but cursed by a people deemed barbaric, backward, and morally flawed, historian Don H. Doyle wrote in *Nations Divided: America, Italy and the Southern Question.* "We have acquired a very bad country," one northerner noted upon visiting the south after unification, "but it seems impossible that in a place where nature has done so much for the land, it has not generated another people."

The rulers and industrialists of Milan, Turin, and Tuscany looked on southern Italian peasants as no better than the livestock with which they often shared their meager homes. The industrialists figured that the southerners were not worthy of roads or factories or any sort of modernizing development. Thus, affluent northerners treated the south like a well-stocked, roadside fruit stand whose honor box they blithely ignored. And southerners got the message: In the absence of national pride, they identified most with their community or at best, their region. They were *Calabresi*, never Italians. Few spoke the traditional Italian language; most spoke the regional dialect, causing more isolation and disunity. They trusted only family, and close family at that, a trait that remains a hallmark of the southern Italian culture. Sometimes, maybe, they trusted the God of the Catholic Church, unless they believed, as many of them did, in the hand-me-down pantheon of homemade saints and pagan deities who were frequently the object of their superstitious prayers, fears, and rituals.

"In the peasants' world, there is no room for reason, religion, and history," writes Carlo Levi. "There is no room for religion because to them everything participates in divinity, everything is actually, not merely symbolically, divine: Christ and the goat; the heavens above and the beasts of the fields below; everything is bound up in natural magic."

This was southern Italy at the turn of the nineteenth century. The Catanosos were among the few who managed to exist beyond the grip of the worst of it all. They had food from their farms and could afford to shop at one of the village bakeries or butcher shops. They had means to occasionally buy clothes from the traveling merchants from Naples passing through the piazza. And in the early evenings before dinner, the Catanoso men would gather with their friends in the piazza near the lone café to talk, play cards, or simply walk arm in arm.

In Gaetano's home, beneath its terra-cotta roof, his parents did their best to shelter their children from the stormy times. Devout and exceedingly pious Catholics, Antonino and Antonina had Gaetano baptized on the day of his birth, so eager were they to wipe away his original sin and declare their baby's devotion to Jesus. Prayer sustained them almost as surely as the crops from their fields. Every evening after dinner, the family would gather to recite the rosary, the children and parents moving strings of glass beads through their fingers to the comforting murmur of Hail Marys and Our Fathers. And each fall Antonino Catanoso made sure his children saw with their own eyes that he not only believed in Jesus Christ but that he was committed to the lessons the Savior preached. Among them, love thy neighbor as thyself. From his first harvest from the fields, Antonino took a generous share directly to the church, where the local priest, his uncle, Don Francesco Catanoso, was a grateful recipient. Antonino also bagged sacks of wheat and corn and stacked them just inside a small barn on his farm. The poor in the village knew that they could come by and quietly take what they needed. The Catanoso children often helped hand over the sacks.

Gaetano's parents viewed him as a bright and capable child, but dreamy and a little on the lazy side, even clumsy. Tales are told of a butterfingered altar boy who when assisting his uncle, *Zio* Francesco, during Mass would sometimes let the Bible fall to the floor, or break the small glass cruets containing the water and wine. As a seven- and eight-year-old, Gaetano didn't show much interest in book learning. So his father, as he'd done with his six other sons, put a hoe in Gaetano's hand and took him out to the fields in the countryside. It was difficult work, even for grown men. The land was rocky, filled with limestone and pockets of clay. The summer sun was merciless. Young Gaetano, stout but small for his age, swung the hoe at the earth until his arms and shoulders ached. The ground refused to yield. After plenty of time for sweaty contemplation, Gaetano began to think that maybe a little bit of book learning wasn't such a bad idea. He recalled telling his father: "It is best I go to school because I cannot work the land." Antonino Catanoso did not argue.

In 1889, at age ten, legend has it that Gaetano "heard the call" to the priesthood. What's more likely is that his father heard that call on behalf of his son. The path to the priesthood in those days was one of the few escape routes from poverty available to struggling families in southern Italy, short of emigration. Parents who could spare the labor of a healthy son would try to enroll him as soon as possible in seminary, where along with regular studies, there was also the promise of regular food and shelter. These were not Antonino's worries. He could provide for his entire family. But in his devout Catholic heart, he relished the thought of a priest under his own roof, especially his most gentle child, for whom farming was too difficult. Gaetano, for his part, was old enough to feel the spiritual tug of his family's piety and began to grasp the very vague notion that God had a plan for him.

So in October 1889, Antonino Catanoso loaded a few belongings into a saddle bag and put Gaetano in a woven basket, called a *pannier* or *gerla*, on the back of the family donkey. Together, they walked the twenty-eight miles down the winding mountain roads from Chorio for several days until they reached the Archiepiscopal Seminary in Reggio Calabria, a small, coastal town just across the Strait of Messina from Sicily. Gaetano could not officially enter the seminary until age twelve. In a little over a year, he learned to do what more than 80 percent of the people in all of southern Italy could not: he learned to read and write.

After Gaetano's seminary training began, with the guidance of older priests and bishops, he worked steadily for a decade to deepen his mind and his soul in matters of Holy Scripture, philosophy, and theology. His training followed the ancient principles first established in the fifth century by St. Augustine, who demanded a vow of poverty, celibacy, obedience, and a strict monastic life for all who would seek to walk in Jesus's footsteps and serve as missionaries of the church. Priestly education grew more focused and rigorous a thousand years later when the Protestant Reformation challenged Catholic religious supremacy in the 1500s. Despite the changes over time, one thing about the training of priests has remained unaltered through the ages, the thing that all good priests absorb as purely and deeply as oxygen and never lose sight of—the ever-present, ever-living model of their spiritual calling, Jesus Christ. The priest not only represents Christ but personifies Him and becomes identical with Him in all his ministerial functions, James Cardinal Gibbons, a noted nineteenth-century American archbishop, once said. The priest, Gibbons added, not only acts with Christ by the authority of Christ in the name of Christ, but his official acts are Christ's acts. His words are the echo of Christ's words.

This is the calling all gifted priests must hear deep in their hearts and understand instinctively, even courageously. Young Gaetano Catanoso did. He read the Gospels closely, committing Jesus's words to memory. He studied feverishly Jesus's example, easily imagining himself amid the poor and disbelieving, slowly coming to understand that he could light and fan a flicker of hope in even the darkest souls through the strength and consistency of his own living faith. He thought about his family up in Chorio, his father working the land, his brothers sharing in the difficult labor. He came to believe that his failure in the fields was a clear message that God had another plan for him. He never doubted it and was grateful.

While at home one summer, still in training to become a priest, he was asked to deliver his first sermon during Mass at St. Pasquale Baylon's, the church in Chorio's piazza. With a youthful enthusiasm rarely heard from that pulpit, the teenage Gaetano seized the church-goers' attention by preaching his devotion to the Virgin Mary and his belief in Jesus as a sacrament. It was for Gaetano a defining moment when the rapture growing in his heart was unloosed on a people for whom joy was as unknown as a pocketful of coins. He saw the way they stared at him, hanging on his words, and how a few of them nodded, crossing themselves as he spoke. The Lord, he believed, was stirring in him, and he would recall later, "It was a beautiful episode, a joyous anticipation of my priestly mission."

That mission officially began on September 20, 1902, when Cardinal Gennaro Portanova ordained a small group of young seminary graduates in Reggio Calabria. Gaetano Catanoso was ecstatic. "So the little donkey made it," he told his friends, foreshadowing a sense of humility that would become one of his most enduring and endearing characteristics. His parents came down from Chorio with several of their children to celebrate the event. Gaetano said to his family and to his fellow seminary graduate, Don Giulio Ziglio, who would remember it years later, "I promise not to deliberately commit any major sin, not even venial, and to be in the presence of God every instant of my life."

Maybe he was flush with the excitement of becoming a priest. Maybe the twenty-three-year-old Gaetano believed he really could live a life of Christlike perfection in such a miserable place during such a miserable time. He did not believe, however, that he could do it alone. He told his family and friends, almost certainly in the figurative sense and having no way of knowing how such words would resonate after his death: "Please pray to the heart of Jesus to make me a saint."

Of course, not everyone can become a saint. Virtuous lives must be lived. Miracles must be performed after death. Earthly advocates, as patient as they are tenacious, must set the wheels in motion. And popes must approve.

But a cause for canonization must start somewhere. And for Padre Gaetano, it started that fall day in 1978. The sun had long disappeared from the Roman sky by the time Aurelio Sorrentino and Giuseppe D'Ascola left their meeting with Pope John Paul II. They were ecstatic, floating on a cloud as they walked across St. Peter's Square, the saints lining the colonnade bearing witness to their excitement.

"The Holy Father could not have been more clear about his intentions for new saints," Monsignor D'Ascola gleefully told his friend.

"Yes," Archbishop Sorrentino said. "It is time for the people of Reggio Calabria to have a saint of our own."

The commission Sorrentino had organized in Reggio earlier that year to research all aspects of Padre Gaetano's life bore down on its work. Less than two years later, on December 5, 1980, Sorrentino sent a petition to the Vatican addressed to the pope. He requested a *nihil obstat* of the Congregation for the Causes of Saints, a proclamation that "nothing hinders" the introduction of the cause for canonization of Padre Gaetano Catanoso in the diocesan court. Sorrentino's commission, known as the Calabrian Episcopal Conference, drafted the following statement for the petition:

"Calabria needs saints who with their life testimony will call the faithful to a more Christian life, more worthy of the fathers who, in the past centuries, gave the Church notable Saints, the last of whom was St. Francis of Paola [*canonized in 1519*]. We are confident that the glorification of Padre Catanoso will generate more abundant spiritual fruits, not only in our churches, but in the Church as a whole, because Padre Catanoso has a message of charity, of love of God and souls, not only for the priests, but also for the faithful."

Pope John Paul II, not yet established as a prodigious saint-maker, must have been intrigued to learn more about that message. He granted approval to officially launch the cause for canonization three days later.

# 2

# A Saint's Mission

The message that would later carry Padre Gaetano to sainthood first emerged in a godforsaken place called Pentidattilo. The tiny village can be seen easily from the Ionian coast. Its boxy, stone houses, clustered on the side of a hill with a tangle of roofs and balconies and stairways, rise from the base of a tall rock outcropping like some medieval wasp's nest. It was a long, tortuous walk to Reggio—about nineteen miles—along dirt roads that curved tightly with steep drop-offs studded in prickly pear and stubby fig trees. The geographic safety that the location provided from pirate attacks centuries ago had long ceased to be of value. Pentidattilo, which traced its history back to the days before Christ, was now simply isolated.

It was March 1904. As Padre Gaetano drew closer, climbing higher and breathing harder with each step, he could not help but notice that the outcropping looming above the village resembled a stone hand with five fingers reaching up to the heavens. When he arrived as the parish priest, that hand was no doubt reaching for mercy. Most villagers were beyond poor. They were illiterate, downtrodden, bankrupt of hope. If God was among them, they paid little attention. The massive brick and stone Church of St. Peter and Paul, built in the 1500s with a tall, spire-topped bell tower, stood empty and cold nearly all the time. The village had been without the service of a regular priest for several years. Faith was adrift. There was much work to be done there.

As the new priest, twenty-five years old and barely five foot four, Padre Gaetano made his presence felt right away. He was a handsome man with a square jaw and broad chin that had a slight cleft. He kept his wavy brown hair short and parted high; he wore round, rimless spectacles. Though he failed in his father's fields, he had grown to develop the body of a farmer, square-shouldered and solid with a barrel chest. Adapting to the terrain, he rarely appeared winded as he strode briskly along the steep and winding paths of the village. Who was this energetic youth in the long, black cassock? the villagers wondered. Despite his age, he looked to some like an ancient patriarch, an old soul, his eyes bright, his face serene, his smile a transparent expression of warmth and empathy. He spoke to the young and old the same, with deep respect and always a blessing and gentle urging to remember God.

"We must give thanks to the Lord both in joy and suffering, in success and failure," he would say, "because all these things are from Him for our sake and our salvation."

In so simple a saying lay a radical idea: Through trust and prayer you can build your faith and soon lift your own life above the muck of despair. It is not the poverty of your cupboards that should concern you most, he implored, but rather the poverty of your souls. Listen to God's law, he would say: God is love, God is charity, God is humility. Learn how to love and serve God and a better world awaits you, he promised.

The villagers must have thought he was crazy. They trusted no one not of their own blood. Why should they? There was no joy in their lives, only suffering. Salvation seemed a dim promise. But Padre Gaetano continued to move among them, his smile capable of warming stone-cold hearts, his own life a transparent example of his preaching. In time they will hear, he believed; in time they will understand.

That was the start of a priestly career and saintly message that would span six decades and lift the hopes and spirits of countless souls throughout the rural reaches of Calabria. His life and powerful example would also work itself into the very character of the Catanoso

family, many of whom came to revere him as a saint long before Pope
John Paul II and Pope Benedict XVI made it official. For his Calabresi
cousins, nieces, and nephews, he was a beacon of light, a point of reference. But there was one family member at the time who missed the
unfolding of this virtuous life: Carmelo Catanoso, my grandfather.

Growing up in a village as small as Chorio where all the Catanosos
were kin, Gaetano and Carmelo surely knew each other as boys from
family gatherings and church on Sunday. But they would not know
each other as men. In 1903—the year before Gaetano headed to Pentidattilo—my grandfather made a decision that led to the first offshoot
of the Catanoso family tree taking root in America. Because of their
relative affluence in Calabria, only a small number of Catanosos chose
to emigrate to either the United States or South America in the early
1900s. Nearly all of those who left stayed gone just a year or so, saved
some money, and sailed home to their families in Italy. Carmelo Catanoso was one of the very few to never return. His decision severed
his connections with all but his immediate family back in Chorio. His
cousin Gaetano faded from his life and would remain unknown to
Carmelo's nine American-born children and twenty-two grandchildren (including me) for nearly a century. But the saint eventually drew
us and our Calabresi cousins back together.

The rending, though, came in the spring of 1903. When he was
just sixteen years old, Carmelo boarded the steamer *Archimeade* at the
port of Naples and sailed west to New York City. I can study the few
details recorded about the early life of Gaetano Catanoso and begin to
understand both the gentle and turbulent tides of his youth that swept
him into the priesthood. What I don't know—can't know—is what
kind of courage was stirring in the teenage soul of my grandfather at
the very same time that enabled him to look at his father and mother,
his older brother, Giuseppe, and his younger sister, Maria, and tell
them: I am leaving here and I am leaving you, most likely forever.

Maybe he was impulsive, adventurous. Maybe he was fleeing the
obligatory seven years in the Italian military that became required of
all able-bodied young Italian men after unification. Maybe he feared
that his father's tailor and barber shop was not enough to insulate him
from the poverty suffered by so many of their neighbors.

Whatever the reasons, Carmelo Catanoso kept them to himself, telling none of his nine children in later years. This was common of so many southern Italians who had succumbed to what was called "emigration fever." They drew a curtain across the past and never romanticized it; they had left for good reasons. Now it was time to write a new story in a new land. Immigrants like my grandfather kept secrets. And they looked in one direction only: forward.

The port of Naples was a place of demarcation, of endings and beginnings. I struggle to imagine the fear that must have seized even the bravest emigrant as he or she joined the crush of fellow Italians as they shuffled in long lines to ascend a gangplank to the unknown.

On the wharves there were "workmen, peasants, women with children at the breast, and boys, still more boys," wrote Italian author Edmondo De Amicis, who made the journey himself. "They had folding chairs. They had bags and trunks of every shape in their hands and on their heads; their arms were full of mattresses and bedclothes, and their berth tickets were held fast in their mouths."

After more than three weeks at sea, Carmelo Catanoso arrived at Ellis Island on April 2, 1903, according to immigration records there. Listed with his name were about a half dozen others from the township of San Lorenzo, which included Chorio. These men were all older, in their twenties and thirties, and had last names such as Scaramazzino, La Bana, Caridi, and Mercurio. Were these Carmelo's friends? His father's friends? Had they traveled together? Was someone awaiting them? The ship's log, all I have to go on, tells only this: The white steamer, built in 1881 in Glasgow, Scotland, was three hundred and fifty feet long and forty feet wide. It carried six hundred and twenty-six passengers, most of them in the cramped, third-class bunks in the fetid darkness below deck.

"It must be confessed that the first descent into these submarine lodging places is deplorably like going for the first time into a prison with its cells," De Amicis wrote. "In those low, narrow corridors, tainted with the reek of bilge-water, came the smell of oil lamps, the fragrance of sheepskins, and the waft of perfume from the ladies." The smells grew heavy and nauseating as the weeks at sea tossed and tumbled by.

Then, America. The year my grandfather arrived, 1903, the country was bursting with promise. Teddy Roosevelt was in the White House. The Wright brothers were busy preparing for their first flight at Kitty Hawk. Henry Ford was founding his motor company in Detroit. Milton Hershey was building his chocolate factory in central Pennsylvania. And hoards of Italian immigrants were underground digging the tunnels for New York City's subway system.

Carmelo Catanoso had not come to America to break his back wielding a shovel. He didn't stay long in New York, which at the time was thought to be populated by more Calabrians than all of Calabria. He lived for a while in Hoboken, New Jersey. And then, no doubt lured by friends and the promise of steady work, he migrated to Philadelphia by 1904 where he took a job at the John B. Stetson Hat Factory on Montgomery Avenue. It was then the world's largest hat-making plant, employing nearly four thousand people capable of producing two million hats a year. Immigrant laborers made felt from the fur of beaver, rabbit, and wild hare. Using a newly mechanized process, they shaped the ten- and twenty-dollar hats into a distinctly American product that would come to symbolize the spirit of the Wild West.

While my grandfather was busy making cowboy hats and developing for the first time the notion that he could control his destiny, his cousin Gaetano, an ocean and world away, was busy making appeals to the people of Pentidattilo to rise above their meager expectations and surrender their destiny to the ways of the Lord.

The mission facing Padre Gaetano was enormous, made all the worse by the long-gathering forces that drove my grandfather and millions of southern Italians to flee their homeland.

For as long as history was recorded in the regions south of Rome, governmental power meant only one thing: oppression. If you go back far enough, nearly two thousand years, you begin to understand the pressure that had built up, like a huge body of water pushing against a weakened dam. When there was finally the means to flee (nineteenth-century steamers) and a place to receive them (the Americas), the dam broke and they left in torrents.

Trouble began with the Roman Empire, which ravaged the south and virtually vanquished the existing cultures of Puglia and Basilicata just above Calabria. It continued unabated with a steady stream of foreign invaders who followed the Romans—the Lombards, the Byzantine Greeks, the Arabs, the Normans, the Catholic Germans, the French, and the Spaniards. More than a thousand years of occupation gripped southern Italy. Some of it was beneficial, like the agricultural techniques brought by the Arabs, or a system of laws brought by the Normans. But it mattered little to the natives. Distrust and disdain for authority came to be written in their genes.

During northern Italy's great Renaissance of the fourteenth and fifteenth centuries, which began changing the world through the artistic genius of Leonardo, Dante, and Michelangelo, life just a few hundred miles south in the *Mezzogiorno* remained virtually unchanged. Self-determination and the flourishing of the human spirit, so buoyant and rampant elsewhere, were thoroughly repressed in the heel and toe of the boot. Two hundred years of Spanish occupation, beginning in the sixteenth century, only ensured that feudal southern Italy remained feudal. Awful roads, few schools, little hope. Corrupt Spanish viceroys cut favorable deals with native landowners who in turn plundered the labor and often the homes of the swelling masses of peasants.

When the last of France's Bourbon monarchy swapped places with the Spanish as the almighty ruler of southern Italy in the early 1800s, meager attempts at development and land reform were thwarted by the kind of corruption and mistrust that was now deeply embedded in the psyche of those natives possessing just enough power to resist. Over time, an entrenched fatalism took hold among southern Italians that could not be undone by whatever fleeting promises shimmered on the horizon of Italy's unified northern and southern halves in the 1870s. The real promise seemed to lie across the Atlantic to the West.

As for the Italian south, Carlo Levi wrote, "No one has ever come to this land except as an enemy, a conqueror, or a visitor devoid of understanding. The seasons pass today over the toil of the peasants, just as they did three thousand years before Christ; no message, human or divine, has reached this stubborn poverty."

This was the world my grandfather fled, along with steamer after steamer of like-minded southern Italians. Between 1880 and 1930, in one of the greatest migrations in world history, four and a half million Italians entered the United States, an astonishing 80 percent from the seven regions south of Rome: Abruzzo, Molise, Campania, Basilicata, Puglia, Calabria, and Sicily.

It usually wasn't the poorest of the poor who crowded the ports at Naples, Genoa, and Palermo to form the exodus; those people were often as empty of will as they were of financial resources. No, it was usually those who could see hard times looming ahead, as well as those with marketable skills such as stonecutting, carpentry, baking, or barbering. They were the ones motivated to change their lives before life crushed them and their families.

Those left behind were, in many ways, like the peasants locked away in isolated mountainside villages such as Pentidattilo. "The life of the men, the beasts and the land seemed fixed in the inflexible circle, hemmed in by the position of the mountains and the passage of time, as if condemned by nature to life imprisonment," wrote Italian author Ignazio Silone.

Wearing the yoke of so many centuries of inequity, the villagers remained secretive and wary, always expecting the worst. They even viewed priests with suspicion, just someone else out to shake them down for money, like their foreign oppressors who taxed their sheep and goats. The social order, such as it was, was often dominated by that unique form of southern Italian governance known as the Mafia. In the absence of a genuine government capable of sustaining any respect for rules or law, the Mafia emerged to supply security to those they favored, to enforce some semblance of order, and to mediate conflicts. This all came at a price, of course, paid in cash. And while the peasants may have silently cheered the Mafia and its tactics in undercutting the official authorities, they were no better off as a result.

Pentidattilo, a village of several hundred souls, wasn't completely without resources. There was a school for small children, though few attended; their labor was needed in the fields outside the village where they plodded down furrowed rows behind the family oxen. Upper grades were harder to get to, a long walk down the hill in the larger

town of Melito di Porto Salvo or even farther off in Reggio. There was a
village pharmacist, and sometimes the *carabinieri*, military police, passed
through on horseback. But the Mafia existed unchallenged, calling the
shots, controlling what little commerce existed. The peasants—often
hungry, always impoverished—were compliant in their ignorance.

L ife began to change, however slightly, in the years after Padre
Gaetano Catanoso's arrival. The young priest was constantly out
in the piazza in front of his church talking with the children, telling
them stories and offering hazelnuts and figs from his pockets. On Sundays and holidays, he would smile gently and say to them: "Children,
let's go to church." And they would follow him inside, where he instructed them in the basics of Catholicism. Soon many would come to
love him. They would be drawn like a magnet to his desire to teach
them. Working the fields with their parents, children would seek relief
by saying, "Mama, let me go to catechism class." A few mothers, when
the fathers weren't looking, nodded and said, "Go."

Padre Gaetano said Mass every day, even if only to a smattering of
old peasant widows hobbling in on stiff legs, dressed all in black. After
Mass, he reserved his mornings for praying the rosary, always the rosary, and hearing confessions. Business was usually slow.

In the afternoons and evenings, he would wander the narrow streets
of the village like a peddler of hope, observing, listening, assessing the
needs. He would seek out the elderly and the sick with his visits. He
spoke to any who did not avert his or her gaze. He carried meager
gifts, perhaps a few coins from his own pocket or a small sack of grain.
Soon he was welcomed into their homes—small, dirt-floored hovels
thick with the smells of garlic and livestock. The fears and strange
beliefs of these people, fueled by their ignorance, broke his heart. So,
too, did the squalor of their lives. If they worked at all, it was only as
day laborers and only for a few months at a time. Mostly there was no
work save for a bit of subsistence farming.

As he listened, Padre Gaetano found himself absorbing their suffering and felt ennobled by it. Tell me more, he would say, unbundle
your burdens. As their innate distrust slowly melted into something

different, many of them opened up, touched in ways they never knew by a benevolent hand of paternalism. They rewarded the young priest in the simplest, most profound way. They called him *padre*, father, never don, which was the formal title given to priests of the day.

The more Padre Gaetano listened to the villagers, the more he realized: If he was to have a chance to bring them to Christ and save their souls, he must first teach them to read. To transform their hearts, he must illuminate their minds. So he pulled together a few books, some pencils, and paper and fashioned a classroom out of a small room in the rectory where he lived just behind the church. He opened a night school and taught adults and older children alike, telling them Gospel stories, coaxing them to laugh, never charging them for the lessons.

As in other parts of the rural Italian south, Catholicism barely had a toehold in Pentidattilo. The villagers clung to strange superstitions. They often appeared devout until it became clear that they worshipped witches and believed in spells and lived in fear of *il malocchio*—"the evil eye." The cow horns they nailed above the front doors of their shacks were there for protection from supernatural forces. Some prayed for miracles to their strange gods to mitigate their suffering. None of this was Christian, let alone Catholic. Padre Gaetano would hear this and gasp, "My God, I must teach them the meaning of holiness."

"Sanctity does not lie in doing miracles," he would tell them patiently. "It consists of detesting every sin, in doing what pleases God. It lies in abiding by the Commandments, in loving God and others for the love of our Lord. It consists of walking in the presence of God. You commit sins when you forget about the Lord. Walk in the presence of God and you will be perfect. God is watching."

One afternoon, Padre Gaetano overheard a young girl tell her brother as he returned sweaty and worn from the fields, a load of firewood on his back, "It's so good you're here; may Jesus Christ be praised!" When the boy managed a smile, acknowledging a lesson of worship they had learned from Padre Gaetano, the priest's heart nearly burst with joy. Illuminate the mind and the heart will follow.

There were practical deeds as well. Padre Gaetano was pleased to learn that the church owned a few acres of land on the edge of the village where wheat was grown. Applying the first lesson learned from his father the farmer, the priest gave away as much of the harvest as he could and sold the rest at a few lira below market value. He then carefully distributed the extra money to several families in need, keeping just enough to support the church and prepare for next season's planting.

This, of course, did not sit well with the Mafia men in town. That the parish priest was challenging their moral authority was bad enough. That he was now cutting into their farm profits went a step too far. One afternoon, while Padre Gaetano was riding on a donkey down to Melito di Porto Salvo to visit with other priests, a Mafia goon sprung out from behind a roadside hedge. He pulled the priest off his mount and struck him hard across the face. *You are reaching far beyond your bounds,* the man warned; *we can make life mighty uncomfortable for you.* The young Mafioso had no idea that the priest he had slapped was coming to embrace suffering as effortlessly as the Mafia embraced crime. Nor would he recognize that the priest's response was entirely in keeping with a key teaching of Jesus Christ: always work to resolve conflict peacefully; repay violence with compassion. So despite his stinging cheek, Padre Gaetano simply brushed off his cassock, straightened his glasses, and promised to pray for his assailant. Then he got back up on his donkey and resumed his journey.

Turning the other cheek, he reserved his rage for the pulpit. "Have you always been blind to the difference between black and white, light and dark, between yes and no, or as you say, between the devil and holy water?" Padre Gaetano roared during a sermon in Pentidattilo, "Do you understand me? Have you not seen those good farmers at Mass on Sunday and how they sit and listen to the sermon, only to leave the pub drunk a little while later, singing blasphemous songs until one stabs another for the smallest of offenses—made ten years ago? This is your influence. Then you put an offering of ten lira or a hundred lira on the statue of Saint Antonio and believe this will clear your sins. It will not. You give something of little value and seek to be forgiven. You fail to understand the very elements of a Christian life."

He would clash again with the Mafia a few years later. A young woman from a poor family in the village had gotten pregnant by the son of a powerful and affluent Mafia chief. Despite their lowly social stature, the woman's parents demanded an immediate wedding. After meeting privately with the couple and discerning their love for each other, Padre Gaetano agreed to marry them at the Church of St. Peter and Paul on the piazza. The night before the ceremony, as the priest was readying the church, the father of the groom showed up.

In the flickering candlelight near the altar, the man slashed at the priest's cassock with a knife he pulled from his pocket. Then he threatened "that wedding must not take place tomorrow, and if it does, you will not exist."

In another church in another village, another priest might have quickly gotten the message, and even worked to strike a deal. We are both men of influence, another priest might have said; if I help you, perhaps you will help me. A church could always use the kinds of things a wealthy Mafia man could provide.

Such thoughts did not belong to Padre Gaetano. He reached inside the torn black cloth near his chest to feel for blood. There was none. Then he fixed his assailant with a steady gaze and made himself understood: "Tomorrow I will celebrate the wedding as planned. Then you can do with me as you wish."

The man's eyes went wide. His threats had never before been met with resistance. "But, Padre, you leave me no choice!"

"Do as you wish," Padre Gaetano went on calmly, "but I ask you now, and I beg you to answer: If instead of being the father of the groom, you were the father of the bride, would you have come anyhow this evening and attacked me like you just did? How can you call yourself a man of principles?"

The man was dumbfounded. Was this priest actually asking him to consider the plight of a lowly peasant family? Was he actually taking the side of a poor, disgraced girl instead of the son of a powerful man? Who did this crazy priest think he was? The Mafia chief turned and hurried out without saying a word.

The next day, Padre Gaetano Catanoso performed the marriage ceremony before a handful of people from the bride's family only. He celebrated with them afterward at a small reception, taking care to wrap a handful of sugarcoated almonds, called *confetti*, in a cloth and slip them into his pocket. The sweet nuts were a traditional gift for wedding guests.

Later that night, the father of the groom came knocking at the rectory door. When Padre Gaetano answered and saw who it was, he bowed his head solemnly and said, "I am ready. Do as you wish."

"Padre, forgive me," the man said quickly, the hostility from the previous night replaced now with humility. "I was up all night, thinking about what you said to me. You were right. My son must take responsibility for his actions and for his family. I don't like what happened, but I will support him."

Padre Gaetano had fully expected the man's knife to reach beneath his ribs this time. He let out a sigh and pushed open the rectory door. With a smile and a wave of his hand, he invited the man inside.

"Please come in. I have saved for you some of your son's *confetti*," he said, producing the sugarcoated almonds. "In a few months, you will bring me *confetti* in celebration of the birth of your grandchild."

In those days, it is possible to see Padre Gaetano almost as a young Jesus Christ, a humble man of such strong and infectious faith that souls were captured in an instant and apostles fell quickly in line behind him. Not in Pentidattilo. Not a chance. From behind the carved, oak doors of his church, Padre Gaetano could hear men in the piazza shouting angrily, cursing viciously. He would push through the doors to see a brawl in progress and plunge into the tangle of swinging fists to separate the thugs. One night while walking in the village, he heard the muffled screams of a teenage girl being assaulted in a nearby alley. Padre Gaetano's intervention, as he led the girl away, earned him a face full of spit from the attacker and an urgent wish that he go straight to hell. Such violence and blasphemy, so chronic and slow to yield throughout the village, wounded him more deeply than any Mafia knife. He headed back to his prayers, listening closely for God's wisdom in how best to carry His flag and fight His fight.

Approaching his thirtieth year, Padre Gaetano sought to temper his frustrations with the hard realities of Pentidattilo by immersing himself more deeply in the wellspring of his own faith—the life and suffering of Jesus Christ. During his morning prayers, in the damp, cool solitude of his church, his mind kept going to a favorite story of his from his seminary studies. The story was of St. Veronica, the woman from Jerusalem who was so struck with pity for Jesus as he lugged his cross that she fell in next to him on his way to Calvary. When Jesus collapsed, blood dripping down his forehead from his mocking crown of thorns, Veronica—filled with compassion and eager to ease Christ's suffering—tenderly wiped his face with her veil. The image of Christ's face was believed to have imprinted on the cloth, and it became one of the most sacred and revered relics in the history of the Catholic Church.

Veronica's act of charity and compassion, her desire to ease Christ's suffering, and the holy relic bearing the bruised face of Jesus came together to form the foundation upon which Padre Gaetano would carefully construct a half century of priestly, saintly service to the poor throughout southern Calabria. It was in Pentidattilo that his soul became enflamed with *il volto santo*, the holy face of Christ, which was captured on Veronica's cloth at the moment of His most intense suffering. Padre Gaetano would, in his heart and in his mind, pray deeply enough to imagine reliving that moment in Jesus's life and feeling that same pain. In the shadows of his own church, with a cruel, needy world just outside its doors, he came to fully grasp the enormity of Christ's supreme act of sacrifice. It was all about reparation—praying and suffering for the accumulated ills of all people and atoning for those sins in the most dramatic way. He was grateful for the example and humbled by it. It became his ardent desire to also atone for the sins of all those around him and, in the process, help alleviate Christ's suffering, just like Veronica.

"The Holy Face is my life. He is my strength," Padre Gaetano came to say again and again as he tried to explain the spiritual forces guiding his life.

As his faith grew and deepened, the mystical nature of the Eucharist, always a cherished sacrament for him, became more powerful than ever. It was as if he were seeing it for the first time. The Holy Face of Christ had been imprinted on Veronica's veil. But to adore the real, divine face of Christ, Padre Gaetano would say, you need only lift that white veil and behold the Eucharist, the body and blood of Christ made real at his altar every morning in the Church of St. Peter and Paul in tiny Pentidattilo. Driven by the core of his Catholic faith, that thin wafer was no mere symbol. He shivered with the realization. The Eucharist was a daily reminder of Christ's suffering and sacrifice, and his continued presence among the faithful. Padre Gaetano came to believe he could do no less than to love with the same kind of intensity that Jesus loved. How else could he soften so many hardened souls?

"Jesus needs many Veronicas for the sins of blasphemy and sacrilege and for the always heavier cross of the poor and the helpless," he would say.

Like St. Veronica herself, Padre Gaetano would fall in step with the many, many poor hobbling all around him. He would wipe their faces of tears and blood. He would love them blindly, radically, unconditionally.

For southern Calabria, the cross proved heaviest on December 28, 1908. A region plagued for centuries by natural calamities such as mudslides and volcanoes had never seen anything as terrible as *il terremoto*, the earthquake that struck that morning and rocked both sides of the Strait of Messina for five days. An estimated 80 percent of all the buildings in Reggio were leveled; in Messina, across the straits in Sicily, the destruction was even worse. The violent, merciless tremors were followed by a tidal wave of epic proportions, drowning two coastal cities that had already been reduced to ruins. The death toll and destruction were so staggering that the pagans could be forgiven for believing that an angry god was punishing them for their sins. Twelve thousand people died in and around Reggio; sixty thousand died in Messina. Many of those who survived, including countless orphans, were crippled with injuries and made homeless. Suffering existed on an unimaginable scale. It remains the worst earthquake on record in Western Europe, and damage was by no means limited to the larger cities.

Up in Chorio, about twenty-eight miles from Reggio, the death toll was less severe, but homes fell apart and the 183-year-old Church of Saint Pasquale Baylon in the piazza collapsed. Sources of drinking water were badly damaged. Travel between villages, difficult prior to the earthquake, was rendered practically impossible. Over in Pentidattilo, the Church of St. Peter and Paul remained standing, but scores of homes did not survive, including the rectory behind the church.

On the morning of the quake, when the earth started to tremble, Padre Gaetano was praying in his room. He suddenly felt compelled to call for his older sister Angela, who was staying with him during a visit. As she entered her brother's room, the ceiling of the room where she had just been collapsed in a crushing pile of stone and plaster. Whether by luck or providence, they both escaped before the rest of the building came down.

Padre Gaetano lost what few belongings he had, yet emerged unscathed in the disaster. Like many of his fellow villagers, he was homeless for days until he was able to take lodging in a ramshackle stone house on the edge of the village.

In many ways, his physical life had been reduced to that of the lowliest peasant. He could have returned to Chorio, where the Catanoso family had the means and resources to recover faster than most. It's likely that such a thought never crossed his mind. In a response of pure humility and obedience that would leave some scratching their heads and perhaps even questioning his sanity, Padre Gaetano felt fortunate to be dragged down with everyone else. God's will, he insisted, was nothing to question; the earth had been shaken for a reason. In the spirit of reparation, in the example of his savior, he would bear the pain for others.

"Suffering purifies us and gives us courage," he would say in the aftermath of the earthquake, "because we feel in that circumstance, in that adversity, that we are not alone, but that the Lord is with us."

Writing about Padre Gaetano years later, Italian scholar and author Paola Dal Toso reflected that the priest lived with the certainty that Divine Providence, the literal hand of God, always emerges in times of need. "With his endless hope and trust in God's mercy," she writes, "he accomplished with unceasing drive and total dedication a series of initiatives the importance of which should not be underestimated, in conditions that others would rationally judge as crazy, sheer madness, folly."

The next dozen years of his life—after the earthquake, through the advent of World War I, and Italy's eventual succumbing to fascism— were marked by intense activity. The need was great and there was little time to lose. Padre Gaetano was not working without a script. The high bishops of Calabria, stunned to witness so many of their best sons and daughters lost to emigration, feared that those who remained were devolving into godless wretches beyond the reach of salvation. Through a "Collective Letter of the Calabrian Bishops," they put out an urgent call to the clergy throughout the diocese to redouble their efforts to educate the villagers in the ways of the church, in the power of the Eucharist, and in the saving grace of God.

Padre Gaetano, who like all obedient priests viewed the bishops as the successors to Christ's apostles, embraced the call. He expanded his night school to teach even more children in Pentidattilo. He scrounged for funds and opened a small orphanage for boys and girls, too. On the back of his donkey, he would ride north into the Aspromonte to his hometown of Chorio and beyond—up to Bagaladi and Montebello, up even higher and farther to Roccaforte del Greco and Roghudi, all tiny, remote mountain villages as poor and forlorn as his own parish. He would come clopping into each village, past piles of rubble and ruins, wearing a smile beneath the broad brim of his black *galero*, the round-topped priest's hat he always wore. Gently, he offered all that he had: hope and compassion.

Small in stature but huge in presence, he would give a spiritual pep talk to the beleaguered local priests, many of whom felt abandoned by the church in these times of great desperation and need. Where were the funds to rebuild the crumbled villages? they despaired. Where was the government? Where was the church of Calabria?

Padre Gaetano would plead with them to be patient. "Hear in your superiors the voice of God," he would tell them. "Love the bishop. Do not cause him any pain. Always obey him, and when you do not know how to act, talk to the Lord and he will enlighten you."

His words came softly in a voice free of conflict and doubt; his eyes glowed only with sincerity. Now was the time for the church and its representatives to stand together, not pull apart, he would gently implore them. Trust in Divine Providence; after all, he did. And pray to the sweet, healing graces of the Virgin Mary and the Holy Face of Christ, those to whom he prayed with a ferocious faith. Then undergirding the pious with the practical, he would offer to assist them in their work, helping with confessions and Mass in the village churches. Sometimes he would even preach the sermon, delivering it as a missionary would with a clear and confident voice filled with passion.

"We often recite the Our Father," he preached in 1915, "but how many of us comprehend the high significance of the words we pronounce? In order to love, it is necessary to understand. Therefore, love increases as the knowledge of what love is increases."

Through his travels and his preaching, Padre Gaetano, though only in his thirties, saw his reputation for holiness spread among his peers in the clergy and the vast diocese of Reggio Calabria with its eighty-three parishes. In all parts of the region, priests and nuns, monsignors and bishops honored him by making Padre Gaetano the priest to whom they confessed their own sins. Just as his spiritual influence extended to reach the peasants who would heed his call, so, too, did it reach the clergy whose suffering was often no less pronounced than those they lived among.

Unwittingly, Padre Gaetano Catanoso was building a foundation of faith and good works upon which a solid case for canonization could be later constructed. Such a case had not been built at the Vatican on behalf of a son of Calabria since the early 1500s. Padre Gaetano knew all about St. Francis of Paola, who was born in a fishing village north of Reggio in 1416. Padre Gaetano prayed often to the last Calabrian saint, whose life story he knew well.

At age thirteen, young Francis—inspired by St. Francis of Assisi who lived two hundred years earlier—dedicated himself to cloistered meditation, utter deprivation, and spiritual leadership. He founded an order of friars who embraced what they called "perpetual lent": frequent fasting, no meat or eggs, strict celibacy, and abundant charity to the poor. Francis built monasteries in southern Italy and France. He was hailed by popes and sought after as a spiritual and political advisor to Italian and French kings right up until his death in 1507, on a Good Friday.

But today, if St. Francis of Paola is remembered at all (his marble statue is among those perched atop Bernini's colonnade in St. Peter's Square), it is for his magical, mystical miracles of a distant, bygone era. Legend has it that he brought forth water from a rock to slake the thirst of Calabrian workers building a monastery. That's a mild one. The medieval monk also tossed a dead fish in that new pool of water, and it came to life. Followers said he could predict future events and read minds. He was seen levitating while deep in prayer. He could hold on to hot coals without burning his palms. And like Jesus, he is said to have cured the sick and even raised a few corpses from death. But his most vivid miracle, the one that earned him the honor of being named the patron saint of boatmen, came in 1464. On trying to board a small vessel to cross the Strait of Messina to reach Sicily, Francis was turned away by the boat's owner. Suit yourself, the monk must have said. Francis waded into the water and spread out his cloak. Then he pulled one side up and attached it to his staff to make a sail. As the wind rose, he and some companions were seen floating safely across the strait. A miracle. At least that's how the story is told. He was canonized in Rome in 1519.

Nearly five centuries would pass before Calabrians could celebrate another local saint. This one, though, was exalted not in medieval magic and myths but in actual deeds during contemporary times. Padre Gaetano's faith was just as strong and his charity just as generous as St. Francis of Paola, or even of Assisi. He believed in the great mysteries of the ancient church and believed, too, in its sainted miracle workers. But his own story was far simpler, far more recognizable, and in many ways, far more believable.

Padre Gaetano never tested his overcoat to see if it might double as a raft. Hot coals would have blistered his skin, had he been foolhardy enough to grasp them. And if he ever laid hands on anyone with the intention of healing him or raising him up, there is no record of it. In fact, he worked strenuously to turn villagers away from their pagan thoughts of witches and evil eyes and gnomes hiding in the woods.

And though his life spanned political times—Mafia oppression, two world wars, and the rise of fascism under the dictator Mussolini—he seemed to float above the twisted and violent repercussions of such inhuman behavior. Spiritually that is, not literally.

For a man so simple and exceedingly humble—"the little donkey of Christ," he called himself—he was in all ways remarkable. Just not in the ways that marked his sainted predecessor, St. Francis of Paola.

"He was a different and extraordinary priest imbued with the light of simplicity, of poverty and charity. He had totally abased himself in the contemplation of the Holy Face and in the love of others," wrote Monsignor Vincent Lembo, a Calabrian priest who knew Padre Gaetano well. "He was different in his constant going out to meet life's defeated in order to console and rescue the part of Jesus he recognized in them in their abandonment and suffering. The young orphans, especially those brought ashore by war or by the ruthless behavior of mankind. The sick, the dying, the old, the imprisoned, the sinners, which he considered the poorest of the poor. This was the privileged space in which Padre Catanoso mainly exercised and condensed his apostolate. His love of God and for humankind indeed was, in his spiritual horizon, two aspects of the same inseparable love."

3

—————

# *In Domino*

On a distant shore at the same time, my grandfather, Carmelo Catanoso, was living a life his cousin could in no way fathom. Every day he was astonished. So much freedom, so much opportunity—if you were smart and worked hard enough to seize it. He did. In 1911 in South Philadelphia, the heart of the city's Italian district, Carmelo met a young woman named Caterina Foti. She would become his wife, and her family would launch his career. Like Carmelo, Caterina was an immigrant, too, a native of Riposta, a fishing village on the northeast coast of Sicily just above Catania. In 1905, when she was fourteen, she had sailed from Messina on the steamer the *Sicilian Prince* to Ellis Island with her widowed mother, two brothers, and a sister.

Caterina's older brother, Giacomo Foti, was already in Philadelphia, having immigrated two years earlier. Giacomo, or Jack, as he came to be known, was industrious and ambitious. He wanted nothing to do with factory work or the urban slums where immigrant workers lived in growing numbers as their population exploded: In 1900, some forty-five thousand recently arrived Italians lived in Philadelphia, more than any other place in America, except for Manhattan and Brooklyn. And they kept coming, settling mostly in South Philly.

Jack Foti figured he could make a good living if he could give the newcomers a taste of what they had left behind. He began importing olive oil in bulk and filling cans one by one, soldering them closed himself. He named the product Rosa, after his wife, and sold the cans to the Italian markets in South Philly. With the success of olive oil sales, he broadened his product line to include tomatoes, olives, and pasta—all grown and made in Italy. Each can carried the distinctive label of four ripe plum tomatoes hanging from the vine against a field of dark blue. Nearly a century later, Rosa Food Products, still operated by descendants of Jack Foti, remains a thriving import and distribution wholesaler of Italian and ethnic foods in the Delaware Valley.

Not long after Carmelo Catanoso and Caterina Foti married on March 31, 1913—at St. Rita of Cascia Church on Broad Street—Carmelo went to work for his brother-in-law Jack as a salesman of Rosa brand products. The warehouse and offices were located then at 1312 Federal Street. Carmelo was a twenty-six-year-old newlywed; his bride was twenty-two. Life in Chorio and Riposta was steadily receding into the past. If either of them had ever harbored any notion of returning to their home villages, they now let those ideas vanish. Caterina's entire family was already in America; Carmelo's older brother Giuseppe, who had emigrated before the earthquake of 1908, had also settled in Philadelphia. The brothers' parents, Antonino Catanoso and Elisabetta Mangiola, journeyed to Philadelphia to visit, but returned after a few months to Chorio to their tailor and barber shop. Carmelo tried to convince his younger sister, Maria Portzia Catanoso, to cross the Atlantic. She considered it, but once she married Bruno Priolo, who had no interest in leaving the village, she and her husband settled in the Catanoso home on a small piazza in Chorio and spent the rest of their lives there.

So as Padre Gaetano was riding his donkey high into the Aspromonte in search of southern Italian souls to save, his cousin Carmelo was settling down with his wife in a South Philadelphia row house at 1520 Dickinson Street and beginning to raise a family full of American children. There would be nine in all, four girls and five boys—born between 1914 and 1931. My father, Leonardo Richard Catanoso, or Leonard, would come in the middle, born December 6, 1920.

The children could understand much of the Italian their parents spoke to each other, but they spoke only English among themselves.

They knew vaguely that they had an aunt back in Italy but had no idea they had so many cousins. And they would grow up knowing nothing about the priest in their family who was working and preaching and suffering in third world conditions as they grew and prospered in the New World.

Like their parents, the children of Carmelo and Caterina Catanoso looked in just one direction: forward.

As Padre Gaetano continued his travels beyond Pentidattilo, he saw the task before him as enormous. "When visiting many isolated towns on the mountains of Calabria and preaching in almost all of the parishes of the archdiocese," Padre Gaetano wrote in *Il Volto Santo* (*The Holy Face*), a newsletter he founded in 1920, "I felt a pang in my heart in seeing so many innocent children exposed to corruption, so many young girls without guidance and without direction in life. I saw too many poor, bare churches and so many tabernacles without their due dignity. Always I saw too many suffering priests without assistance."

The living conditions in southern Italy were bad enough without the compounding burdens of an earthquake and a war sweeping Europe. Wherever he traveled, wherever he looked, the needs of the people seemed only to multiply. If he ever questioned God's judgment, or perhaps even God's existence in the face of so much suffering, he kept such thoughts only to himself. Outwardly, always, he radiated compassion and understanding. There's no way to know whether he questioned his own faith, but it's clear that no one who knew him ever questioned it. He gave them no reason to.

There were a few orphanages operating in Reggio during these times, but most required a subsidy of some kind before accepting a child. When Padre Gaetano opened his orphanages, first for girls, then later for boys, he never inquired about money. "Bring me the child. *In domino*," he would say, always in God. When the nun running the house complained, he would smile and tell her: "Don't worry, the Lord will provide." And invariably, the support came.

He would call for such support wherever he preached: "With Jesus, let us turn our eyes to the youth and abandoned children. Truly our hearts ache at the sight of so much misfortune. Today, humanity is more morally sick than ever."

Somehow, this societal sickness made him that much stronger. Padre Gaetano's daily, intense meditations inflamed him with certain concrete beliefs, all centering on the reality of Jesus Christ living and working, moment to moment, in the priest's own life. This unshakable faith was a source of great joy amid so much deprivation. With Jesus as his model, he viewed himself as a creation of infinite love. And like the biblical disciples before him, he felt compelled to shoulder an enormous responsibility as well. He saw the face of Christ in each face of the suffering poor, and instinctively, he reached out to help them. He provided the practical necessities—schools and orphanages and gifts of food. But it was their souls he most sought to nourish in a pitched battle against indifference, paganism, and increasingly, fascism. He would seek to arm them and convert them by simply bringing Jesus to life for them, just as Jesus lived in him.

That's why it enraged him to see damaged and ill-tended tabernacles on the altars of so many village churches; it was in the tabernacle that Jesus waited. And that's why Padre Gaetano was so determined to support those priests who were struggling with their own parishes and often their own doubts; it was during the consecration of the Eucharist in every Mass, he would stress, that the humble priest holds the awesome power to bring Christ to life. When Christ lives, there is hope. To Padre Gaetano, nothing was more important. He would say that just as the archangel Gabriel sought the Virgin Mother's consent for Jesus to become incarnate, now at Mass, Jesus awaits the priest's consent to descend onto the altar as the body and blood incarnate. Padre Gaetano found the anticipation of the consecration thrilling. He said Mass every day, *every* day, and heard confessions daily, too.

"All of the priest's life should be nothing more than preparation and thanks for the Holy Mass," Padre Gaetano would say. "We adore Him with remote preparation, ensuring that our lives are pure and virtuous. We adore Him with immediate preparation, by meditating to consider the great action we are about to perform on the altar and by dismissing all thoughts of the world."

Outside of Mass, of course, there was much worldly work to do. He put his newsletter, *Il Volto Santo*, a folded leaflet really, in the hands of those who could read, which usually meant those with means. In that way, he could raise awareness of the needs of the poor and also the poor priests. He had little boxes made of polished wood and cardboard. An image of the holy face on St. Veronica's cloth covered one side, an image of St. Anthony covered the other. Along with copies of his newsletter, he put the boxes in churches, shops, spinning mills, any place of business that would have them throughout the diocese. A message on the box urged people to drop a spare coin inside whenever they could. He did this for years and thereby became known as *parroco delle cassette*, "the parish priest of the boxes."

"I would remind everyone," he later wrote, "that alms giving has never made anyone poorer, but rather, it can enrich you."

Early on, the funds were used to support an orphanage founded by his close friend and mentor, Don Luigi Orione, as well as the Institute of Poor Clerics in Reggio, which Padre Gaetano helped establish. This organization offered relief to struggling parish priests and also provided the means for young men from poor families who heard the call, as he had, to enter the priesthood. With an ever-expanding multitude of souls to salvage, the church needed as many priests as it could attract. He was determined to clear a path for those eager to follow.

"Let us call upon all our energies to give the church many holy priests," Padre Gaetano wrote in his newsletter. "Especially in our farms we can find the best flowers waiting for the pious hand to pick them and transplant them to our Lord's gardens."

One of the many young men who heeded his call, who sought to match his priestly devotion, was his own brother, Pasquale Catanoso, twelve years younger than Gaetano, the eighth of nine Catanoso children born in Chorio. The younger brother went on to become ordained and lead parishes of his own in southern Calabria.

Pasquale, or Pasqualino as he was called, knew his older brother Gaetano, in almost all circumstances, to be a serious man with a serious message. But Pasqualino knew, too, and spoke lovingly of his brother's childlike nature, his beaming smile, his ability to tell a good joke. Even on their mother. One afternoon, while returning to Pentidattilo after a visit to Montebello just up the mountain, Padre Gaetano's donkey got skittish while crossing a rushing stream and refused to budge. He tried to dismount to pull the stubborn beast across, but his foot caught in the stirrup and he tumbled into the water. A farmer who saw the mishap invited the soaking-wet priest home and loaned him a dry change of clothes—a coarse, brown work shirt and some pants. When he arrived back at the rectory in Pentidattilo, his mother was already there for a visit. She was stunned at the sight of her son in lay clothes. "Mother," he explained with mock seriousness, "I don't want to be a priest anymore."

In July 1921, Monsignor Camillo Rinaldo Rousset, the archbishop of the diocese of Reggio Calabria, called on Padre Gaetano to move down from Pentidattilo to the bustling town of Reggio on the coast. Monsignor Rousset needed someone to take over as priest of St. Mary of the Purification, known also as Candelora. More than a decade after the earthquake of 1908, the reconstruction of Reggio's commercial district and waterfront was well under way, though many of the outlying town's residential areas still lay in ruins. Candelora, a struggling parish in the center of town, endured challenges of its own. When Padre Gaetano arrived, the church was little more than an oversized hut standing amid the rubble just a few blocks up from the coast. He rebuilt the congregation little by little, just as he raised funds to slowly rebuild the church brick by brick.

Now forty-two, he was in the prime of his life. Diocese leaders were impressed with the deep humility and spiritual fortitude of this priest from Chorio. They gave him more and more opportunities to touch more and more people with his special grace. In 1922, Padre Gaetano was named chaplain of the hospital in Reggio, where he visited and prayed with the sick and dying. He served as chaplain of the prison there, too, going weekly to hear the confessions of inmates and urge them to give their lives over to the Lord. He was also made spiritual director of the Archiepiscopal Seminary, where he received his own religious training as a boy and young man. There he would influence generations of Calabrian priests, instilling in them the special joy and privilege he experienced in following Christ's life of service while trusting God with all his heart.

That same year, he made a special pilgrimage to the southern Italian region of Puglia on the Adriatic side of the country. Like Catholic faithful all over Italy at the time, he was intrigued by the fantastic stories of a Capuchin priest who appeared to carry the stigmata—the constantly bleeding, unhealing wounds in the hands, feet, and chest in the same places where Jesus was pierced and bled during the crucifixion. The Capuchin priest's name was Padre Pio, nearly as famous and notorious then as he remains today.

In those days, newspapers carried stories of Pio's extraordinary holiness and claims of miracles he performed. In San Giovanni Rotondo, where Pio lived, an old beggar, crippled from birth with two club feet, used to drag himself about on his knees using short crutches. One day when the man called out to Padre Pio for a blessing, the priest turned and said, "Throw away your crutches." Townsfolk were stunned to witness the man do as he was told, then rise up on his deformed feet and walk upright for the first time. Such miraculous stories swept through Italy like wildfire, and Padre Pio found himself attracting crowds of believers as well as skeptics.

Certain Vatican officials, who seemed to fear his widening popularity, were dubious of Pio and his stigmata, not to mention his so-called miracles. He was frequently investigated and told to keep his wounds covered. In 1922, the Congregation of the Holy Office, the Vatican's arbiter on matters of faith and tradition, warned that Padre Pio's miraculous powers could not be confirmed and that the faithful should not see him as a living saint with supernatural powers. That view would change over time, but back then, the Vatican seemed intent on containing the growing cult surrounding the bearded priest.

But Padre Gaetano was drawn not merely by the rare, bloody spectacle of Pio's wounds. He was drawn to size up his peer's message and spirituality for himself. "I need to seek Padre Pio's opinion regarding the work I am contemplating in my heart," Padre Gaetano wrote. Thus he was among the multitudes that traveled to see Padre Pio up close. En route, he spent the night curled up on some piled-up sacks at the train station in Naples. Whether he got near enough to speak with Pio once he arrived in San Giovanni Rotondo is unlikely; there's no record of him having done so. But he probably did get to hear Pio preach during that pilgrimage in 1922. A few years later, Padre Gaetano's dear friend Don Orione (a priest who would also go on to be canonized by Pope John Paul II) gave him as a gift a black *zucchetta*, a priest's cap worn by Padre Pio, which Gaetano treasured like a holy relic. Padre Pio's fame would continue to escalate the rest of his life and beyond as he became one of the world's best-known contemporary saints, a living miracle worker. Meanwhile, Padre Gaetano would return to the relative obscurity of southern Calabria and his diligent work among the poorest of the poor.

As he carried out his priestly duties in Reggio between his church, the seminary, the prison, and the hospital, Padre Gaetano never forgot his own people, the peasants living in the far-off mountain villages. World War I was over, having brutalized Italians in the north far more than in the south. The fascists, dedicated to the dictatorship of Benito Mussolini, were taking over all levels of government, even at the local level, and promising change. The people were heartened at first, and hopeful. But as always in southern Italy, nothing changed. Despair only deepened with new disappointments. On January 17, 1923, Natale Catanoso of Chorio, a nephew of Padre Gaetano, wrote an angry letter to the township mayor that captured the desperation of the times:

We demand of the illustrious mayor of San Lorenzo to tell us if he intends or not to start up the lights of this town, which have been out since the month of June of last year. The people pay taxes and how! The people are tired and sick and can no longer tolerate the sluggishness of those who are supposed to help us. We ask again, signor mayor, to repair the streets of the area. They are abandoned, dirty and ill maintained. When will you decide to help us? Another important need is to repair the schoolhouse, which has been reduced to a miserable hovel, an indecent, ruined shack with broken windows. The poor little ones are numb in the cold and the teachers are all sick. Signor mayor, act at once. The public has patience, it is true, but this patience does not want to be, and should not be, betrayed.

Unlike his relatives, Padre Gaetano never involved himself with secular politics. He remained focused on the poor and what he himself could do to assist them. If someone came begging at the rectory, he would give them what money he could. Once a nun scolded him for giving away grocery money needed at the church, but he told her not to worry as he went off with his ever-present rosary to pray. When a benefactor arrived a few hours later with a generous donation, Padre Gaetano smiled knowingly at the nun. *"In domino,"* he would say, a Latin phrase that would become his motto.

Spiritually, he drew inspiration from the stories that the Virgin Mary had appeared as an apparition in places such as La Salette and Lourdes in France during the mid-1800s and in Fatima, Portugal, during his own time, in 1917. The message the Virgin delivered during those mystical appearances was always the same: repent for the accumulated sins of mankind. He took such messages to heart. In his daily prayers to the Holy Face, to the mother of God, and to St. Veronica, he offered himself as a humble recipient of their love who was devoted to the reparation of sin. This became the centerpiece of his interior life.

Padre Gaetano would still travel out to the mountain villages to see the peasants when he could, though less frequently now. When he did, he deployed some creative tactics to lure the peasants away from their superstitious ways of practicing religion. Together with the local priest in the village, he would do a bit of playacting in the church or even the piazza. Wearing an old, muddy overcoat, Padre Gaetano would take on the role of an ignorant farmer being told by the local priest that he must attend church every Sunday and be absolved of his sins so he can accept the Eucharist during Mass.

"I cannot be bothered by church," Padre Gaetano would say, speaking in the dialect used by the peasants. "I must work and tend to my farm. I have no time for church and I have no interest."

In hearing the doubts of faith and realities of village life, the peasants would be drawn in to listen closely. Crowds would gather.

"I have no sins to confess," Padre Gaetano would go on. "I do not kill and I do not steal. I have nothing to take to you in the confessional."

The local priest would then carefully explain the difference between the farmer's earthly concerns and his spiritual ones. He would discuss the need to follow all of God's commandments, not just a few. And he would stress that just as the poor farmer must feed his family with bread, so must the farmer be nourished by the word of God. The poor farmer's soul depended on it, as did his shot at eternal life in heaven. Thus enlightened, Padre Gaetano, the playacting farmer, would nod vigorously that he understood and that he had every intention of following the local priest's wishes. Some of the peasants would scoff at the act and turn away, but some would stay for the Mass that always followed, as Padre Gaetano slipped back into his cassock.

The greatest limit to this kind of outreach was simply that Padre Gaetano could only be in one place at a time, touching only so many people. To serve more people in his way—humbly, patiently, generously—he needed assistance. By the mid-1920s, he began speaking to the various established orders of nuns in Reggio to gauge their interest in joining him in his mission work. Invariably, they would return his questions with ones of their own: What were the conditions in the villages? Would they have a comfortable place to stay? What kind of support would they receive? Padre Gaetano answered candidly. And when the nuns realized the misery and poverty they would encounter and live amid, they politely declined to leave Reggio.

Padre Gaetano was discouraged at first. And with good cause. He found he simply could no longer do what he had always done before. He had the will, but no longer the stamina. In 1929, at age fifty, he was diagnosed with diabetes, which sapped his strength and gradually eroded his health the rest of his days.

Thus, founding his own special order of nuns, as quickly as possible, became evermore important to him. But there were both obstacles and resistance. Where would he find the women to establish his order? How would they be trained? And where, in such desperate times, would he find the money to build or buy the facilities the nuns would need to fulfill their mission, like schools and orphanages? During this uncertain period, he sought the help and advice of his dear friend Don Orione. A northern Italian with sweet eyes and a boyish smile, Don Orione had come south to help in Reggio and Messina in the aftermath of the earthquake. He befriended Padre Gaetano while he was parish priest in Pentidattilo. The two priests would become extraordinarily close and joked once that they would later become "neighbors in paradise." Padre Gaetano learned the art of organizing institutions from Don Orione, who had vast experience in creating orphanages, boarding houses for the elderly, and congregations of nuns and priests in both southern and northern Italy and overseas.

With Don Orione's encouragement, Padre Gaetano began to envision founding an order of nuns of his own made up of young women already living in poverty in the mountain villages. Some in the church questioned whether the humble priest, who often struck them as childlike in the simplicity and purity of his beliefs, had the savvy and guile to recruit, train, and supervise a widely dispersed network of nuns and then run the always-political gauntlet of church regulations and expectations to win authorization for the order. Even his younger brother the priest, Don Pasquale Catanoso, implored protectively: "You're crazy. Give up this idea."

Padre Gaetano did not concern himself with such doubts. After all, Calabrians are renowned for being hardheaded, and when coupled with his unshakable faith, he believed there was nothing he could not accomplish.

He looked at Pasquale and said, *"In domino, semper in domino,"* and plunged ahead.

His nuns, he believed, should be "women who know how to speak to their own, who love the Lord deeply, who don't ask if there is a house or garden in town where they are sent, who go without taking anything, who sacrifice themselves, who suffer, who help the church."

To them, he would say, "Your place is wherever others have refused to go, among the humblest and poorest people."

With his spiritual guidance and the innate skills and faithful commitment of these special nuns, he believed he could create an entire order made up of many St. Veronicas, filled with love and compassion and eager to wipe the sweat from the brows of their suffering neighbors. It took ten years to bring to fruition this "tiny mustard seed" of an idea, as he called it. But on December 2, 1934, Monsignor Carmelo Pujia, the new archbishop of Reggio Calabria, approved the founding of what would become Padre Gaetano Catanoso's everlasting legacy: the congregation of the Sisters of St. Veronica of the Holy Face.

At the time, Padre Gaetano was fifty-five years old, well past middle age. His once broad shoulders were now slightly hunched, and what was left of his hair had gone white. With his eyesight weakening from his diabetes, he took to wearing thick, horn-rimmed glasses. He couldn't walk without a cane, and his joints constantly ached from years of hiking steep mountain roads. But physical pain was something he had come to relish. He ate only enough to sustain himself. And he took to sleeping atop a cilice, a sturdy metal band of barbed spikes that could also be worn around his waist, against his skin, under his cassock. As if his personal deprivations and daily meditations on Christ's passion were not enough, he insisted—as other devoted holy men of the time did—on being reminded of and sharing in Christ's physical suffering even as he slept.

"Suffering purifies and sanctifies us," he would say in the spirit of reparation. "It brings God's mercy to us."

In a sense though, despite his advancing age and mounting health problems, he was getting a second wind, a second calling. His mother had died earlier in 1934 at age eighty-two, and his father, living with him at his church in Reggio, was eighty-six years old and frail. Padre Gaetano no doubt gave increasing thought to his own mortality as he knelt each day in the chapel of his church to pray the rosary. The opportunity to form an order of nuns to carry on and extend his mission and message gave him renewed vitality.

So he returned to the remote Aspromonte villages, traveling the winding roads of dirt and gravel to still-isolated and impoverished places like Bagaladi, Bivongi, and Roghudi. He met with peasant families and inquired about their older daughters. Dressed in his dusty, tattered cassock, and broad-brimmed hat, he spoke in the mountain dialect, his voice strong and sure, his eyes aglow. Many of the fathers, whose deep lines in their faces and cracked, calloused hands underscored the harshness of their lives, turned him away, even ran him off.

But many listened and sensed an opportunity, whether spiritual or practical. The priest explained what he needed. He hoped the young women—mostly teenagers, some a bit older—would be literate and possess skills that they could teach, skills like reading and writing, sewing and embroidery. But he didn't turn away those who could do none of that. That's because he looked, too, for a gentleness of soul and a spark in their eyes that suggested they were eager to serve a family much larger than their own. And to these recruits, these novices, he promised nothing but the privilege of doing God's work in following the lessons of God's own son.

In many ways, he was naïve and idealistic, to a fault as it would turn out. Trouble was looming. But he never wavered from his vision, which he trusted as God's vision, too.

"The nuns I wanted," he would say, "were to be rich in their poverty and without pretensions, being content with everything as a gift of the Lord. I took them from the ordinary people, simple souls, and I sent them out like that, like the apostles of Our Lord, with nothing, into the villages that most had need of them."

Of course, he knew the villages well. He knew the small stone houses shared by children and animals alike; the communal ovens where peasant women waited in line to cook dinner; the patches of farmland that barely underwrote survival. He had been born in such a place and had visited many, many others over the previous three decades. And in doing what he could to teach these young women to become sisters, Veronican Sisters of the Holy Face, he prayed for and implored them always to live the spirit of obedience, sacrifice, and humility. Jesus did. As best as he could, Padre Gaetano did, too. And he expected his sisters to do the same. Among these virtues, he prized humility above all else, warning often that "a grain of pride can destroy a mountain of sanctity."

"Be like violets," he told his nuns. "The violet is a flower that does not stand tall. Its petals face downward. It hides beneath the leaves. But it gives off a delightful scent."

He did not, however, intend them to be invisible. There were too many war orphans, too many disconsolate priests tending shabby churches, too many lost souls, too many old people dying alone.

At the time Padre Gaetano was gathering scores of Veronican sisters and preparing them simply and quickly for this mountain mission work, Benito Mussolini was midway through his reign as Italy's ironfisted dictator. The son of a northern Italian blacksmith and anarchist, Mussolini came to power in 1922 in the aftermath of World War I, where a marginally victorious Italy did not receive the territorial gains she expected through the Treaty of London. As a newspaper editor with a gift for charismatic oration, Mussolini learned the power of propaganda and how to manipulate a populace tired of war and fearful of the tides of socialism and communism then sweeping Eastern Europe and Russia. A weakened King Emmanuel II invited Mussolini to become prime minister to avoid the threat of an Italian civil war. Initially, Mussolini's self-styled fascism sounded promising—universal suffrage, land for the peasants, strong foreign policy. But it proved corrupt and stifling virtually from the start. He pledged to restore order and stability and bring Italy to greatness through unbending, unquestioned dictatorship. State control was absolute over corporations, capital, and people, from the cities to the villages, from the north to the south. Opportunistic thugs posing as local politicians enforced the new law of the land, often cruelly. Freedom of speech and assembly were strictly prohibited. The right of workers to strike was eliminated. With the help of secret police, dissent was brutally crushed along with the spirit of those still waiting for enlightened, humane political leadership. Oppression, once again, settled over the country like a heavy, dark cloud, landing heaviest in the south.

The fascist government's motto was simple: "Everything within the state, nothing against the state, nothing outside the state." The masses were told to "believe, obey, and fight." Mussolini did manage to boost factory production and agricultural output, and, yes, he did take credit for the trains running on time. But these were grim consolations for the vast majority of Italians. Life barely improved.

Mussolini was savvy enough to mend the rift between the papacy and the Kingdom of Italy, estranged since unification in 1870. That's when Italy's new rulers confiscated all lands owned by the papacy, which retreated behind the walls of the Vatican and refused to recognize the legitimacy of the newly unified Italian government and its king. In February 1929, through the Lateran Agreements, Mussolini pressed for a bargain, and the papacy, led by the admired and strong-willed Pope Pius XI, benefited enormously. To buy peace and lure Italian Catholics to his side, Mussolini declared Catholicism the only religion of Italy, mandated Catholic education in schools, and consented to church outreach. With the pope agreeing to give up all territorial claims to Rome and any lands beyond, Mussolini established the Vatican City as a sovereign state with the pope its recognized international leader, possessing full diplomatic rights. In return, the Vatican recognized the legitimacy of Mussolini's tyrannical government.

It may have been a deal with the devil, but Pope Pius XI got plenty of what he wanted, most important, international prestige and the right to send ambassadors anywhere in the world. Mussolini gained as well—mostly in a power grab with imperial aspirations that eventually led to his downfall in 1943. But having successfully dealt with the papacy problem, *Il Duce*, as he was called, went on in the following decade to double the size of his military, invade Ethiopia and Albania, cozy up to Adolph Hitler and his Nazi regime, and in 1940, join his crazed, murderous ally by entering World War II on the wrong side of history.

Down in Calabria, the people looked upon Mussolini's rule with some sense of hope at first. A trickle of public works projects—a few new roads and some new schools—fed that hope in the 1920s. But it didn't last. Idealistic government leaders in towns such as San Lorenzo and Melito di Porto Salvo became disillusioned and passed quietly to the opposition. The peasants merely resumed their age-old apathy and listlessness. It was their fate to suffer, they long assumed, like over-worked farm animals entirely lacking free will. For those who hadn't escaped to America, life was the same: hard. And when the Allies' bombs began raining on southern Italy in the early 1940s, life got harder still.

"Without fear of being accused of exaggerating," Padre Gaetano wrote, "we can state that we are faced with a disastrous present state of morality. The individual is demoralized. The family is in disarray. Society is in a constant state of upheaval. Iniquities are added to iniquities."

Paola Dal Toso explains that Padre Gaetano recognized the complex nature of the times he was living in, but his response, his message to his flock, was uncomplicated and consistent throughout the years.

"He was definitely not an intellectual, or a man of thought deeply rooted in the humanities," Dal Toso writes. "He was not the protagonist of an imposing social action, nor a revolutionary given to protest and demands. And yet he was a true priest, different, extraordinary, an ideal example of the good shepherd—perennially simple, poor, and capable of great charity."

But even the pure of heart, an uncompromised holy man, an eventual saint, can fall into trouble and despair. As Mussolini marched Italians headlong into another world war, Padre Gaetano faced his greatest crisis.

# 4

## Crown of Thorns

The archbishop of Reggio Calabria in the early 1930s, Monsignor Carmelo Pujia, was a great admirer of Padre Gaetano. He was proud of the priest's service and steadfast character. His trust was such that he made his confessions to Padre Gaetano, who heard similar emotional outpourings regularly at *il Duomo*, the enormous, Gothic-style cathedral in central Reggio. The cathedral had been rebuilt after the earthquake, just up from the waterfront.

For years, Monsignor Pujia had been struck by Padre Gaetano's determination to pull together this new order of nuns for its far-reaching mission of mercy. He offered his counsel and encouragement. In August 1934, when the archbishop was eighty-one years old, he went further— he offered his verbal approval to proceed with the founding, followed by his written approval at the end of that year. The founding of the Veronican sisters, and the idea that they would be made up entirely of peasant girls from the poor mountain villages, was a great story, even then.

The story, in fact, was written up in a local newspaper in Reggio Calabria. Not long after, a clipping made its way to the Vatican, to the Congregation of Religious Institutes, the office that retained for itself the authority to review applications and grant approval of religious orders within the Catholic Church. This was serious business, and it was how Padre Gaetano's troubles began. Requirements for the aptitude of novices and their spiritual formation were strictly spelled out by the Vatican for all those called to establish and serve in new orders. The novices needed to be carefully recruited and educated, not only in reading and writing, but also in theology and church service. It took little effort to discern that Padre Gaetano had not followed church rules in founding the Veronican sisters. The Vatican and its authoritarians were not happy. Regardless of Padre Gaetano's intentions, church officials could point to too many examples of orders being launched recklessly with no real religious foundation. In some circumstances and other orders, girls had been recruited, perhaps even captured, who were too young and too naïve to understand the commitment they were being asked to make. Some were mistreated. The church intended to guard against such abuse. Its spiritual credibility was at stake.

Thus, the elderly Monsignor Pujia was called on to explain his hasty decisions and was then reprimanded severely for failing to obtain the proper authorization before approving the new order of nuns. The old priest was mortified and wounded. He apologized profusely, arguing with due respect that he had been acting in good faith and in accordance with the pressing spiritual and social needs of his diocese. It did little good. When Monsignor Pujia died on August 20, 1937, the matter of congregation approval of the Veronican sisters was far from resolved.

The Vatican did not, however, order the Veronican sisters to disband. And Padre Gaetano, though he hungered for the kind of imprimatur that would make the sisters worthy in the eyes of his beloved church, forged ahead. He continued to distribute his wooden and cardboard alms boxes throughout Reggio and in all the villages where his nuns were preparing to work. Enough money came in for him to purchase small, one-story buildings in far-off places such as Bivongi and Roghudi to open nursery schools where there had been none. By 1940, with the country fully immersed in war and with more orphans being made every day, he had thirteen such shelters operating on meager budgets around southern Calabria, mostly in the mountains, as well as a few on the Tyrrhenian Seacoast in villages such as Scilla and Palmi just above Reggio.

"Ensure attendance at the nursery schools," he implored his sisters regarding those for whom he prayed the hardest—the children, the most innocent victims of the war. "Insist politely to the parents that they send the children. Always remember, it is among the children that one can breathe the most oxygenated air."

Service and outreach, however, was uneven at best in some locations. Despite the promises of newly recruited sisters, many washed out or fled before becoming full-fledged nuns, particularly the youngest teens. Padre Gaetano had underestimated the need for competent screening of novices and the amount of spiritual education it would take to transform them and develop their commitment, just as Vatican officials had feared. He described many of these mountain girls as "poor, really poor; ignorant, very ignorant." His own emotions ran the gamut. He preached often that patience is a virtue that must be practiced daily, and though he typically displayed the patience of a saint, his voice would rise and his temper would flare often enough to remind the nuns that this holy man was indeed human. There were other problems as well. In one particularly remote village, funds were so lacking that some of the nuns fell ill from hunger, forcing the founder to pray: "Lord, the sisters, they are your children, too, and you must provide for them." Mostly, though, the news that another young woman had left the sisterhood—either from deprivation or lack of commitment—reduced him to tears and the fear that he was failing, failing God.

Weary and heartsick, but far from despondent, Padre Gaetano made a special request in 1940 of the new archbishop of Reggio Calabria, Monsignor Enrico Montalbetti. He asked permission to retire as the parish priest of Candelora in Reggio, which he had led since 1921. At age sixty-one, and increasingly ailing from his diabetes, he wanted more time to focus on his troubled order of nuns. Thus he asked that his younger brother the priest, Don Pasquale Catanoso, be appointed to succeed him. It was not out of family favoritism that he requested Pasqualino, he explained. His brother, then forty-nine, was in far better health and had recently demonstrated his courage and spiritual commitment as a chaplain in northern Africa with invading Italian troops. "He is the best choice," Padre Gaetano said, and the archbishop agreed.

It wasn't exactly that he was slowing down. Padre Gaetano remained the chaplain for both the hospital and the prison in Reggio, making weekly visits to say Mass and hear confessions. He also heard confessions each day at the cathedral in the center of the city. Nuns and priests and parishioners of all kinds sought him out as their sole confessor. "At his feet for confession, or close to him, heart to heart, you were driven to tell him everything, to confide in him, and to pour into his good heart your own happiness, hopes and sorrows," recalled Don Basilio Guzzo, a Franciscan priest in Reggio. "He sympathized with and understood everything. He was dominated by Christ's charity."

Padre Gaetano also remained the spiritual director of the Archiepiscopal Seminary of Reggio, a position he held from 1922 to 1949. There he influenced scores of young priests who absorbed his teachings and living example and went on to become monsignors, bishops, and cardinals serving throughout Italy over the next fifty years or more.

"I had the great fate to be called to the priesthood," he would tell his seminarians. "The priest is 'alter Christus,' another Jesus. Between the eternal Father and man is Jesus. Between Jesus and man is the priest. For the priest to be like Jesus, he must live for others. He must always pray, never tiring. Jesus would pray entire nights. He worked all day, but during the night, He rested by praying. And so must you."

Even with all these responsibilities, his order of nuns remained his greatest concern. Monsignor Montalbetti said of Padre Gaetano, "The congregation was the joy and crown of the father, a crown of thorns for the trials to which he was subjected."

Whether intentionally or not, the archbishop applied some of the prickly thorns himself. A native of Venice, tall and erudite looking with wispy white hair and large, oval glasses, Monsignor Montalbetti carried himself with a regal bearing. He was drawn quickly to Padre Gaetano's goodness, and like his predecessors, the archbishop made the priest his confessor. But perhaps he pitied him, too. Some caught hints of northern Italian superiority, especially when he suggested that Padre Gaetano relinquish his supervision of the Veronican sisters and allow the order to merge with the better established and better trained Sisters of Maria Bambina, an order founded in and run from Milan. This was, to Padre Gaetano, unthinkable. Yes, there were problems with many of his mountain novices; the youngest were ill suited for the rigors of mind and spirit that were required to promote religious and social progress. But he believed fervently in his founding vision of the order and was determined to see it through.

"I wish for my sisters to be the last ones, the ones left aside, those not taken into consideration," he would say. "These missionaries of the Holy Face must be the ones who help the poor, who teach the Gospel to the children, who assist the dying, who help the old and sick priests, who pray always and do not leave Jesus alone as a prisoner of love inside so many desolate churches."

Padre Gaetano was known throughout his life for his unblinking obedience, at all times, to his superiors. In what for him amounted to a screaming, fist-pounding revolt, he told Monsignor Montalbetti in regard to his merger idea, "Excellency, let me think about it."

The moment was described as "a dagger to the founder's heart," and the archbishop no doubt sensed that. After a long silence from Padre Gaetano, he never suggested the merger again, choosing instead to help draft the first constitution for the Veronican sisters that would begin to establish the training they would require to receive Vatican authorization.

But there were daggers elsewhere. Several priests in the diocese made it clear to their brethren that Padre Gaetano was on a quixotic mission that was surely doomed to fail, possibly bringing embarrassment to the Calabrian clergy. The money he was raising was being wasted, they argued; they could make far better use of it in their urban parishes. Such criticism prompted Padre Gaetano, in 1941, to write a close friend: "I have my share of troubles. We are on the open sea. I have against me some of my dearest friends. They say that I am crazy. *Deo gratias*. Pray for me." (Looking back on that period, his friend Monsignor Vincenzo Lembo would say, "Indeed he *was* crazy, but crazy for God, like all great Saints are.")

Padre Gaetano clearly needed a respite, a change of scenery. At the height of these challenges, the Brothers of Divine Providence invited him to Tortona, just outside Genoa in northern Italy, to pray at the tomb of Don Luigi Orione, who had died a year earlier, in March

1940. Don Orione had been his confidante during the planning stages for the Veronican sisters. Padre Gaetano felt a profound loss after his friend's death and hastened to make his travel plans. The brothers did something else as well. Don Orione had been an acquaintance of Pope Pius XII, and the brothers, whose order was founded by Orione in 1898, were able to arrange an audience with the pope for Padre Gaetano during his travels. They viewed it as a golden opportunity for the Calabrian priest to plead his case for the Veronican sisters directly to the Supreme Pontiff himself.

Returning from Tortona by train on September 11, 1941, Padre Gaetano stopped in Rome and made his way to the Vatican for his special appointment. It is remarkable that the pope made time for such visits. Having assumed the papacy in 1939 on the eve of World War II, Pope Pius XII found the war a near-constant preoccupation. His controversial position of neutrality was under relentless siege. Critics whispered then, as they shout today, that Pius was a Nazi sympathizer and a Hitler enabler who was indifferent to the plight of European Jews. That fall, Harold Tittman, the U.S. delegate to the Vatican, asked the pope to publicly condemn the atrocities of the Holocaust. But Pius insisted on remaining neutral, saying privately that he feared that such statements would only endanger Catholics in German-held lands. As devastating as such positions appear in hindsight, history also records that Pius gave secret approval for the safe sheltering of thousands of Roman Jews in church properties throughout the city.

At the appointed time for private audiences that late summer day in 1941, the pope's secretary introduced an elderly, balding priest dressed in a black cassock who, while leaning on a cane, walked past a set of medieval-garbed Swiss guards. Padre Gaetano's heart no doubt raced as he crossed the room with a smile of pure reverence. He was overwhelmed to be in the presence of such holiness. There in his high-backed, thronelike chair sat the Bishop of Rome, the Vicar of Christ, the Successor to the Prince of the Apostles . . . the pope, his holy leader. Pius looked exactly as Padre Gaetano imagined—hollow-cheeked and serious, his penetrating eyes framed by round, gold-rimmed glasses sitting atop a classic Roman nose. He was dressed in papal white with his ankle-length simar and short, white cape, or *mozzetta*, over his shoulders. All this white made his gold pectoral cross, hanging from a thick, gold chain, stand out even more. The pope sat amid the trappings of a king, and he played the part, holding out his right hand so that Padre Gaetano, who had dropped to his knees, could kiss his bulbous ring. As the priest rose to his feet, Pius asked the reason for the visit and what request his visitor might have.

The door was opened, but where to start? With the chronic poverty and ignorance afflicting the peasants of the lower Aspromonte? With the difficulty in gathering trained nuns to live and serve in such poor, forgotten areas? With a plea for understanding of the late Monsignor Pujia's well-intentioned approval of the founding of the Veronican sisters, which so angered the pope's bureaucrats?

Unfortunately, none of those questions came immediately to mind. Padre Gaetano was unable to become in that moment something he was not—a political operator, a deal maker, or a peer seeking a favor. It was not in his heart. When he got himself to speak, he said, "I ask only your blessing, Holy Father, for me, my nuns, the children of my institutes, and those who are dear to me." Pope Pius XII did so, lavishly, perhaps even gratefully given the worldly demands on him at the time. And the old priest left.

When he returned to Reggio, Padre Gaetano's church friends and Monsignor Montalbetti, the archbishop, were eager to hear about his papal audience, eager to learn if the crisis of authorization had been resolved. He could only laugh at his own meekness and tell them, "As soon as I exited the room, I remembered about the matter of the approval of the congregation. But by now, the opportunity had passed and there was nothing to be done. But—I received the pope's blessing from the pontiff himself. And for me, one of the Lord's little donkeys, that is enough."

# 5

# *Americans*

The row houses in South Philadelphia were casting long shadows as Carmelo Catanoso walked up Dickinson from the trolley stop on Fifteenth Street. He had left in darkness that fall morning in 1926 to catch the train across the Delaware River to southern New Jersey. That day he had been to Vineland, Bridgeton, and Millville, towns brimming with Italian immigrants and Italian-American grocery stores. As a salesman for his brother-in-law's wholesale import company, Rosa Food Products, he knew all the stores in Cumberland and Camden counties. A new grocer he called on in Vineland wanted to know why he should stock Rosa canned tomatoes. Carmelo was not a talker, not prone to waving his arms and making a fuss. Five foot six with broad shoulders, he cut a professional figure in his brown wool suit. His thick, curly brown hair was piled high and brushed over, and he pinched up the corners of his mustache with wax. He may have come from the land of poor peasants, but he never thought of himself that way.

*"Mi lasci spiegare."* Let me explain, Carmelo began to tell the grocer in Italian. "The San Marzano tomato is the best in the world. It is grown in the rich soil outside Naples, which is nourished by the lava of Mount Vesuvius. You know the area, no? Now, the tomatoes ripen on the vine and are packed with no salt. None. That makes them less fibrous, easier to cook down into sauce. *Ecco*, let me show you." Carmelo peeled back

the lid of the can to reveal the pungent, bloodred fruit nestled in its own pulpy juices. The grocer lifted one out with his pocketknife and slit it in half on the counter. *"Bene, bene,"* he said, nodding his head. "Send me three cases."

As Carmelo approached his three-story house at 1520 Dickinson Street, he saw his two oldest sons, Anthony and Leonard (my father), running with the kids from the block, kicking a ball in the last light of the day. Leona was sitting on the marble stoop out front, cradling her baby brother, Joseph. Little Mary was next to her, tugging on the baby's leather shoes. The eldest of the children, Elizabeth and Bessie, not yet teenagers, were inside helping their mother with dinner. It was Monday night. That meant Caterina Catanoso, pregnant now for the eighth time in the last fourteen years, was preparing a kettle of thick escarole soup made with chicken stock and flavored with garlic, flecks of beaten egg, and little hunks of ground beef. Mary spotted her father approaching. She told Leona and called out to her brothers, but none of the children rushed down the street to greet him. They waited. Carmelo was a hard worker and a solid provider; he was not effusive with his children. *Buona sera, Papa,* they said as they stood together when he reached the stoop, Anthony and Leonard itching to get back to their game. *Buona sera,* he said, leaning over to rub the baby's cheek.

Carmelo Catanoso could take great pride in this scene. A big family. A house big enough to hold them. And a pantry stocked well enough to keep them fed. He was nearly thirty-nine and had spent more than half his life in America. When he landed at Ellis Island as a sixteen-year-old, sailing right past the Statue of Liberty, he probably thought, as many Italian immigrants did, that she was merely waving, "Hello, have a nice visit!" He would stay a few years, he figured, save a small fortune, and return to his family in Chorio to find a bride. It would not have been unusual. Of the four and a half million Italians to arrive in America between 1880 and 1924, at least two million of them returned. For many of those, tenement life in the sad urban slums of Boston, New York, and Philadelphia had been more miserable than the villages they left behind in Italy. But once Carmelo quit his monotonous, low-wage job in the Stetson Hat Factory in South Philly and began working as a salesman for his in-laws, the Foti family, the real promise of America opened up to him like the genuine meaning of Lady Liberty: If you worked hard and lived frugally, you would be rewarded. Unlike in Italy, where the notion of getting ahead was as foreign as good government, Carmelo could dream of a better life for himself and his family. More important, he could actually see a way to get from here to there. He gladly became a naturalized American citizen on June 14, 1922, forever turning his back on his homeland.

That night, after dinner, after the children had gone to bed—the four girls in one room, the three boys in another—Carmelo spoke with Caterina of his dreams, and his concerns. He was ready to be his own man, he told her, ready to run his own shop. Don't get me wrong, he explained, the Fotis have been most generous. For years, in fact, he and his in-laws ran a side business from the front parlor of the Dickinson Street house—the Riposta Loan Company, named after the Sicilian fishing village from which the Fotis emigrated. They hired a secretary, Mary D'Angelo, to keep track of the five- and ten-dollar loans to their Italian neighbors, paid back at a rate of fifty cents a week. The extra money earned in interest, split among the four owners, eased Caterina's worries when shopping for meats at Bonelli's on Hicks Street or milk and cheese at Abbots Dairy on Tasker. It also helped make possible the dreams Carmelo was now describing.

He had found a two-story bungalow on New York Avenue near Eighteenth Street in North Wildwood. The shore town near the southern tip of New Jersey was becoming more than a sleepy fishing village. Now it had Victorian-style hotels, a raised wooden boardwalk along the beachfront, and a growing population. Having both grown up on or near the sea in Calabria and Sicily, Carmelo and Caterina took their children to the seashore of Wildwood every summer, eager to get away from the city's fetid heat and happy to see their children playing in the sand and surf. Unlike "America's Playground" at the time, Atlantic City, which was thirty miles north and much more developed, the five-mile-long barrier island of Wildwood offered pure opportunity. Irish, Swedish, and increasingly, Italian families lived there year round and more were moving in. The summers were always busy with day-trippers and vacationers riding the train from Philly to the depot on Seventeenth Street and New Jersey Avenue.

Nowhere on the island could you find an Italian-American grocery. Carmelo knew the business as well as any other; he wanted to open the first one. He told Caterina that the two-story bungalow on New York Avenue was one block from the sound, or canal as they called it, two blocks from the rail depot, and four blocks from the beach. *Perfetto.* The house could be raised up and the store could be built underneath. Jack Foti, his boss and his wife's older brother, had agreed to loan him the money to make it happen.

Slow down, Caterina protested, fixing the combs she used to keep her short wavy hair in place. She was a stout and proud woman with a round face and soft eyes, just over five feet tall. Caterina was close to her brothers and sister, their children, and her many cousins. They all lived in Philly, and their house on Dickinson was where the family always gathered. She was not ready to leave. But Carmelo had worries besides his dreams. The neighborhood around Dickinson was changing. The more prosperous Italians were moving to bigger houses across town. Racial tension was building as black families moved in and gangs of kids were forming. Knife fights were not uncommon. "How many times," he asked his wife, "do we need to see blood washed from our sidewalk?"

And then there was Anthony, the oldest son, whom everyone called Tony. He was a smart kid, the only one in the family with a knack for learning and speaking Italian. But trouble chased him down like a pushcart peddler after an elfin pickpocket. Carmelo had found cigarettes in Tony's coat. The boy was ten, mind you. He knew his son's black eye was from a fistfight, not a football game. And now he was in a gang, the Hicks Street gang, a pack of young Italian hooligans who confronted the new gang of black kids in the neighborhood every chance they got. The strap Carmelo used to discipline his son, grabbed from the back of the basement door, was hardly a deterrent. He shouldn't have been surprised. Tony, like all his children, was half *Calabrese* and half *Siciliano*, wild and hard-headed times two.

Carmelo had made up his mind. "This city is no longer the place I want to raise my family," he told his wife. "We are Americans now. We have choices. We are going to move."

Caterina! I need a chicken!" Carmelo called up while leaning out of the side door of the North Wildwood Italian-American Grocery. Caterina, who had spent the morning doing laundry by hand, had cleaned the kitchen after lunch, and was now slicing carrots and potatoes in preparation for dinner. She dropped what she was doing. Coming down the side steps of the house, which was perched atop the store, she walked into the backyard to the chicken coop and cornered a clucking, darting, white-feathered bird. Laughing gulls, like beach buzzards, hovered in a slow circle above. The warm, summer afternoon smelled of salt air. With one swift motion, Caterina rung the chicken's neck on the way to the open garage where a large kettle of water was kept over a low boil. Soon she had drained the chicken of its blood, dipped it in the boiling pot, and stripped it of its feathers. Carmelo was waiting to wrap it in brown paper. Inside the store, the place was bustling. Customers perused the fruit and produce stands out front under the broad canvas awning. Grapes, for local Italians to make their wine, overflowed their crates. Inside, they wandered the three aisles stacked with cans of tomato sauce, jars of olives, and boxes of pasta, most of them Rosa brands. They lined up at the butcher counter for fresh seafood and meats.

Carmelo and Caterina Catanoso moved their family to North Wildwood, New Jersey, in the summer of 1927, shortly after their eighth child, Charles, was born. The store was a success from the start. In many ways, it insulated the family from the hardships of the Great Depression. There was always business in the summer, even during the worst of times. Small annual bank loans, diligent savings, and food from the store sustained the family, even if it was only beans and macaroni, the rest of the year, all the way through the 1930s. They were never rich; clothes passed from sister to sister, brother to brother until they disintegrated into rags. But they were never poor, either.

Carmelo saw to it that the store helped others as well. He "sold" food on credit to his customers who had no jobs and no money. He carefully listed the credits alphabetically on index cards in file boxes, trusting that those neighbors would pay up when the hard times passed. Many didn't. But still, the store managed to remain afloat. Carmelo took care of the butchering, a skill he taught himself. He made sausage, too. In the busy summer months, he added a second butcher. His work-force, though, consisted mainly of his children, all of whom dutifully swept the floors and stocked the shelves. On weekends, when other kids in the neighborhood were organizing football and baseball games, the Catanoso kids were with their father, working. And none worked harder than Leonard, my father. Carmelo would rise at 6:00 A.M. and Leonard would be right behind him, squeezing out of bed between his three brothers, who all shared one cramped room on the third floor of the house (the ninth and final child, Peter, came in 1931).

After a quick breakfast of hot chocolate and toast, Leonard would join his father in the store downstairs. He was the athlete in the fam-ily, strong and lean, the star of his junior high school's football and basketball teams. Helping unload the bread truck from the Marine Bakery at 6:30 and stack the racks with warm loaves was no trouble for him. Then he would dash out back to gather eggs from the chicken coop. By seven, when the store opened with his father behind the cash register, Leonard had washed down the sidewalk out front and swept the aisles clean inside.

During the day, even when he was as young as twelve years old, Leonard would climb behind the wheel of his father's Ford panel truck and drive it a few hundred feet to the back of the property. That's where a small warehouse stood. He would load it with boxes of dry goods or wheels of hard cheese and then pull back up to the store to unload. He learned to drive that way; all the kids did. Sometimes, when Tony was with him, they would linger in the warehouse a while and "test" the cheese. They would carefully cut a long plug out of the middle of a wheel of provolone, eat the ends, and replug the hole. They never got caught.

Meanwhile, Carmelo didn't just wait for business to come to him. Customers would phone in their orders and he would pack them in boxes and send Tony or Leonard off to make the deliveries. He also arranged to stock the galley kitchens of fishing boats that would leave from Cold Spring Harbor in Cape May for two weeks at a time on mackerel runs. The brothers filled the Ford with voluminous orders of steaks and chops, loaves of bread, and crates of fruits and vegetables. Then they went along with Carmelo on the ten-mile drive down Route 9 to deliver the provisions boatside at the docks to the fishermen. Often, they made another stop. There was an Italian shoemaker who lived across the street from the marina. When Carmelo would deliver groceries there, the shoemaker—in old-country commerce at its best—would pay him, not in cash, but in shoes for the children.

For hours during the day, particularly in summers, father, sons, and daughters worked side by side—mostly in silence. Carmelo was strict and demanding, and the children did not ask of him that which he could not give—warm, physical affection. They got that from their mother in loving, open-armed abundance, and it instilled in all the children a fierce devotion. Carmelo had become, whether he recognized it or not, the traditional American father: quiet, hard-working, and aloof. Rarely did he attend church. They were a Catholic family, of course, and the children were all baptized. At a time in Calabria when his cousin Gaetano was immersing himself in the depths and devotion of an ancient religion and bent on saving souls, Carmelo dutifully sent his children to St. Ann's Church on Atlantic Avenue in Wildwood every Sunday but remained back at the store, bent on providing for his family.

Carmelo was not a storyteller, either. He didn't regale any of his children with tales from Chorio or of his crossing the Atlantic to start a new life. He did belong to a couple of Italian-American clubs in North Wildwood. Maybe there, in privacy shrouded by home-made wine and cigar smoke, he talked about Chorio or the impact of Mussolini's fascism on his relatives back home. But with his children, *niente*, nothing. They barely knew they had an aunt, Maria Portzia Catanoso, in Calabria. They had no idea they had scores of Italian cousins. This was typical of many immigrant parents, who turned away from their past like a bad memory, blocking it out altogether or guarding it like a haunted secret. Either way, they were Americans now, and Americans looked forward.

There was one stark, daily reminder of the family's immigrant origins: Antonino Catanoso and Elisabetta Mangiola, Carmelo's parents from Chorio. Twice they came to visit the family in South Philly. When they planned to visit a third time, Carmelo told them flatly: I cannot afford to keep paying your way back and forth. If you come again, you must plan to stay. They did. Initially, it was thought that the parents would move in with their eldest son, Giuseppe, who still lived in Philadelphia with his wife and one daughter. They certainly had room. But the wife, Giuseppe's second, absolutely refused; she threatened to leave her husband if he took in his parents. He didn't fight her. Reluctantly, Giuseppe informed his brother of the bad news, to which Carmelo said, I'll take them.

It wasn't easy, especially for Caterina. There were now thirteen people living in the four-bedroom bungalow above the grocery store on New York Avenue. Each meal was a multigenerational banquet, played out three times a day in two languages. At the long, dining room table, order ruled. Carmelo insisted that the children speak only when spoken to. More and more, they spoke only English. The parents wandered in and out of both Italian and English. The grandparents spoke only Italian, mostly dialect. Worse, they dressed like ancient museum pieces from an unknown world, always in black, always formal. The grandfather was small with narrow shoulders and a white mustache; the grandmother retained hints of her youthful beauty with smooth skin and long, silver hair always braided and wrapped in a bun. Elisabetta's ankle-length dresses were puffed up with five layers of petticoats, which served as secret chambers for hidden oddities. She would reach somewhere down inside and pull out a piece of hardtack to offer one of the grandchildren. They thought it would break their teeth. Mostly, the old couple spent their days in their bedroom, saying their prayers. The children found their grandparents strange and kept their distance. Only Tony, the oldest son, talked to them very much—honing an ear and knack for speaking Italian that would serve him well later. But like his siblings, he never asked much about where his grandparents came from or what they left behind. They were a bridge to a past that the children had no interest in crossing. Still, Carmelo insisted on respect, even to the point of having his children line up on holidays to kiss the hands of their grandparents. They hated it.

They weren't crazy about being Italians, either—which surely wiped out whatever interest they might have had in their cultural roots. North Wildwood had plenty of Italians, immigrant families named Versaggi, Cafiero, Olivieri, Sicilia, Mattera. But there were far more families with names like Baker, Davis, Colson, Dietrich, McGlinley. The Italians were the last ethnic group to arrive, and given the usual prejudices of the American immigrant pecking order, the most reviled. "Get over here!" young Charlie heard the father of one of his neighborhood friends growl when they were all swimming in the canal down the street. "I don't want you playing with those dirty dagos."

Leonard and his older sister Leona were often taunted on the way home from Margaret Mace School by an Irish bully who kept shouting "dago" and "wop" at them. When Leonard finally had enough, he took off after the kid, who plunked him on the head with a rock. Bleeding, my father attacked and was joined quickly by Leona, who dropped her books and was one step behind. Brother and sister flailed at their provocateur, pinned to the sidewalk, until he promised to stop his taunts. Tony, now a skinny teenager, was the real family enforcer; he would "fight at the drop of a stick" to defend himself or any of his siblings.

Still, the persistent sneers and catcalls of prejudice had a way of burrowing deep inside, producing a nagging feeling in the pit of their stomachs. They wouldn't say it aloud, but the children were embarrassed by their ethnicity. They cringed when their parents spoke Italian to them in front of their friends. They did their best to brush the curls out of their dark brown hair. They wanted to be Americans. Only Americans.

# 6

## *World War II*

In the winter of 1941, the Catanoso family in North Wildwood, New Jersey, had fallen into a comfortable rhythm. Carmelo was fifty-three years old, Caterina nearly fifty. They had survived the Depression largely intact. Carmelo's mother had died the previous year, but she had been in her nineties. His eldest daughter, Elizabeth, had recently married a fine Italian young man and was living just up the coast in Sea Isle City. Leonard, my father, at the middle of the nine children, was halfway through his sophomore year as a physical education major at Penn State College in central Pennsylvania. This was a profound achievement. Not that my father wasn't college material. He was a hard worker, just like his father. But he was also a diligent student, something his father had never been. In fact, neither Carmelo nor Caterina had completed much more than a year or two of formal education back in Italy and none in America.

But Leonard was fortunate. He had a mentor, Elwood Chester, the principal of the junior high school and one of the most influential men in town. Mr. Chester thought the world of my father and made sure he kept his grades up. He was the one who planted the seed about going to college. Penn State was his idea; he had a friend there who helped my father get admitted. Carmelo and Caterina were dubious. Nine children. Who can afford college? But they saw Leonard's determination, respected it, and didn't stand in the way. With a mixture of confusion and pride, they watched their son follow a uniquely American path.

Remarkably, at five foot six and barely 130 pounds, Leonard had been offered a football scholarship based on his daring runs as a halfback for the Warriors of Wildwood High School. This was years before Penn State, then a rural outpost in the middle of the state with about sixty-seven hundred students, became a football factory. In 1939, my father's scholarship essentially meant he was given a job making a few bucks waiting on tables at the McAllister Hall dormitory on campus. He needed the job, as most students did in the aftermath of the Depression. Tuition was $69 a semester, plus $10 a week for room and board. Students were issued ration stamps for scarce items such as sugar, butter, coffee, and beef. Even though his sisters Leona and Mary silently yearned for the opportunity, Leonard was the only one of his siblings to go to college. And he paid his own way—with the help of the meager salary his father offered at the grocery store, but mostly from sneaking off to work as a lifeguard on the North Wildwood beach patrol during the summer. Football, though, didn't suit him. He went to one practice and felt dwarfed by the other players. He opted for gymnastics, soccer, and lacrosse, all of which he played at the varsity level. He was also in the Army ROTC. With World War II underway in Europe, ROTC was compulsory for all freshmen and sophomore men on campus, which came to resemble a military base as students in uniform marched in formations between classes.

The rest of the family continued to live at home above the store on New York Avenue. Now they numbered eleven. After the store was closed for the day, after the dinner dishes were cleaned and put away, they would gather around the console model RCA radio in the living room and listen to programs such as *The Shadow Knows* and *The Lone Ranger*. Peter, the youngest, "the little king" as his older siblings called him, curled up happily on Carmelo's lap. The usually distant family patriarch tended to show the baby of the family uncommon affection. Meanwhile, the newsreels at Hunt's movie house on Atlantic Avenue in Wildwood brought reports of the war in Western Europe. But

President Roosevelt seemed intent, at least in early 1941, on remaining neutral. Even though Mussolini decided on behalf of Italy to enter World War II on the side of Hitler's Third Reich, North Wildwood was a long way from all that trouble. There, life was good. But for the Catanoso family, it was about to come off the rails.

On Wednesday, February 12, 1941, the family gathered for a big Italian dinner—spaghetti with tuna fish gravy (Italian-Americans still call tomato sauce gravy). Carmelo enjoyed two large helpings and complained afterward of indigestion. Yet he and Caterina had promised to visit their new in-laws in Sea Isle City and so they made the thirty-minute drive from North Wildwood after dinner. On the way home, just as they reached the northern end of the island, Carmelo began to feel a tightness in his chest. The pain grew so sharp so fast that he clutched his hands over his heart. Caterina, trying not to panic, leaned over to steer the car the last mile to their driveway beside the store. She helped her husband out of the car and up the side steps, shouting for the children to come quick. Tony, the oldest son, was at a junior high school basketball game a few blocks away, and Bessie was chaperoning Mary at a dance at the community hall at St. Ann's Church. Leona, then twenty-two, and Joseph and Charlie, both teenagers, charged downstairs from their bedrooms to help their father. He was on the living room floor. After they got him to the couch, the drama intensified. It's indigestion, Caterina insisted. All that tuna fish gravy he ate. But Carmelo kept writhing and moaning in pain. Leona ran to call Dr. McCloud, their regular physician. He wasn't in. She called Dr. Cohen, who rushed right over. He knew immediately what was happening: heart attack. Dr. Cohen filled a long needle with adrenaline, opened Carmelo's shirt, and pushed the needle into his chest. Maybe he was gone already, maybe not. But Caterina shrieked in Italian, "You're killing him! You're killing my husband!" When she started after the doctor, her children rushed to head her off. She was sobbing in Leona's arms when Tony got home. By then, it was all over.

The next morning, the day my father began hitchhiking his way home from State College, Pennsylvania, Charlie came downstairs to someone banging on the kitchen door. It was Tony Finacaro from the Marine Bakery. What the *hell* is the matter with you people, he ranted, waving his arms. It's seven o'clock. The store isn't open. I've got a delivery here. "Mr. Finacaro," Charlie said softly, his voice cracking, tears rolling down his cheeks, "my pop died last night." The bread man gasped as he brought his hands to his face. Then he did something Charlie never forgot. He took off his snap-brim cap and threw it down on the landing. *Sonuvabitch!* he yelled and began to sob himself.

The obituary in *The Wildwood Leader,* under the headline "Carmelo Catanoso, Grocer Here Dies," said my grandfather was "prominent in Italian-American circles in Cape May County and well known to scores of residents throughout this area." It also noted that he was a member of the North Wildwood Fire Department, the North Wildwood Republican Club, the Italian-American Citizens' Club, and the Sons of Italy.

Carmelo was buried in the Catholic cemetery in Cold Spring near Cape May on February 14, which was also Padre Gaetano Catanoso's sixty-second birthday.

Trouble, which Carmelo had always been able to hold at bay, now stalked the family. Caterina agonized over how she was going to take care of her children, her ninety-five-year-old father-in-law, and now the grocery store. Don't worry, Ma, Tony told her; I can handle it. His troublemaking days were behind him. He had been working with his father ever since he dropped out of Wildwood High during his sophomore year, after plunking the shop teacher on the head with a block of wood intended for a classmate.

Leonard said he would withdraw from Penn State, immediately, and work with Tony at the store. But Leona, his closest friend and confidante, wouldn't hear of it. "You're going back to college," his sister insisted, and he went until he finished.

Things got worse still. That summer, Caterina was in a terrible car accident that hospitalized her for months with a badly broken leg. By the end of that awful year, 1941, she was still recovering as the United States entered the war—against Italy, no less. Soon her four oldest sons would join the military to serve their country. They were, after all, Americans. By 1944, she was proud of the four blue stars she displayed in the living room window overlooking New York Avenue (better than gold stars, which were hung when a family's sons were killed in action). But the absence of Tony, Leonard, Joseph, and Charlie over the next several years proved too great.

For nearly two decades, she and her family had been sustained by and lived happily above her husband's immigrant dream come true, a successful American business. But the bills piled up. The loans Carmelo took out to float the store between summers came due. Caterina couldn't keep it going and was forced to sell.

Meanwhile in Italy, it wasn't long before the problems besetting the Veronican sisters were overshadowed by the escalating nature of the war. In 1943, British and American forces, sweeping upward from Libya, invaded and occupied Sicily and began an episodic bombing campaign of southern Italy. On January 31, a British reconnaissance plane mistook a police-escorted procession of dark-colored vehicles for a military convoy moving along just outside Melito di Porto Salvo on the southern tip of Calabria. A burst of machine-gun fire strafed the lead car, killing everyone inside. The victims were not Mussolini's armed guard. They were clergymen from Reggio on a pastoral visit to the cathedral in Anna. The archbishop of Reggio Calabria, Monsignor Enrico Montalbetti, then fifty-three, was among the dead. By 10:30 that night, word reached the seminary in Reggio about the deaths. Don Giuseppe Agostino, a young priest who was supposed to accompany the archbishop that day, received the startling news. Not knowing what else to do, he woke Padre Gaetano, who also lived at the seminary. Noticing Don Agostino's agitation, the older priest responded, "Remain calm. Everything is a mystery. *In domino.*"

Together, they went out on foot to inform Monsignor Montalbetti's mother.

"It is late and you have not retired for the night," said the mother, Carolina Portman, answering her door. "Has something happened?"

Rather than explain, Padre Gaetano bowed his head and said barely above a whisper, *"In domino."* Clutching her hands to her heart, the woman understood at once. "God is passing through my life," she moaned and invited the priests inside her home. There, in a small chapel, she fell to her knees and, with anguished cries, prayed for nearly an hour. To the young priest with him, Padre Gaetano urged, "Remain still. Don't move. Adore God in this moment and take example from this great mother."

"At times he seemed naïve," Don Agostino recalled later, "but instead he had a shrewd depth. So it could be understood that his was a suffered peace, a word matured in silence, a smile born of real passion."

Returning to the seminary in the middle of the night, the two priests roused the others to meet in the chapel, where Padre Gaetano led them in prayer. "He had such a presence," Don Agostino recalled. "That evening remained with me as a vital lesson on the meaning of faith."

The war put Padre Gaetano's faith in perspective. Another errant bombing attack in May 1943 struck the seminary, located just behind the cathedral in Reggio. Six seminarians and three priests were killed. Padre Gaetano was uninjured but not unaffected. His heart shattered at the sight of so many innocent lives lost all around him. His young nephew, Natale Catanoso, and his teenage friend, Bruno Mangiola, were living at the seminary at the time and fled together right after the bombing. They took the first train from Reggio to Melito di Porto Salvo, then walked the remaining ten kilometers up to their homes in Chorio. Neither would become a priest.

The new archbishop of Reggio, Monsignor Antonio Lanza, a native of Cosenza in Calabria, arrived in August 1943. He quickly enlisted the assistance of Padre Gaetano to help hold the diocese and its frightened parishioners together during the worst of the war. Monsignor Lanza, young looking with straight dark hair and an open face, developed a great affection and admiration for Padre Gaetano. And so, with his background in teaching theology and canonic law, the archbishop set about to get the Veronican sisters properly educated and trained.

Padre Gaetano resisted at first. "Yes, Excellency, my sisters lack an education, they lack training," he told Monsignor Lanza. "But, Excellency, they have humility and a spirit of sacrifice." It wasn't enough for the archbishop, and it wasn't enough for the Vatican, if it was ever going to grant its spiritual recognition of the order. Drastic measures needed to be taken. In 1946, Monsignor Lanza undertook the painful step of removing Padre Gaetano as the sisters' leader and spiritual guide. He believed it was the only way to resolve the impasse over Vatican authorization. Padre Gaetano was crushed. But in keeping with his disciplined spirit of obedience, he accepted the decision and what turned out to be a five-year separation from his beloved nuns.

"The Lord is always with you; do not be daunted or afraid, but have faith," he wrote to two of his Veronican sisters: "One of our great servants of our Lord, Don Orione, would always say, 'Ave Maria e avanti!' Hail Mary and go forth. So it behooves us now to repeat that, not once, but a thousand times."

Padre Gaetano was severely tested during this forced separation. Monsignor Lanza called on a Benedictine nun from Rome, Mother Raffaella, to move to Reggio to oversee the religious education of the existing Veronican sisters, as well as those new to the order. She worked from the Monastery of Visitation in Reggio, a kind of seminary for nuns. To keep the "Padre Catanoso shelters" open in the villages, the nuns were called to the city in groups of twenty, in a rotating fashion, for a period of training. They attended lectures. They studied Scripture. They learned about the liturgy and the elements of the Mass. They read and prayed and sang. This educational process, which lasted about a year, was not nearly so rigorous as that prescribed for male seminarians. Still, the idea was to prepare their minds and souls for a life of Christian service.

Mother Raffaella was by most accounts horrid. Stern and sharp-tongued, she belittled many of the peasant novices, reducing them to tears. When the sisters weren't studying, she put them to work as if they were actually training to become chambermaids. Those who complained she rebuked as cowards. And she spoke not at all about their mission in the mountain villages, as if the Veronican sisters' reason to be had ceased to exist.

This was a cruel lesson for Padre Gaetano as well, who learned from his priest friends about the conditions at the monastery, located just a few blocks from the seminary where he lived. They urged him to report Mother Raffaella's abuses of authority to Monsignor Lanza, but for several years, he remained silent. This was God's plan, he believed; it was happening for a reason. His rosary, a band of thick, delicately carved wooden beads, was seldom out of his hands. Suffer and offer, he prayed throughout the day. And when he visited the nuns, which he was permitted to do, he encouraged them to do the same. Suffer and offer. Most did, but several of the novices refused to endure the mistreatment. They dropped out and returned home.

After a couple of years, Padre Gaetano broke his silence, urged to do so by his close friend Monsignor Italo Calabro, the vicar of the cathedral in Reggio. To the archbishop, Padre Gaetano said, "It is good that they receive their spiritual formation at the monastery, but they also must prepare to leave the monastery and reenter the world in order to bring Jesus to the youngest and the poorest. They must descend from Mount Tabor to return to the roads of Palestine."

Monsignor Lanza listened patiently and agreed that a change was needed. He sent Mother Raffaella back to Rome. In 1951, Padre Gaetano was gratefully reinstated as the leader of the Veronican sisters. He was seventy-two years old, recently retired from his position as spiritual director of the seminary, and ecstatic. Along with his most seasoned and trusted nuns, he would resume his recruitment of new novices to the order and oversee their education at the monastery. Because of the established reputation of the Veronican sisters, and despite their travails, young village women eager to become nuns would make their way to Reggio to appeal to Padre Gaetano for acceptance into the order.

Following his retirement, he had taken to living in the Santo Spirito district in Reggio, a mile or so up the city's winding streets from the cathedral. It was a crowded, shabby-looking neighborhood. It is where the city's poor, working people lived in three- and four-story apartment buildings made of drab cinder block. This suited Padre Gaetano fine, as did the neighborhood's name, Holy Ghost, to which he had dedicated his entire life. With his constant alms-box collections and generous support from Catanoso relatives and affluent parishioners, he was able to purchase a corner property there that contained little more than some sheds and a modest house big enough for him to share with several of the older sisters, including his first mother superior, Sister Anastasia Mazzeo. These landholdings became the first Mother House for the Veronican sisters. Padre Gaetano envisioned later building a large Mother House for all his nuns, an adjoining nursery school, and eventually, a church in honor of the Holy Face of Christ. He viewed these plans, these prayerful dreams, as his life's crowning achievement.

But now, in the 1950s, he was saddled by advancing age and infirmities. Stiff from arthritis and nagged by a painful hernia, he still said Mass every day, though now while sitting down in the small, makeshift chapel across from his room. With a plain, wooden kneeler next to his desk in the same room that held his iron twin bed, he still heard confessions. He still made appeals to his supporters and relatives for the financial assistance of his nuns and the building plans he had in Santo Spirito. And he still received visits from Catanoso family members every Saturday, serving as their moral and spiritual counselor. The gentleness of his spirit seemed only to deepen. Seeing the end of his days in the not-too-distant future and believing that, God willing, a place awaited him in heaven, he laughed more heartily and smiled more radiantly, reclaiming the childlike simplicity for which he was known as a young priest.

"He appeared almost as a Biblical figure in his old age, as he lived with dignity even within his poverty," his friend Monsignor Vincenzo Lembo wrote. Indeed, Padre Gaetano accumulated few possessions in his life beyond some books, a few colorful priestly vestments of white and purple and trimmed in gold, and the glass and silver altar vessels he needed to say Mass and offer Holy Communion. He also had several sets of rosary beads. As he did with money his entire life, he gave away most of his belongings to the church several years before he died. He wanted only in his final years to be available to those he loved and those who needed him.

Visiting him in his room in those twilight years was a memorable experience. Don Giuseppe Agostino, who was with Padre Gaetano the night Monsignor Montalbetti was killed and who later went on to become the archbishop of Cosenza, made frequent visits. The priest's small room, he said, with its plain plaster walls and a marble floor was a "joyous shelter, a mysterious habitat." When he would arrive, Padre

Gaetano would be seated in a wooden armchair leaning over his desk. He used a magnifying glass, along with his glasses, to read from the papers and leaflets scattered about. A silver crucifix on a pedestal sat on the far corner of the desktop. There were alms boxes piled there, too, and a strange item that fascinated adults and frightened children—a human skull, a stark reminder of the brevity of life.

"This room was like a harbor for so many shipwrecked souls, a safe landing of truth and peace for lost men and priests longing for authenticity," Don Agostino wrote. "On the kneeling stool, when I would confess, the sunken, empty orbits of the skull appeared to me like an opening to the final mystery of humanity. In fact, Padre Gaetano used to tell us, in pointing to the skull, that death opens us up to life, showing us those orbits as openings to the world beyond."

Once, when Don Agostino walked across the room to open the window above the bed, he noticed a barbed-metal cilice partially visible beneath the sheets. "I understood then that my spiritual father was crowned with the cross," he wrote. That elective, self-induced pain—so difficult for outsiders to understand—illustrated the determination of the priest to live in all ways through Christ. If Jesus freely chose death to atone for the sins of mankind, then Padre Gaetano believed that he, too, should suffer, even as he slept, as an act of reparation for the collective sins of mankind during his lifetime.

"He carried the pain of many, everybody's pain, his family's pain, the pain of his close friends, even those who did not understand him and often amused themselves by pitying him," Monsignor Lembo said. "He was old, but years don't matter when you have a child's heart. Serenity sparkled in his eyes. You could say he had the gift of joy."

There was a transformation taking place, though not in how the elderly priest conducted himself. Over the decades, that never changed. No, the change came in the way he was viewed by those close to him. Their reverence and respect was evolving into something reaching a higher realm. Monsignor Aurelio Sorrentino, a seminary student of Padre Gaetano's who would become the archbishop of Reggio Calabria-Bova and initiate his mentor's cause for canonization, said, "My impression when I was with him was to be in front of a saint, a saint in the truest sense of the word."

Four of the five Catanoso brothers became World War II soldiers, and all of them survived. (Peter, the youngest, just missed the war, but signed up for the Korean conflict as soon as he could.) My father was the first one enlisted, in February 1942, when he was a junior at Penn State in ROTC. He graduated in June 1943 as a first lieutenant in the U.S. Air Force. He was twenty-two and went immediately into bombardier training, first in B-17s, then in B-29s at bases in Alabama, Texas, and Louisiana. The war ended before he could be sent overseas. His younger brother Joseph, drafted in June 1943 when he was eighteen, saw plenty of action as a technical sergeant in the U.S. Air Force in the Japanese theater. He was a flight engineer in B-24s and flew on twenty missions out of Guam and Okinawa, praying that the Japanese "Zeroes" wouldn't blast him out of the sky. On August 6, 1945, while returning from a bombing run on Nagasaki, he looked out to see the most amazing, puzzling sight—an enormous mushroom cloud rising over Hiroshima. Back at the base, his crew was let in on the secret. They had witnessed the devastating plume of "Little Boy," the first atomic bomb. A week later, Charlie, who enlisted as a seaman first class in the U.S. Navy in June 1944 when he was seventeen, landed with his crew at Pearl Harbor. He was to be part of the naval assault on Japan, a guaranteed human slaughter. It never happened. The Japanese soon surrendered.

Tony went on to have a war experience that influenced him far more than any of his brothers. It profoundly changed the way he viewed himself and his place in the continuum of an immigrant family. He spent more than a year in Italy, much of it in Sicily. There he discovered the famous warmth and humor and simple goodness of the southern Italian people, in a sense, his people. For the first time in his life, he became a proud Italian American. And years later, after he knew he had a genuine, canonized saint in his family tree, he told me with the kind of spunk and sincerity that put a youthful sparkle in his eighty-nine-year-old eyes: "I received the first miracle."

Tony didn't want to go to war, and he didn't enlist. His mother needed him more at home, he figured. But he didn't get to decide. He was drafted and joined the U.S. Army as a corporal in February

1943. He was twenty-six. While in basic training in upstate New York, the officers scanned the recruits for special talents. Tony's soon surfaced. He was friendly and outgoing. Of more strategic importance, he could speak and understand Italian fluently. This, Tony realized, might keep him out of the infantry and off the front lines. He wrote home to his sister Leona with a frantic request: Send an Italian dictionary fast. She did.

In early 1943, General Dwight Eisenhower had drawn up elaborate plans to invade Sicily along with his British allies. There were three goals: remove the Vermont-sized island as a base for enemy shipping and aircraft, set up an occupational government to establish civil affairs, and eventually, knock Italy out of the war. Communicating with Italian sympathizers was of paramount importance to the plan. Translators were thus a hot commodity. Tony was tapped, along with about 250 other young Italian-Americans. After further training in Newport News, Virginia, the translators, hundreds of soldiers, and two Irish-American priests packed onto a huge transport ship, the USS *Mariposa,* for the six-day crossing of the Atlantic. They landed first in Casablanca, Morocco, where they spent several weeks in sand-blown tents. Then they moved on to Tunisia, which offered the shortest route across the Mediterranean from North Africa due west to Sicily. There they joined tens of thousands of soldiers preparing for the single largest amphibious assault ever attempted, larger even than the epic D-Day assault on Normandy the following year.

Operation Husky, which launched the Allies' Italian campaign, began on July 9, 1943. It was made up of American, British, and Canadian forces called the Allied Fifteenth Army Group. The size of the combined landing-force flotilla was staggering: more than eighty thousand soldiers, seven thousand vehicles, three hundred trucks, six hundred tanks, and nine hundred pieces of artillery carried by nearly twenty-six hundred vessels. Tony found himself on an open-air transport ship that, like the others, was tossed like a cork during the windy, stormy crossing. Scared, puking soldiers dubbed the forty-mile-per-hour gales "Mussolini's wind." Tony was soaked to the skin as German bombs sent up geysers all around. He and a friend crawled under a truck and prayed to Jesus.

American forces landed in Gela on the southern coast of Sicily on July 10 and immediately pushed inland. British forces landed to the east near Siracusa; the front was a hundred miles long. Initial German opposition was fierce. But after only a few days, Axis soldiers began to retreat. The Germans mostly escaped, the Italians mostly surrendered. General George Patton, who commanded the American Seventh Army in Sicily, took about a week to secure the western half of the island for the Allies, including the port city of Palermo on the northwest coast. The British Eighth Army, under the direction of General Bernard Montgomery, took a few weeks longer to secure the eastern half.

At the same time the Allies pursued their ferocious ground and aerial assault on Sicily, they bombed Rome for the first time. The effect was immediate. On July 25, 1943, Italian King Vittorio Emmanuele III forced Mussolini from office and placed him under arrest. Italy could not, however, remove itself from the war so easily. Much of the country still lay in German hands; Hitler turned his forces mercilessly on the Italians for another year. But the fascist era was over. Italy surrendered to the Allies.

During the bloody month of July 1943, Tony didn't fire a shot. He didn't carry a gun. That wasn't his job. As a translator, he was an important component of AMGOT—the Allied Military Government of Occupied Territory, which would bring order to the island in the coming year, as well as schools, public works, and commerce. Initially, Tony reported to Colonel Charles Poletti, the former lieutenant governor of New York State, whom the army appointed assistant administrator of Sicily based in Palermo. But Poletti spoke Italian well. He sent Tony on to Canicatti, a hill town and former fascist stronghold of about thirty thousand people near Agrigento on the southern coast. The town's architecture bespoke its former wealth. There were centuries-old castle ruins and three monasteries, a baroque fountain in the town piazza, and handsome churches, such as Chiesa di San Diego, decorated with eighteenth-century frescoes. The farmland surrounding the town was rich as well. Canicatti farmers produced the popular grape *Italia* for table wine. And given the moderate year-round climate, blood oranges, peaches, plums, and nectarines grew in abundance. Tony stood on the edge of the town in the aftermath of Operation Husky and saw smoke still billowing from bombed-out buildings. But there was beauty as well, the kind he had never seen before.

In Canicatti, Tony worked directly under Major Edgar Johnwick, a public health officer from Gainsville, Florida, who was now in charge of AMGOT's control of the Agrigento region. Johnwick didn't speak a word of Italian. When Tony met him in the former fascist headquarters building on the piazza, the major told him: no more salutes; I can't operate here without you; we're equals. That suited Tony fine. Never much for following rules, he wasn't crazy about military protocol. Until he was forced to care.

Shortly after his arrival in Canicatti, Tony was working in the second-floor office on the piazza when he heard a commotion out on the street. He wandered downstairs and suddenly found himself face to face with the surly and powerful General Patton himself, sitting in the back of a Jeep, his ivory-handle pistol at his side, waiting on Major Johnwick. Tony snapped to attention, but he might as well have been standing naked. "*Soldier*, where's your helmet?" the general demanded. As Tony began to stammer and point upstairs, Patton bellowed: "If I *ever* catch you without your helmet again, I'll have you *court*-martialed!" Tony was already halfway up the stairs.

Major Johnwick had enormous responsibilities over eight communities in the region. He was charged with rebuilding schools and reestablishing a rule of law. He had to root out existing fascists and turn them over to the military. He had to deal on an almost constant basis with aggrieved local aristocrats and even Mafiosi, all of whom wanted a place in, or a piece of, the new system. Tony was in the middle of it all, the bilingual conduit, leaning to his left to listen, turning to his right to translate. It came easy to him; he never realized he knew the language so well.

Six decades later, when my uncle Tony would tell me these stories in vivid, flawless detail, it wasn't his work with AMGOT that he wanted most to share. By then, Canicatti had mellowed in his mind's eye into something akin to the sweet, idyllic Sicilian villages portrayed in Italian films like *Cinema Paradiso*. The scenes he described suggested as much.

During his time there, he lived on the second floor of the four-bedroom rooming house that the Americans had taken over. Early one morning Tony awoke to someone in the alley shouting, *"Latte, latte!"* Sounds good, he thought. Maybe he'd go down and buy a bottle. But when he pushed open the shutters and looked down, all he saw was an old farmer walking along, tugging a cow and a goat. What's going on? Then a woman came out of the house across the alley with two jars and he got his answer. The farmer stopped the animals, bent over, and yanked until he filled one jar with warm cow's milk and the other with just-as-warm goat's milk. Tony smacked his head in amazement as the farmer began calling again, *"Latte, latte!"*

Tony moved easily among the locals and nearly always felt comfortable, almost at home. A soldier friend of his, Leonard Volante, once wrote Tony's mother saying: "Your son has many friends and is well liked by all; the Italians here come in search of him, big shots, too, mayors, lawyers, professors, barons, and dukes, etc. Yes, he's quite a boy—he's alright."

Of course, if not for his ever-present Army uniform, Tony could pass for a local, what with his olive complexion, dark eyes, and wavy brown hair parted in the middle. Early on, he befriended a *Canicat-tinese* about his age named Stefano Mundo who had dropped by the AMGOT office looking for work. Tony received permission to hire Stefano as his driver. He also served as a kind of local consultant. "That's the best trattoria in town," Stefano pointed out. "And stop overpaying the barber. He closed his shop for a week after your last haircut."

Then there was the matter of so many funerals. Every day, it seemed, a parade of mourners, all dressed in black, would make their way weeping and praying through the center of Canicatti, trailing a slow-moving hearse with its curtains drawn. Looking out from his office window, Tony figured another war victim had passed. But after a couple of weeks of near-daily funeral processions, he wondered if maybe the town had been hit by some type of epidemic.

"Stefano, what's going on?" Tony asked. His driver wouldn't say much. He wasn't a snitch. But he didn't lie when Tony wondered aloud if he should request an investigation. Within a week, AMGOT investigators stopped a procession and opened up the back of the hearse. There was no coffin. Rather, the hearse was stuffed with crates of wine, sacks of dried beans, and boxes of shoes all stolen and being smuggled out for sale on the black market in a nearby town. The ringleaders were locked up and just like that, the "mortality" rate in Canicatti improved.

Tony would laugh at such antics and might have chosen to look the other way had he been in charge. He liked these people. They could use a break. Besides, they reminded him of so many Italian families he knew back in North Wildwood. He empathized with them, too. In his travels outside Canicatti in the fall of 1943, he witnessed plenty of examples of extreme poverty and squalor. It was shocking. This is what his father hadn't told him about. This, he realized, is what drove Carmelo from Calabria and the Foti family from Sicily. Tony wasn't much for writing, but when he came across a twenty-verse poem called "Panorama of Sicily," he typed it up and mailed it home to his sister Leona.

> Castle and palace, opera house, too,
> Hotel on a mountain, marvelous view.
> Homes made of weeds, brickets and mud,
> People covered with scabs, scurvy and crud.
>
> A beauteous maiden, a smile on her face,
> With a breath of garlic fouling the place.
> Listless housewife, no shoes on her feet,
> Washing and cooking out in the street.

Such dismal scenes could easily be set aside in the evening. On warm, balmy nights beneath a sky blanketed with stars, Stefano would walk over to Tony's rooming house and call up for him to join the passeggiata—the evening ritual common to most Italian towns and villages. Every night, the locals would come out to walk aimlessly on the cobblestone streets through the town center for the simple pleasure of being together. Parents carrying babies. Little kids chasing around. Old folks tottering on stiff legs. And Tony—in the middle of a half dozen paesans, swaying arm in arm as they cantered along. He may have been an American soldier, but he felt every bit an Italian. Sometimes he'd tip his head back and lead them in some folk song they had taught him the night before. As Tony sang, they all staggered and laughed like lifelong friends. Tony could hardly believe that just a few months earlier, they had been considered the enemy.

By the end of 1943, Tony had been transferred to AMGOT headquarters in Palermo. He was made the chief receptionist of the allied military. All appointments with the brass had to go through him. He was still a corporal, but his stature had grown. He traveled the island a lot and was often given the freedom to do as he pleased. Once when serving as a translator near Mount Etna on the southeast coast, he drove down the volcanic mountain to the fishing village of Riposta, where his mother was born. He couldn't find anyone who knew the Foti family. But it got him thinking. The Catanoso family was just across the Strait of Messina in Calabria. Somewhere. He remembered his father's only sister, his aunt Maria, still lived there. He just didn't know where.

Back in Palermo at breakfast one morning, Tony was talking with his pal John Giordano, an Italian-American soldier from West New York, New Jersey. "Where's your family from?" Tony asked. Calabria, his friend said. "Mine too," Tony said. Knowing they had relatives so nearby pulled on them like a magnet. "We should go find them," Tony suggested and his pal agreed. Naturally, Tony had a friend who looked after the motor pool of military vehicles. That morning in early February 1944, the friend looked the other way as Tony picked out a Jeep, grabbed several containers of gasoline, and took off with Giordano. AWOL.

By late afternoon, the two Italian-American soldiers in their olive green U.S. Army uniforms had crossed the Strait of Messina by ferry and landed in Reggio Calabria. Giordano knew exactly where his aunt lived. They drove straight to Villa San Giovanni, just a few miles north. He was immediately mobbed by relatives. So much crying and screaming and hugging. Tony stood on the edge of the scene and took it all in. Beautiful, he thought. He pulled Giordano aside after a while and told him, "I'll come back for you in a few days, I've got to go find *my* aunt now." The problem was, he didn't know where to begin to look.

Tony drove back to Reggio and wandered around. It was raining and getting late. He had no idea the city was teeming with Catanosos. He didn't know that Padre Gaetano, his father's cousin, was living at the seminary in the center of town. The two would never be any closer. But Tony would come to believe later that the future saint must have had a hand in what happened next.

It was dark now and Tony was drawn to the light of what looked like a friendly trattoria on a side street. He stepped inside and was seated alone in the middle of a cozy room filled entirely with locals. He ordered a plate of macaroni; it was green, made of fava beans because wheat was in such short supply during the war. While eating, he made small talk with the waiter and told him of his quest. The waiter turned and waved over a middle-aged man dressed nicely in a wool jacket and tie, a professor at the local university. "Maybe he can help you," the waiter said. Tony doubted it, but he didn't mind the company.

"*Parla italiano?*" the professor asked as he took a seat, then inquired where the soldier lived in America. Tony thought about saying North Wildwood but figured the man may have heard of Philadelphia. He told him that.

"Well, if you're from Philadelphia, you must know my brother." Oh, sure, Tony thought to himself; there are only a few million people in Philadelphia. "His name is Silvio Smorto."

Tony sat up straight. Smorto? You mean the guy who owns the real estate business on Ninth and Mifflin?

"*Sì, sì,* that's my brother!" the professor said excitedly.

Tony was stunned, but he had more news. His father Carmelo had been close to the Smorto family in Philly for years; Silvio Smorto, known as Sam in the States, was Tony's godfather.

"*Mama mia!*" the professor shouted as he pounded the table. "That's incredible!"

With that, Professor Alfredo Smorto bounded from his chair and threw his arms around Tony, kissing him on both cheeks. Then, with his hands cupping Tony's face, he announced to everyone: "This American soldier is family!" And the whole place erupted, converging on Tony as if he alone had just liberated Italy. They hugged and kissed him and clapped him on the back. *Cugino!* they kept saying. Cousin.

When the din subsided, Tony reached out for Alfredo Smorto in the crowd and pressed him with the only question that was important to him: "Do you happen to know, by any chance, where I might find my aunt, Maria Catanoso? She is my father's only sister and I've never met her." The professor was on a roll. Or maybe he was a divine intercessor for a relative-priest across town.

"Maria Portzia Catanoso? Of course I know where you can find her. She lives in Chorio with her husband, Bruno Priolo. They are my friends. I live in Chorio, too!"

The next morning, when Tony awoke at the British headquarters of AMGOT in Reggio where he spent the night, he looked outside to see Alfredo Smorto, dressed in the same wool jacket and tie, sitting in the front seat of his jeep. The ride up to Chorio through farmland and along steep, winding roads should have taken an hour. With the deliriously happy professor, it took twice that long. Every time Smorto saw a farmer chopping into his field or a shepherd tending his goats, he would direct Tony to pull over. "This is my cousin!" he would shout.

Finally, the tiny village of Chorio came into view—a small cluster of low-slung row houses tucked in tightly between the side of a mountain and a bend of the river Tuccio. So this is where Pop was from, Tony thought. This is what he left behind.

He was directed first to the professor's mother's house. People came out to witness the commotion. Who was this handsome American soldier, the first anyone could remember setting foot in Chorio? A son of the village, they learned. Word spread rapidly. People poured out of their houses. It all felt surreal to Tony. He was as far away from home as he had ever been in his entire life, but it was like coming full circle. The father had left this place in 1903; the son had returned.

As Alfredo Smorto led Tony down a few short alleys to a piazza ringed with unadorned two- and three-story row houses made of block and stucco, a growing crowd of locals had formed a procession behind them. The professor went to a corner house and called up, "Maria Portzia, there's an American soldier here to see you!" From inside the second floor, Tony could hear her say, "Go away. I don't know any American soldiers."

A few moments later, though, when she came down and opened the door, she laid eyes on a stranger who looked entirely familiar. She gasped and put her hands to her mouth. She had not seen her brother Carmelo in more than forty years. And now, in the body of this soldier who was red-eyed and trembling, her brother seemed to be staring back at her. She pulled Tony in close as the crowd pressed in around them, cheering and shouting. He could feel her tears on his face.

Tony did not have the heart to tell his aunt that her brother had died a few years earlier. He lied about that, saying Carmelo was fine. He left that detail out of the long letter he wrote home to his mother describing the amazing reunion:

"In a few minutes, the whole town was in the house. I think everyone was crying with joy and they were asking me questions a mile a minute. Well, to make a long story short, I think that the three days that I spent there were the happiest days that I've put in during my time in the army. I never knew we had so many relations. I could not count them all and they all remembered father, Uncle Joe, and the old folks."

During those three days, Tony was treated like a king, or more accurately, like family. At night, he slept in the thick feather bed that his father slept in as a boy. He was surprised to see that Maria had photographs of Carmelo's family back in North Wildwood, which her brother had sent. And Tony worried about the family's obvious suffering as a result of the war.

"Mother, will you do me a favor and draw $100 from my money in the bank and send it to Aunt Maria, for they can certainly use it. They need clothes more than anything else, but they must wait until after the war before they can get any. Well mother, writing this letter to you is like a dream. I cannot express how I feel toward Aunt Maria and Uncle Bruno. It only makes me think of home and how much I miss the dearest mother in the world."

My eighty-nine-year-old uncle Tony wiped tears from his eyes as he shared this story with me practically a lifetime after it happened. "I wouldn't take a million dollars for my memories of that time in Italy," he told me. As for his return to Chorio when he stepped across the bridge of time to reconnect the Italian and American Catanoso families, he said simply, "It was a miracle."

Padre Gaetano Catanoso did not receive a miracle on March 25, 1958, just the answer to his most ardent prayer. Nearly a quarter century after the founding, the new archbishop of Reggio, Monsignor Giovanni Ferro, was cleared to give Vatican-sanctioned approval to the Congregation of the Sisters of St. Veronica of the Holy Face. At last, his beloved nuns were officially recognized as a mature and spiritual group that understood its mission and carried it out faithfully with love and devotion.

*"In domino,"* Padre Gaetano said upon being told the news.

In time, the Veronican sisters would grow to number several hundred. They would live and work in some two dozen communities throughout Calabria, running what were called "Padre Catanoso shelters." These were seen as pioneering efforts in the impoverished region, as the shelters were used, depending on village needs, as nursery schools or orphanages, vocational training centers or old-age homes. As always, the nuns worked closely with the local parish priest to make sure the often rundown churches and tabernacles were properly cared for.

As the nuns' reputation grew, so did their mission field. Veronican sisters would later establish themselves in other parts of Italy, such as Rome and Salerno, and as far away as the Philippines and Tanzania, where schools named for Padre Gaetano would open. They still operate today.

In the final years of his life, more good things happened. Shortly before the nuns received their Vatican approval, ground was broken in Santo Spirito for the large Mother House for which Padre Gaetano had spent twenty years raising funds. The nuns, wearing their black habits, helped push wheelbarrows and lug bricks to lay the foundation. At the same time, an architect in Milan had been commissioned to draw up plans for the adjacent sanctuary, which Padre Gaetano saw in his mind's eye as being "big and beautiful, full of light with wide windows, to be used by the faithful of the area." There, his decades-old message of charity, mercy, and abiding faith in the saving grace of the Lord would live forever in those called to come inside.

On February 14, 1959, Chorio witnessed another Catanoso home-coming. It was perhaps the largest celebration ever seen there. A hobbling Padre Gaetano, wearing his galero and a long black overcoat, was taken to his native village to celebrate his eightieth birthday. He was swarmed by his nuns and happy villagers. A brass band paraded around the piazza. There was even a candle-topped birthday cake. St. Pasquale of Baylon, the village church that fell in the earthquake of 1908 and had been rebuilt in 1931, was packed with hundreds of people, front to back. Catanoso relatives, most of whom now lived in Reggio, occupied several rows of pews.

Padre Gaetano took to the pulpit and basked in the reflected glow of so many admiring and grateful faces. He was grateful, too. He recalled a life lived in faith, which began just a few steps from this church. He spoke of his great fortune to have been called to the priesthood. He spoke of his immense pride in the work of his Veronican sisters. And he reminded everyone of an essential truth he had witnessed again and again during some of the worst of times in recent Italian history: "Everything is possible through Christ," he said, his voice ringing with vitality.

In all ways, the old priest, the living saint whose miraculous powers had yet to be proclaimed, was *molto contento*, very happy.

# PART II

# *Family*

## MIRACLE STORY—SISTER PAOLINA

In the early morning darkness of April 4, 1963, a nun kneeled at the bedside of Padre Gaetano Catanoso to pray. The eighty-four-year-old priest had died peacefully an hour earlier. At the time, his bedroom had been crowded with scores of Veronican sisters, church leaders, and relatives. Now the last person had left and the room was empty.

Sister Paolina Ligato had been waiting patiently for this moment. A native of tiny Montebello in the Aspromonte, she was forty-two years old and had spent half her life in service to the poor as a Veronican sister. Half her life she also had suffered the crippling symptoms of acute bronchial asthma. Her work as a kindergarten teacher was frequently curtailed by a plague of coughing and gasping for air that left her feeling listless. Medicine did little good; the pain was relentless. Whenever she saw Padre Gaetano, she would plead, "Padre, please, you must cure me of this disease so that I can better do your work." He would smile, bless her for her commitment, and say: "Suffer and offer, dear sister, suffer and offer." For more than twenty years, she did.

Perhaps Sister Paolina's patience stemmed from her knowledge that Padre Gaetano, while still alive, did not possess the power to rid her body of disease. Only a saint, working as God's intercessor, had that power. But after his last breath, she had no doubt that Padre Gaetano was indeed a saint, so she prayed: "Padre, now that you are in heaven, you must obtain for me this miracle."

Moments later, while still on her knees, she felt what she described as a warm shiver pass through her body. She had never felt anything like it before. She rose and leaned over to kiss the priest's hands, still holding a rosary. She went off to bed. When she awoke several hours later, she felt another strange sensation, one she recognized from long ago—the ability to breathe deeply without fighting the urge to cough. She took another deep breath. And another. Easy. And painless.

*My God*, she thought.

A few days later, when Sister Paolina visited her doctor, he was surprised to see her doing so well. Her color was good. Her spirits were high. She was filled with energy. But she was missing something. The doctor listened to her lungs. He ran some blood tests. He compared the new results with those of her last visit a few months earlier. He was confused. Sister Paolina showed no signs of having asthma. Even more confusing, she showed no signs of ever having *had* asthma. It's as if you have been cured, the doctor told her.

In October 1995, five Roman doctors comprising a committee of the *Consulta Medica* of the Vatican's Congregation for the Causes of Saints studied the medical records of Sister Paolina Ligato. They scrutinized the history of her illness and the treatments she had received. They sifted through a small pile of lung exams and blood tests. Their knowledge of asthma told them that someone as severely ill as Sister Paolina had been should have lung scars and lesions from her condition, even after her symptoms had disappeared. There were none. In fact, thirty-two years after the nun kneeled at Padre Gaetano's deathbed, she was still alive, still working and still breathing as if asthma had never afflicted her.

Dr. Raffaello Cortisini, a respected heart-and-lung transplant surgeon in Rome, rendered the unanimous opinion of the committee: Sister Paolina's cure was medically inexplicable.

A month later, a special Theological Congress of the Congregation for the Causes of Saints rendered its spiritual judgment. There was a clear cause-and-effect link between the nun's prayers and her immediate and lasting cure. In the eyes of the Vatican and ultimately Pope John Paul II, Padre Gaetano Catanoso had, through the divine powers of the Lord, performed his first miracle.

# 7

## Going Back

The train ride from Rome to Reggio Calabria took six hours. I had no idea what to expect. It was two days after Christmas 2003, and Termini was packed with travelers, mostly Italians grappling with luggage, gift boxes, and small children. Absorbed in a cacophony of voices we could not understand, my wife, Laurelyn, and I were keen to keep our three daughters between us as we moved through the jostling throng, pulling our bags behind us. We walked for what seemed like blocks along the length of the Eurostar until we found the first-class cars.

"*Ecco, ecco*," an Italian in work clothes yelled to me from the door, reaching out for our bags. I handed them up to him, then paid the ten euros he demanded, not realizing he wasn't a porter, just a local working the hapless in the crowd. We were an easy target.

Finding our seats in the open car and settling in facing each other, Rosalie, my middle daughter, asked, "Nervous, Dad?" I stared at her for a moment.

It was a fair question. I *was* nervous, more nervous than I could remember. We were all together, heading into unknown territory, emotional as well as geographical. We were in Italy, just a couple of days into a two-week vacation, and it would have been so easy for us to head north from Rome to the tourist-friendly locales of Florence or Siena or Venice. We were going in the opposite direction. But why?

For some romantic vision of a family reunion with absolute strangers with whom I shared only a last name? I wasn't certain they even welcomed our arrival. To kneel in the church of a saintly relative I knew virtually nothing about? I had drifted away from the church years ago.

"I'm not nervous at all," I said calmly. "This is going to be fun."

For Laurelyn and me, this was our second visit to Italy. Our first trip had been nineteen years earlier on a two-month honeymoon adventure in the fall of 1984. Clad in matching hooded Woolrich jackets, we trekked from the cathedrals of London to the mosques of Istanbul. Back then, as naïve coach-class Eurail travelers, we had spent ten of those days during a cold, rainy November starring in our own version of an Italian highlights reel—the Grand Canal in Venice, Giotto's Arena Chapel in Padua, everything Michelangelo in Florence, and a close-up view of a young, vibrant Pope John Paul II at the Vatican auditorium. I knew then that I had relatives somewhere in Italy, but as a twenty-four-year-old newlywed, I didn't have the nerve to seek them out. Next time we come, Laurelyn and I vowed, we'll be braver. We'll find them. We'll be ready then.

We were older now, making good on our promise, with our daughters Emilia, Rosalie, and Sophia along for the ride, doing something that no American Catanoso had done in more than thirty years. We were heading south, farther than Naples, beyond the Amalfi Coast, into the very toe of the boot of Italy to a place I could only picture as gray—Reggio Calabria. It didn't feel dangerous exactly, just vague, distant, perhaps a little grim. But the magnetic tug of family is hard to resist. This is especially true of second-generation Italian-Americans eager to connect with relatives their parents had no interest in knowing. At least I had some prodding—a message in a bottle set adrift by electronic means. The e-mail had surfaced at work.

"I found your name on the Internet," Giovanna Catanoso had written in mid-2002. "Perhaps we are related." I responded with a few details and a picture. "I showed everyone your photo," she wrote back. "There is no doubt. We are related."

Soon Giovanna sent me a letter in her best English. "My grandfather came to USA in 1912, he was already married and left Italy, his wife and a little baby, my aunt Nini." At the outset of World War I in 1915, she went on, the Italian government called out to all Italians abroad, particularly in America, and issued an ultimatum: return home immediately and fight for your country, or your country will bar you from ever coming home again. "My grandfather returned and went to war. He conceived my father during Christmas leave, went back to the front and died. My father was born in 1917, Sep. 24, when his father was already dead since January, 1917."

In those few simple sentences, I learned more about the Catanoso immigration experience than I had ever known before. Such drama. Such courage and tragedy. Along with her letter, Giovanna sent a photocopied diagram of a Catanoso family tree; she was a cousin. And there were so many more, branching out for generations in names I had never seen before. One name was marked in yellow, Gaetano Catanoso, the third of nine children of Antonino and Antonina Catanoso. Giovanna had drawn an arrow to the highlighted name of her great-uncle. In parentheses she wrote, "The saint."

More than anything, the saint in our family was the unseen force pulling us down to Reggio Calabria. True, Giovanna had invited us to visit. But when we started planning an Italy vacation in early 2003 and told Giovanna we wanted to come right after Christmas, we practically stopped hearing from her. A bad sign, I thought. Maybe she didn't want to see us after all. I wondered: How would I feel if a family of strangers who didn't speak English decided to visit us for a couple of days in Greensboro, North Carolina, where we lived? Ambivalent.

As Laurelyn and I struggled to work out the itinerary of a two-week vacation that would span the length of the Italian peninsula, we saw that Reggio just wasn't on the way to anywhere we wanted to go. It would take a day in train travel alone just to get there. That mixture of anxiety and logistics made my vision of a grand family reunion seem more like a mirage.

But just when we would come close to deciding "Let's just skip it," we would think about Gaetano Catanoso. How many people can claim a near saint in their family? If we were going to fly all the way to Italy, we agreed that it was important to at least visit the priest's church in Reggio. We could learn firsthand about this miracle-making relative and pick up some relics and prayer cards for my mother and my aunts back home in New Jersey, good Catholics all. Such religious mementos would mean the world to them.

I remember well first learning about Gaetano Catanoso. It was a spring Saturday in 2001, a year before I had been unexpectedly contacted by Giovanna Catanoso. The mail had just arrived. I was standing in the kitchen, taking a break from mowing the lawn, when I spotted an envelope from my mother. She had sent me a couple of photocopied pages with a yellow Post-it note attached. "Came across this article on Gaetano Catanoso," she wrote. "Thought you'd enjoy it." The pages had been sent to her by relatives in Philadelphia a couple of years earlier. She had not felt any urgency to send it to me sooner. Attached was a card the size of a large postage stamp. It showed an older, bald-headed priest in a long, black robe kneeling at an altar with his hands clasped, his eyes cast upward in prayer. Beneath this illustration was the name "Beato Gaetano Catanoso." I recognized neither the name nor the title. The text on the back was in Italian. Who was this guy? And what was he doing with my last name?

I started to read the enclosed pages: "The following is a rather general translation of the document received regarding the proposed movement for the elevation of Blessed Gaetano Catanoso to sainthood."

Catanoso? Sainthood? What is this? More to the point, *who* is this? I thought about my dad and his four brothers and four sisters. Fine folks, every one of them. But not a saint in the bunch. Besides, maybe Catanoso is a common name in Italy. Maybe this Gaetano Catanoso isn't even related. I had no idea.

I read on: Born in 1879 in Chorio. Ordained in 1902. Founder of an order of nuns. Tireless advocate for the poor. Died in 1963.

The timeline then jumped ahead twenty years to a passage that struck me as beyond belief: The cause for sainthood began in 1980, and in 1990, it was accepted by none other than Pope John Paul II. And then this: "Gaetano Catanoso was credited with having performed a miracle shortly after his death, curing one of his nuns of a chronic bronchitis."

I read that passage over several times, but it wasn't really sinking in. A miracle maker? In our family? Could this really be possible? How come I had never heard of this person before? And even if I had, my Catholic moorings were so tenuous that I had little means to make sense of something so incredible. None of those misgivings changed the apparent facts, which I learned as I continued reading. On May 4, 1997, without a single American Catanoso knowing about it, Pope John Paul II beatified Gaetano Catanoso in St. Peter's Square in the next-to-last step before canonization. Tens of thousands of people attended. Then there was this postscript. Blessed Gaetano needed another miracle attributed to him to be made a saint. Apparently, one was not enough. The note concluded: "As a family member bearing the Catanoso name, married or otherwise, it would be a great and holy accomplishment if someone on this side of the ocean would be the recipient of such a cure."

I folded the pages and put them back in the envelope. I tossed it back on the stack of bills and catalogs and junk mail. I went back to mowing the lawn. It would be several years before that innocuous introduction took hold and led me and my family to Termini in Rome for a morning train en route to Reggio in December 2003. Just a few months after that trip, with my older brother stricken with cancer, we would all be praying to Gaetano Catanoso for one more miracle cure.

What if nobody's there, Dad?" Emilia asked as the Eurostar moved closer to our destination. The thought certainly crossed my mind. I had let Giovanna know by e-mail a month earlier that our train would arrive at 4:15 P.M. at Centrale station in Reggio. She never responded. A few weeks before we left, I heard from another cousin, Daniela Catanoso, who said she looked forward to meeting us in Reggio. But she didn't respond either when I e-mailed her about our arrival time.

"It doesn't really matter," I told Emilia, even though I thought otherwise. "I have the address to the hotel and I have Giovanna's phone number, Daniela's, too. If nobody's there, we'll get a cab and just give them a call later. No big deal."

For a moment, I put my worries aside to take in the view from the tall train windows. With the density and antiquity of Rome far behind us and the steam from Mount Vesuvius outside of Naples a distant sight as well, I was stunned to see a landscape that, while not rounded and rolling green like the famous hills and valleys of Tuscany, was verdant, rugged, and striking in its own ways. Vineyards spread out for acres as old men worked the rows, tending the dormant winter vines. We saw sheep farms and olive groves on the nearby hills as well as in the valleys that fronted the gray, craggy mountains beyond. And on the other side, the Tyrrhenian Sea stretched out as vast as an ocean. We could see fishermen in small boats just off the coastline.

As beautiful as the natural features were, the man-made structures were much less so. Most buildings near the train tracks were squat cinder-block boxes painted pale yellows and greens and lacking molding or trim around the doors and windows. Too often we'd see small apartment buildings or flats that had been framed out enough to suggest a two-story structure, but whose open walls and absence of construction materials indicated a stalled project. It wasn't like that around Rome. I thought about my grandfather, Carmelo Catanoso. This was the south. Lots of farms and fish, but few factories and few jobs beyond what the land and sea could provide. No wonder he left.

Sophia interrupted my daydreaming. She was hungry. Rosalie and Emilia were, too. They each requested a croissant. My Italian was strictly limited to the few greetings I learned as a kid from my maternal grandfather, Giustino Giandomenico, my namesake: *Buon giorno, come sta? Sto bene.* I reached for the palm-size phrase book we'd brought with us and practiced saying, *"Quanto un cornetto?"* How much is a croissant?

The Eurostar had been filled to capacity when we pulled out of Rome, packed almost entirely with Italians traveling after Christmas. With each stop, far more people got off than on. As Sophia and I walked past those who remained, I saw mostly young mothers and fathers with characteristic dark hair and olive complexions. Their children, playing at their feet, looked up at me with deep brown eyes. These faces all looked familiar, like the faces I was surrounded by as a boy growing up in North Wildwood, New Jersey. I felt comfortable amid these strangers. And as long as I kept my mouth shut, with my brown-eyed daughter at my side, I probably seemed just as familiar to them—another Calabrian heading home for the holidays. That was sort of true, wasn't it?

In the dining car, I imagined that I really *was* an Italian. I saw the croissants stacked up in the glass case. The young man behind the counter asked, I assumed, what I wanted, so I spit out my newly polished, *"Quanto un cornetto?"* There, I'd said it. Not bad. But I was immediately thrown off. He answered straightaway, apparently understanding what I had said. I froze. I stared at him blankly, biting on my lower lip. "Dad!" Sophia implored. "Say something!"

My cover was blown. My own curly hair and Calabrian nose were a thin disguise. I was just a hapless, monolingual American. "I don't know what he said," I whispered out of the corner of my mouth. The waiter sized up the situation with a nod and tapped quickly at the register. He tore off a paper receipt. One euro, ten. Red-faced, I handed him the money. "Thank you," I said, taking no more chances.

B y 3:30, we were past the regions of Campania and Basilicata and deep into Calabria. Reggio was just a little farther. The view from the window couldn't distract me any longer. We would be there soon. As we began pulling our things together and brushing the crumbs off our clothes, I could feel my heart beating a bit harder in my chest. Whether or not this was a good idea, we would soon find out. Whether our long-lost relatives cared enough to meet us at the station, well, we would find that out, too. I was hoping that Giovanna would at least have time to have dinner with us.

"Okay, this is it," I told Laurelyn as we gathered our bags and hauled them onto the platform at Centrale, the train station in Reggio. Every one of the few dozen people still left on the Eurostar after the six-hour run from Rome seemed to step off the train and fall directly into the welcoming arms of family members. Everyone except us. We stood there alone amid our small pile of suitcases and backpacks wondering what to do next. I looked around for a familiar face, but now, all those people who a little while ago resembled neighbors

from my childhood just looked like strangers in a strange place. Oh,
well, I thought. I slipped my hand into my pocket to finger the piece
of paper I had with the phone numbers I would need later.

Just then an older lady, not quite five feet tall, ambled up to me.
Her brown hair was thin and short and her eyes were confident behind oversize glasses.

"Catanoso?" she asked, beautifully enunciating every syllable.

"Yes."

"*Pina* Catanoso," she said, before reaching out with soft hands to
kiss me on both cheeks.

I could hear Laurelyn gasp in that way she does before she starts to
cry. As Pina moved to kiss Laurelyn, a younger, dark-haired woman
was standing behind her, her daughter Daniela. After a warm hug, both
Pina and Daniela turned and looked behind them. "Giovanna Catanoso," they both said, introducing my smiling pen pal as if she were a
new actor taking the stage. She came forward with her arms out.

"Giovanna!" I said excitedly, tears clouding my own eyes as Laurelyn and I wrapped her in a hug as well. Giovanna's sister, Paola, was
there, too, using her Minolta camera to record what felt like a historic
event.

"Hello, hello!" she said waving and snapping photographs.

As I introduced my relieved and smiling daughters to these relatives, it struck me that we were the first Catanosos from America to
set foot in Reggio Calabria in more than thirty years, the only ones
other than my Uncle Tony and his wife to ever do so. Of course they
were looking forward to our visit! Of course they would be at the
train station! Of course they were ready to pull us into their lives as if
we had lived across town, not across an ocean! The four of them had
brought three cars, two small Fiats and a Renault, to ferry us and our
luggage to our hotel. Giovanna took our bags. Laurelyn and the girls
rode with Paola. I rode with Daniela while Pina, who didn't speak a
word of English, sat quietly in the backseat with a contented grin on
her face, her hands folded serenely on her lap.

Daniela's English was quite good, and our disjointed conversation
bounced all over during the short ride to the hotel. She is an attorney
in practice with her uncle, Piero Catanoso. Criminal and civil work.

Yes, the north and south of Italy are quite different. Reggio doesn't have a great reputation. The Mafia, you know. It's bad, but it's getting better now. Young people, they don't like to stay here. Not enough opportunities. They leave when they can, for Rome or Milan. Same old story.

I wanted to take each one of those thoughts and dive into the middle of it, ask a million questions, learn as much as I could, make up for two generations of absentia. But now we were in the lobby of the hotel, a babbling knot of giddy, familial exuberance.

"Do you have any plans for dinner?" Giovanna asked. As a matter of fact, no. "That's good," she said. "Dinner is at nine. There will be twenty-five of us."

I was pretty sure I hadn't heard her right. "How many?"

"Twenty-five," Paola jumped in, her eyes aglow, "but that includes all of you!"

Again, I was reminded of my needless worrying. Italians, it was becoming clear, do not share the American penchant for confirming every last detail. They note what they need to know and go about making plans. But I did have one question.

"The only thing we really *need* to do while we're here is visit the church of Father Gaetano. When is it open?"

"We can go any time," Paola said with a laugh. "It's our church! For Catanoso, it's always open." Then, putting her thumb to her ear and pinkie to her mouth, she pantomimed, "You call up and say, 'Catanoso,' and they open the church!"

We had all been together not more than thirty minutes, and everything felt so easy and relaxed. A six-hour train trip seemed to have spanned a gap of a hundred years. We were amid Catanosos in Calabria.

While in Rome, we had stayed at a luxury hotel near Piazza della Repubblica, checking in on Christmas Eve. It was a grand and elegant place. The doormen wore capes and top hats. The lobby was ringed with Corinthian columns of red marble. There were statues parked in hallways as wide as a Roman alley. And in our adjoining rooms, chandeliers with yellow Venetian glass hung from the ceilings. Each evening, our beds would not only be turned down, but silk mats would be laid out by the bedside with terry cloth slippers.

We laughed and marveled at all this luxury. At breakfast one morning in the sumptuous lobby, as a harpist played nearby and not one, but two handsome Italian waiters catered to our whims, I thought I might as well share with my daughters a bit of wisdom from a noted American philosopher. "Girls," I said in a low voice of utter sincerity, "always remember the words of Sophie Tucker: 'I've been rich and I've been poor. Rich is better.'" The girls giggled as they sampled the scrambled eggs with salmon.

These guilty pleasures were solely the compliments of a writing assignment from a magazine back home. And we did our best not to appear like a family of bumpkins who had won a radio call-in contest. "Stop staring at the frescoes on the ceiling," I'd say teasingly. "Act like you *belong* here." I then reminded the girls that the splendors of our grand Roman hotel would pass soon enough and would not likely follow us to Reggio.

They didn't.

At the Hotel Lungomare, one of the finer hotels in Reggio, the three stars on the sign are purely relative. Our third-floor room was slightly larger than our bathroom back in Rome. There were cold marble floors instead of Oriental carpets. Plain white walls instead of oil paintings in gilded frames. And the girls groaned at the sight of the sleeping arrangements: metal bunk beds crowded against a double bed that filled all but the edges of the room. Emilia and Rosalie quickly claimed the bunks.

"Where am I supposed to sleep?" whined Sophie with the alarm of a youngest sister imagining herself forced to sleep on the hard floor. I pointed to the middle of the bed. "Right between us," I told her, meaning me and Laurelyn. "Don't worry about it. We didn't come here to hang out in a hotel."

"Good thing," Emilia grumbled as she swung her suitcase up onto the top bunk. "When are we going back to Rome?"

As our daughters took turns in the bathroom, Laurelyn and I stepped out on the narrow balcony. The evening was turning colder;

it was December 27. The white, billowy clouds that lined the sky were just starting to darken. "We're going to be surrounded by Italians all night," I said. "I hope the girls do okay."

The previous night in Rome, we had dinner at a popular pizzeria in the Trastevere neighborhood. The place was packed with locals wedged in at marble-topped tables set in long rows. We got seated right in the middle of the loud, arm-waving chaos, the only nonlocals. Just as I was thinking what a great cultural experience this was for the girls, I noticed them hunched up and leaning in on one another, their faces a similar mask of concern bordering on fear. It was clear that our daughters preferred their foreign encounters at a more comfortable distance.

"Last night was pretty hard for them," Laurelyn said. "We'll see what happens."

Giovanna met us back in the lobby of the hotel, eager to show us her city. Wearing a long gray coat over a maroon sweater, she greeted us all with kisses to each cheek and an easy smile, totally relaxed. Her English was pretty good, though far from fluent. She would pause and often drag out a long "ahhhhhh" while searching for the right words, which sometimes didn't come. We were grateful for whatever English she could muster.

"Reggio has changed a lot in the last few years," Giovanna said, as we walked along the waterfront toward the center of town. "It used to be ugly down here, all rocks and rubbish and railroad tracks. But now it is very beautiful."

In fact, it was stunning. What had been a shabby rail yard a decade ago was now the pride of Reggio, an exquisitely designed walkway that takes full advantage of the city's most enduring asset: its seaside location and postcard-perfect views of the northeast coast of Sicily. The *lungomare*, a wide boulevard built with cobblestones and square blocks in a smart array of geometric designs, hugs the curve of the coastline and is perched just above the sandy beach. It plays out at two levels, with wrought iron railings to lean against and admire the view, and plenty of stone benches. Fan-leaf palm and orange trees fill a long, narrow park between the *lungomare* and Corso Vittorio Emmanuele, the main street along the waterfront. Ficus and magnolia with huge, gnarly trunks stand two stories tall. And way off in the distance, looking southwest across the Ionian Sea below the strait, we could see the steaming, snowcapped peak of Mount Etna in Sicily, at nearly eleven thousand feet, Europe's tallest active volcano.

"We used to have to take the ferry to Messina if we wanted to shop or have things to do at night. Now people in Messina come to Reggio," Giovanna said, her soft, high voice ringing with pride.

She directed us to a small, brightly lit gelato stand in the shade of one of those house-size ficus trees. Inside, Calabrian men in their thirties wearing white short-sleeved shirts and boat-shaped paper hats stood ready to scoop balls of gelato from aluminum tubs. A rainbow of creamy colors was arranged beneath the glass case. The flavors bore such beautiful names: *fragola* (strawberry), *stracciatella menta* (mint chocolate chip), *mirtillo* (blueberry), *frutti di bosco* (wild fruit). Giovanna recommended the *gianduia* (chocolate hazelnut), and we happily followed her lead. As I handed the girls their cups with tiny, flat plastic spoons, Giovanna slipped over to the register to pay. I quickly produced a handful of euros, but she waved me off.

"It's okay," she insisted, looking at us as if she still couldn't believe we had materialized, all five of us, in her city.

We walked a block up to Corso Garibaldi, Reggio's main commercial stretch. It was night now, and as far as we could see, the street was alive with bright lights from stores and cafés. Big white stars were strung to hang over the center of the street. Ornate streetlamps complemented perfectly the 1920s architecture, a kind of aesthetic that reminded me of New Orleans with second-floor balconies and fancy iron railings. I was prepared for Reggio to be poor and shabby. What surrounded me did not fit the mental image I had been carrying in my head for months.

And then there were the people. Hundreds of them, filling the street and sidewalks, walking slowly, leisurely, anything but purposefully. I checked my watch: 7:15, a time when most American families are settling down in front of the television after having finished dinner. Who were all these people? Were they tourists?

"No, they are locals," Giovanna explained.

The *passeggiata*. It was like being back in time sixty years in the center of Canicatti with Uncle Tony and his Sicilian buddies. Families, often three generations, walked together. Old men, sometimes arm in arm, talked excitedly with their hands as they went along. Little kids scrambled around, some riding small bicycles. Teens sauntered in packs, girls often holding hands. All this closeness and touching is a distinctly Italian trait, signifying friendship. Before long, Emilia and Rosalie linked arms as they walked, their long, curly hair and good looks turning the heads of the Calabrian boys who no doubt assumed that my daughters were locals.

Soon the crowd parted just enough to make way for a Santa Claus riding a scooter and pulling a homemade wagon made to look like a sleigh. *"Buon natale! Buon natale!"* he shouted.

Giovanna laughed and grabbed her cell phone, again. It had been ringing every few minutes. The callers must have all asked the same question because her answer was always the same: "Yes, they are here!" Everyone in town seemed to know that Giovanna's cousins from America were visiting for the weekend.

"Antonio! Antonio!" Giovanna called out to someone she spotted in the crowd. It was a friend of hers. "Come meet my cousins!" Another block, another set of friends, more introductions. Now our own group started to get bigger. Somewhere along the way, Paola, Giovanna's only sibling and closest friend, joined us with two of her children, Frederica and Mario. They were thirteen and eleven, nearly the same ages as Rosalie and Sophia. With silky brown hair, dark eyes, and friendly smiles, they were both gorgeous. They offered handshakes and cheek kisses. I gave them American-style hugs.

"Speak in English," Paola playfully instructed her kids. "Show your cousins what my tuition payments go for!"

Just as I was having to abandon my misconceptions of Reggio, I was doing the same about the Catanosos of Calabria. I knew so little about them, and my reading on southern Italy in preparation for this trip suggested a land of mostly peasants and poverty. But Giovanna worked at a bank and had a law degree. Paola was a pharmacist and owned her own store. Daniela, who met us at the train station, was an attorney in practice with her uncle. It got me wondering: If my grand-father fled this place a century ago, was it really to escape poverty? Were the Catanosos of his generation, the descendants of my hosts, as poor as the vast majority of Calabrians at the turn of the twentieth century? As we walked along the Corso, I just didn't know.

At 9:00 P.M., we arrived at a restaurant on Via Torrione called *I Tre Farfalli*, Three Butterflies. Inside, the warm air smelled of sim-mering tomato sauce and frying garlic. It had a homey feel, exposed brick walls covered with family photos and rustic beams crossing the ceiling. Our waiter, wearing a heavy cable-knit sweater and jeans, directed us to a set of tables that had been pushed together near the far wall to accommodate twenty-five people. I was nervous and excited; my daughters were hanging close behind, mostly nervous, I'm sure. The first guest came through the door.

"Hello, I'm Justin Catanoso," I said to a dark-haired woman who appeared to be about my age and who practically marched right up to me.

"*Ciao*, Caterina Catanoso," she said with a huge smile and kisses on both cheeks.

Something about hearing my surname spoken so beautifully, so confidently by someone I didn't know, but who looked entirely fa-miliar, startled me. It was—wonderful. Caterina was followed by her sisters, who both introduced themselves, the lilting sound of their names rolling off their tongues like types of pasta: Antonella Cat-anoso, Patrizia Catanoso. Husbands and teenage children followed the sisters. Their names came one after another—Vincenzo, Orazio, Domenico, Salvatore. I quickly lost track of who was with whom. And still there were more and more Catanosos: Gabriela, Michela, and Irene, joining Giovanna, Paola, Frederica, and Mario who had come in with us.

"*I had no idea we had so many relations,*" my uncle Tony wrote his mother from Italy in 1944. Sixty years later, I found myself thinking the same thing. My heart was pounding. Every one of these cousins came close and stared at me hard, like some kind of museum exhibit. Several said something in Italian, which Giovanna interpreted: "They say you look like a Catanoso."

Of course I do! I *am* a Catanoso! In fact, I was a new branch sprouting from the old family tree right before their eyes. I wanted to shout. I wanted to cry. I wanted to wrap my arms around all of them and jump up and down. More family was arriving, including Daniela and her teenage nieces Giorgia and Alessia. A tall and handsome man wearing the most stylish clothes of all wandered in last with his girl-friend, his teenage daughter Simona, and his sister Caterina.

"George Clooney!" Paola called out. "How are you, George Clooney?"

He rolled his eyes dramatically and said, *"Bene, bene. Non c'è malle."* With his dark eyes, close-cropped hair, and square jaw line, he bore a slight resemblance to the American movie star. But Giovanna assured me that that's not why he was invited. His name was Bruno Calarco, but his mother was a Catanoso. He was family.

The next several hours went by in a blur of raised wineglasses, broken English, fractured Italian, and plate after plate of Calabrian delicacies that seemed catered from my mother's kitchen in New Jersey, where Sunday dinner back home usually entailed a traditional macaroni dinner with browned meatballs and sausage simmering in tomato sauce all afternoon. As more than two dozen of us began settling in around the banquetlike table, Rosalie and Emilia were waiting for me. "Where are you sitting? We want to sit next to you," Emilia insisted. She seemed to be getting a flashback from the crazy Italian crush in Rome the night before. As I started to explain that I, more than ever, needed to be sur-rounded by these Italians, Paola came to my rescue.

"Come with me," she said, leading my three daughters to the far end of the table to sit with her and her children. Before long, Paola was writing out Italian phrases on a napkin. "Now look closely," she told them in mock seriousness. "Here is how you tell your parents you have an Italian boyfriend. But *here* is how you ask for the Italian boyfriend you really want! See the difference?"

The food came right away. No menus, just an array of plates filled with thin-sliced hams and salami, risotto, *frittelle* (zucchini flower fritters), *frittata* (onions and eggs with capers), grilled eggplant, and mounds of olives and cannellini beans. Jugs of red wine were within everyone's reach. Every time I drained my glass, Caterina's husband, Vincenzo Infortuna, would refill it with a cheer, *"Salute!"* He knew no English, but we talked as best we could, trading an Italian-English dictionary back and forth. Laurelyn was absorbed in her own attempts at conversation, and occasionally, we would glance down the far end of the table, only to see my daughters eating and laughing comfortably with their new cousins.

The appetizers were followed by oval platters of rigatoni, in both a hearty tomato sauce and white cream sauce. It crossed my mind that my mother might actually *be* in the kitchen. *"Mangia, mangia,"* Vincenzo said as he spooned the macaroni on my plate. Amid the steady din of conversation and laughter, Giovanna told me, "We are all Catanosos here, but we are from different branches of the family. There are cousins here that I don't see very often. Most live here in Reggio, but some are here from Milan visiting family. It really feels like Christmas."

After we agreed to pass on the meat course and head straight to gelato and espresso, the waiter handed the check to Bruno. He began doing the division in his head. The men came together, handing Bruno euros of different sizes and colors. They never let me see the bill. They waved off the money I had in my hand.

"You've come a long way," Giovanna said, translating the words bouncing back and forth, "but they all say, 'When we come to America . . .'"

It was nearly midnight and I figured we'd start saying our good-byes. Not yet, not this crowd. Bruno suggested we all gather for a group photograph down on the waterfront, and no one hesitated. Soon this giddy gathering of Catanoso cousins was walking the five blocks down through the center of the city to the *lungomare.* We headed straight for the grand monument to Vittorio Emmanuel III, a modern marble arch with a bronze statue of a warrior whose back is to the Strait of Messina. Bruno interrupted a teenager who had been making out with his girlfriend behind the statue and asked him to take the photograph. We crowded in together, four rows deep. *"Formaggio!"* we shouted as the photos were taken.

Before we headed back to our hotel, finally calling it a night, I asked Giovanna if she would get everyone's attention.

"Please tell them thank you for making us feel so welcomed. This evening has exceeded our expectations." Giovanna's translation prompted a burst of cheers and clapping from the group, now circled around us.

My new pal Vincenzo, with whom I had exchanged maybe a half dozen words over the last three hours, threw an arm around me. In that moment, he felt like my best friend in the world.

# 8

## A Family Baptism

A few nights earlier, on Christmas Eve back in Rome, I had sat with dozens of Italians for midnight Mass in the cathedral Santa Maria degli Angeli on Piazza Repubblica. There I wrestled with twin aggravations. The Italian words of the local priest were entirely lost on me. And the ways of the Catholic Church, both here in the capital of Catholicism and back home in America, had long been lost on me as well.

I had not regularly attended Mass since childhood when my mother forced me and my three siblings to accompany her and my father to St. Ann's Church in Wildwood. I was baptized there. I made my first confession and first Holy Communion there. I was even confirmed there. But those sacraments, taken mostly with my boyhood friends and celebrated with family parties at the house, failed to hook me and pull me into the mystical core of the faith. When I didn't marry a Catholic, it was easy to drift even further from the church and its many rules, which I found so alienating. There was something I could not deny, though, if I ever stopped to think about it. My young soul had absorbed and retained a few remnants from those early years that I never shed, despite decades of doubt and cynicism and just plain distance. Somewhere deep down, I continued to carry a simple though often wavering belief in an all-powerful God. And I still said the few prayers taught to me as a child, though usually only at night when restless or worried. That's about it. Tender shoots from a seed planted long ago arrested in their development.

All this seemed terribly unfortunate as Giovanna Catanoso drove me in her tiny Fiat up through the narrow, curving streets of Reggio to the hilltop district of Santo Spirito and the church of Padre Gaetano Catanoso. It was Sunday, December 28, the ninety-fifth anniversary of the earthquake that had destroyed the city. Though no one else mentioned it, that epic event was on my mind that morning. Going to Mass? It never really occurred to me to go, even to a church in Reggio made extraordinary by a miracle-making relative. To me, this was a journey of familial significance, not spiritual. True, Padre Gaetano had been beatified by the Supreme Pontiff of the Roman Catholic Church, assuring the faithful that the humble priest now lived in heaven. But his life, message, and miracle making are not what resonated with me. Only the fact that he was a Catanoso did.

Laurelyn and the girls, who were riding with Daniela in her Renault, were waiting outside the church when Giovanna and I arrived. I got out at the curb and stared, feeling too excited to move. Emilia walked a short distance down the left side of the church's gated courtyard to snap a picture. "It says VIA CATANOSO!" she called out, describing the street sign attached to the side of the building.

The church was plain and more modern than I had imagined—boxy with a smooth stucco exterior painted a pale yellow. Olive trim accented the arched windows and a four-story bell tower with rectangular openings on four sides rose above the sanctuary. Laurelyn waved me into the courtyard, which occupied a corner space between the church and the Mother House for the Veronican Sisters of the Holy Face. There in the center of the courtyard, looking out over the neighborhood and perched atop a round, cement pedestal, stood Padre Gaetano Catanoso in bronze, the patina leaving him a dark, drab green. He looked younger than in the photos I had seen and was wearing a long cassock that flared out at the bottom like a bell. He was smiling sweetly and his hands were at his waist, the thick beads of a rosary woven through his fingers. I snapped a photo and kept moving, following Giovanna and Daniela up a short flight of outside steps to the doors of the sanctuary. As I entered, I didn't dip my fingers in the dish of holy water at the entrance and cross myself; I didn't say a prayer. It didn't occur to me. I just gawked like a tourist in a museum.

The space was gorgeous, intimate, and bathed in an ethereal glow of sunlight filtering through stained glass. The entire altar wall was filled with a tall, modern mosaic of a crucified Christ hanging above a robed woman holding up a cloth with the suffering image of Christ's face on it. It was St. Veronica.

In the back of the sanctuary in a corner chapel, though, was a truly stunning sight: Padre Gaetano himself, or at least his remains, lying in a glass-sided tomb that doubled as an altar. The tomb was lit from within and we could see that the body was dressed in a white priestly robe stitched with red trim, the hands together at the waist, again with a rosary between the fingers. The head was propped up on a gold pillow, and there were red satin slippers on the feet. We were somewhat prepared for this sight, having seen a small image on the Internet when we were planning the trip. Such tombs, with the visible remains of long-dead religious heroes, are not uncommon in Italy. We had seen from a distance the remains of a centuries-old pope at St. Peter's. But we could walk right up to Padre Gaetano.

He looked pretty good, actually, especially for someone who had died forty years earlier. We all inched closer, preparing to look away if need be. It wasn't necessary. While his remains were indeed inside the robed, body-shaped vessel, his head and hands, the only body parts showing, were clearly the end result of a skilled artist working in wax. It was quite a sight and I tried hard to clear my head of my racing thoughts to somehow make a deep, profound connection to what I was seeing.

"He looks like my dad, don't you think?" I whispered to Laurelyn.

That's the best I could do. But what did I expect? It wasn't as if I were so moved by the solemn, holy aura of this relative and this sacred place that I felt compelled to fall on my knees and confess three decades' worth of foul language, white lies, and letting my eyes wander when clearly, darn it, they should not have. It wasn't as if I were so overwhelmed by the guilt associated with my lapsed Catholicism that I vowed to have my daughters baptized—maybe even right there at the marble baptismal font in the back of this beautiful church. It wasn't as if I had decided, unequivocally, that each and every one of us would attend Mass every Sunday, starting the next week.

Now *that* would have been a miracle. Despite my mother's prayers, even before she knew we had such a well-placed relative, my soul was pretty much sealed off from that happening. This guy was a Catanoso. He was born in the same village as my grandfather. Given his broad, square chin and rounded forehead, he looked, in more than a few photos I had seen, a lot like my father, and in some others, just like Uncle Tony. The proud and satisfying call I was hearing most clearly was to family, not faith.

I believe I can be forgiven for that. If faith can make you feel a part of something bigger than yourself, so, too, can an Italian family bearing the love of the ages.

We lingered at the church for two hours, meeting several of the nuns and visiting the modest museum exhibit to the life of Padre Gaetano in the basement. There were dozens of black-and-white photographs on display under glass. There he was with his nuns, with a group of orphan boys, with his brothers and sisters and nieces and nephews. His face was open and honest. His smile was radiant. He seemed like a very nice man. We learned from Sister Felicidad, a young Veronican sister from the Philippines, that the second miracle, the one necessary for sainthood, was being investigated by the Vatican. She was quite sure that the canonization could come in a few years. We'll see you in Rome! we promised.

But now it was time to leave. Daniela took all of us back downtown to the apartment she shared with her mother, Pina, for Sunday lunch. Given the dinner of the previous night and our fascinating church visit, our weekend in Reggio had already been an unparalleled success. And it wasn't over yet.

When Daniela opened the door to her second-floor apartment on Via Possidonea, the roar from those crowding the narrow foyer knocked us back a step. There were at least thirty people there, maybe more, all clapping, all cheering, all Catanosos—and most of them new faces. We were hugged and kissed and swept into a small dining room set with three tables—two long, rectangular tables for seating, the other for staging the meal. Laurelyn and I were directed to sit with the older adults, mostly my parents' generation. Our girls were seated behind us with cousins closer to their age, each of whom tried to speak what little English he or she knew.

It looked as though Pina had spent days preparing this meal, which was carried in from the kitchen in a steady procession by several nieces. The women did all the serving; the men and boys waited to be served. The meal unfolded over the next several hours, one amazing course after another, starting with grilled eggplant in homemade olive oil, a peppers-and-eggs casserole, sun-dried tomatoes, and thick slices of salami. The macaroni—rigatoni like from the night before—came with both homemade tomato sauce and tuna-and-olive-oil sauce. When Laurelyn and I asked for seconds, our table fell quiet and a dozen faces seemed to stare at us with the same expression: Don't you realize there are at least four more courses coming?

My eyes were drawn to an older relative at the far end of the table. He was quite handsome with gray wavy hair, rimless glasses, and a courtly bearing. His name was Piero Catanoso, Pina's brother. He was the uncle who was Daniela's law partner. Their office was in the adjoining room of the apartment. Piero was, I would learn later, the family patriarch, the shining sun around which every other planet in the family naturally revolved. With his hair and eyes, Piero, I told Daniela, could have easily passed for one of my father's brothers. When she translated my remark, the look Piero gave me was that of father to son. He waved me over to formally introduce himself; and I returned the favor, paging through a palm-size photo album I was carrying. I showed him pictures of my dad and his four brothers and four sisters, Piero's relatives back in America. A few moments later, Piero and I stepped out on the nearby balcony for a photo of our own. Posing for Laurelyn, Piero put his arm over my shoulder as if it were the most natural thing to do. I raised my hand to his back. He made me promise, through Daniela, to send him a copy of the photo. Welcome to the family, he seemed to be saying.

The food kept coming—spicy sausages and thin-sliced pork, baked fish, and pan-fried potatoes. We tried everything, passing the wine (which only added to the rising din), marveling at the scene this had become. More relatives had arrived, grabbing plates and squeezing in wherever they could. Caterina Catanoso, the first relative to introduce herself to me at the restaurant the night before, was among the latecomers. She had a bottle of Catanoso-made red wine from Catanoso-grown vines. "For you to take home," she said in Italian. Bruno, the George Clooney look-alike, had also arrived with his daughter Simona.

During dessert—Italian cream cake with candles for the birthday of Piero's beautiful daughter Claudia—another newcomer arrived, Sergio, a handsome young cousin in his thirties with thinning hair and a clever smile. He quickly became the center of attention in the crowded room, poking an aunt, teasing a cousin, playing the clown. In my small album of photos, I had several shots of Laurelyn playing music. She has an acoustic band back home, and there were photos of her playing her Martin guitar and wearing a Western shirt and cowboy boots. At some point, Sergio disappeared from the room and returned carrying an old beat-up guitar. He made a great show of tuning it and attempting to strum it, and then he walked across the room and handed it to Piero. He played a few chords, shook his head, and handed it back to Sergio. What was going on?

By now, Sergio was standing next to Laurelyn, who was sitting pretty much in the middle of the room. He took the guitar back from Piero, held it up like a scepter, and presented it to Laurelyn with an elaborate bow. The room erupted in applause. Laughing, Laurelyn put her hand over her heart as my suddenly mortified daughters, who had been transfixed by everything that was going on, all started to shake their heads, *No, Mom, Don't!* Laurelyn caught my eye across the room where I was taking pictures. Of course she had to play, we both agreed with a fleeting glance. The moment was too charged, too perfect, too filled with overflowing emotions of love and laughter.

Reluctant at first, Laurelyn played a few modest bars of "Silent Night," hoping to draw the crowd in. She tried to hand the guitar back to Sergio, but he crossed his arms and swung his shoulders away from her. A Christmas carol would not do. That's when a chant rising to a roar in accented English started: *"Kahn-tree muus-eek, Kahn-tree muuseek!"* My daughters were laughing now, relaxed, enjoying it all.

Laurelyn relented, playing one of her own songs, an upbeat country tune she calls "Bluebird."

Over the next half hour or so, Laurelyn and Sergio traded the guitar back and forth, swapping songs and laughs. Once while she was playing, Sergio pulled Piero's wife, his aunt Adriana, from her chair to dance in small circles. They both mocked each other with their eyes as they spun round and round. Meanwhile, the food hadn't stopped. Out came fresh pineapple and dates and bowls of fennel, along with fresh Christmas cookies, liquors, and homemade limoncello. And finally—*finally*—this rolling, rollicking banquet ended with what tasted like the best coffee I had ever had.

Late in the afternoon, as darkness was coming on, we forced ourselves to leave with hugs and kisses and promises to write, promises to visit us in America. Two of the teenage cousins, Simona and Giorgia, pantomimed tears rolling down their cheeks.

Our tears, though, were real. I may not have baptized my children as Catholics a few hours earlier in Padre Gaetano's church. But just as my uncle Tony had been sixty years earlier in the village of Chorio, we were now fully, euphorically baptized as Catanosos of Italy right there in Pina's dining room.

# 9

# *Alan*

What is a miracle, really? It is a term we toss around with the ease and lightness of a Frisbee. It's a miracle that I wasn't late for work. It's a miracle that that beautiful shirt I wanted so badly was still available and even on sale. It's a miracle we weren't all killed on the highway that rainy night.

Was it a miracle that my family and I were gathered up into the arms of a host of ancestral strangers and embraced with unbridled, unconditional love? No. These are, after all, Italians, an entire people who have set the standard, worldwide, for what it means to be hospitable. And when you consider that the Catanosos are southern Italians, where devotion to family takes precedent over virtually everything else in life, then the reception we received, while in no way predictable, was at least entirely understandable, explainable.

No, a real miracle is something that is difficult to understand and impossible to explain through ordinary means. It is never luck, never a coincidence. It is, as St. Thomas Aquinas says, "beyond the order commonly observed," like Lazarus rising from the dead or the multiplying of loaves and fishes. It is divine and supernatural, gilded by grace and understood only through faith. Or to bring the matter closer to home (the Catanoso home), it is an Italian nun, kept from carrying out the work of her spiritual mentor because of a crippling lung disorder, recovering quickly, entirely, in the hours after her mentor's death.

Jesus performed his miracles, we are told, to convince a doubting world of his holiness and closeness to God. Padre Gaetano Catanoso orchestrated his first miracle for the bronchitis-stricken Sister Paolina Ligato, his nuns will tell you, as a way of signaling that he was exactly where they prayed he would be.

To understand the power of saints, earthly servants of God who earn their distinction only after death, is to believe in their ability to intercede on God's behalf from heaven. Saints—be they St. Anthony, St. Therese of Lisieux, or St. Gaetano Catanoso—are not the miracle makers themselves, the church tells us. They are God's middlemen. They are intercessors on His behalf.

Shortly after Laurelyn and I returned from Italy with our daughters, my family in America took a keen interest in miracles, and in Gaetano, in ways we never had before. We needed one. And we needed him.

In the winter of 2004, my brother Alan was busy designing and building a small office addition at our campground, located on the mainland near the island resort of Avalon, New Jersey. My family has owned and operated the business for more than forty years. Back in the mid-1960s, Alan and my oldest brother, Lenny, driving a bulldozer and dump truck long before they were old enough to get a driver's license, had helped our dad carve a lucrative summer business out of the ninety acres of woods along Route 9 in a spot (hardly a town) called Clermont. Renovations always occupied the off-season. A few years back, Alan, four years my elder, was forty-eight. He was the third of us four kids, a big, strong guy, five foot ten, heavyset with dark, curly hair and a dense mustache that leaned toward red. The campground project he was working on required carpentry and electrical work, Sheetrock and finishing, even some built-in furniture, like desktops and cabinets. Alan could do it all.

As the work progressed through January and into February, he noticed a problem with his coordination. He had trouble swinging a hammer precisely. He couldn't hold his balance on a ladder. His eyesight was troubling him, too. Double vision would come and go. Alan made accommodations. He got some help to finish the project. My parents called me often with their worries and concerns about Alan's health. My older sister Marlene called, too. Whatever was afflicting Alan, however, did not come as a complete surprise to him. He often feared that he was living on borrowed time.

As a family, we have always been extraordinarily healthy. My parents and my aunts and uncles have lived long lives unhobbled by diseases and infirmities until well into their seventies and eighties. Lenny, Marlene, me, and all our first cousins have been similarly fortunate. All of us except for Alan. We all got the mumps and chicken pox as children, but when Alan got them, they hit him harder and lasted longer. He was the only one of us with childhood allergies. As a teenager, he lost most of a summer to mononucleosis, while the rest of us went blithely on with our routines. Then things got really serious. In the fall of 1976, while he was a twenty-one-year-old senior at Penn State University, Alan noticed that he was having trouble hearing out of his right ear. There wasn't any pain, just an absence of sounds. A plane would fly overhead and he would see it well before he heard it, I remember him telling us.

Home for Thanksgiving, Alan visited our family doctor in North Wildwood, who referred him to a specialist in Philadelphia. The specialist found a mass in Alan's right ear that was as bad as anything he had ever seen. It was pressing on Alan's auditory nerve and reaching into the brain. This doctor called it an acoustic neuroma, dangerous but not malignant. He urged my parents to fly Alan across the country to the House Clinic in Los Angeles, perhaps the nation's best center at the time for ear surgery. They never hesitated. I was too young to understand or even recognize the fears my parents must have harbored. But they made the arrangements and went. My father stayed long enough to get my mother and Alan settled, then returned home; it was summer and his campground business was in full swing. My uncle Tony and aunt Phyllis flew out to be with my mother until my father could return.

The surgery went longer than expected. The tumor was more complicated than originally diagnosed. But the surgeon deemed the operation a success. The tumor cost Alan the hearing in his right ear, which was anticipated, and also some facial paralysis, which was not. His natural smile was reduced to a half smirk. My sister, Marlene, ran to her bedroom in tears when she first laid eyes on Alan after he returned home. "You never told me he was going to look like that," Marlene sobbed as my mother tried to calm her.

But at least the tumor was gone. The surgeon said he had removed everything he could and prescribed a four-week regimen of radiation to kill off any cells possibly left behind. It never occurred to my parents to question why radiation was necessary if the tumor wasn't cancerous. It was 1977, a time when doctors were still viewed as gods and medical information was solely the province of medical professionals.

"They never used the word *cancer*," my mother recalled. As far as she was concerned, her prayers to her favorite saints—St. Jude and St. Anthony; she didn't know about Padre Gaetano—had been answered. Alan was going to be okay.

Radiation was scheduled at Jefferson Hospital back east in Philadelphia, where my parents took turns making the two-hour drive, five days a week for a month, from our home at the shore. Alan sat in a sterile room by himself wearing a lead vest that fit him like overalls. The tip of his nose and the bottom of his right ear lobe were marked with faint, blue tattoo marks. That's how the radiology technician took aim, blasting Alan with megadoses of radiation. The therapy was far from subtle or precise and the long-term effect of such dosages was ill understood at the time. Like most young, otherwise healthy postop patients, Alan's head was hammered with as much as five thousand rads—two to three times more radiation than cancer patients receive today in the latter stages of their illness. His hair fell out for a while, but only over his ears and along the back of his head. My teenage memory of him was of someone zonked out on the living room couch when he wasn't throwing up.

"This is not fun" was the worst complaint I ever heard him utter.

The summer passed and Alan got up off the couch and finished his last semester at Penn State. He was one of those guys who always had a plan, always knew where he was headed. With his agriculture degree in hand, he returned home to join my brother Lenny in the greenhouse and landscaping business they had taken over from my father on New York Avenue in North Wildwood. Dad started the business in 1951, eight years before I was born, just around the corner from where he grew up. He gave the Garden Greenhouse & Nursery business to my brothers so that he and my mom and sister could concentrate on running the Avalon Campground. I worked in both these businesses as a kid, always feeling more like an indentured servant than a willing employee. I started writing for newspapers in earnest when I was a sophomore at Wildwood Catholic, covering high school football, cross country, and basketball for the *Wildwood Leader,* which came out every Thursday. Weekend games paid four dollars a story, lousy pay even in 1975. But it kept me from having to pot tomato plants or weed under the benches at the greenhouse after school and on weekends.

My brothers, though, gladly took on the challenge of running a business they had toiled in with my father since they were little. They worked insanely hard, something else they inherited from our father. They clashed a lot, too, as brothers in business are prone to do. But they seemed to know when to back away when things got too hot. Alan liked to needle Lenny about his short temper, calling him Mister Get-Me-a-Bigger-Hammer. Lenny would ride Alan for his grumpiness, a mood that seemed constant given his half grin that looked mostly like a frown. Mister Happy, Lenny called him.

Lenny, four years older than Alan (and eight years older than me), was the creative, extroverted half of their partnership. He was the outside guy, enthralling doctors and CEOs from the Philadelphia Main Line with his landscape visions for the yards of their million-dollar vacation homes in Avalon and Stone Harbor. He was a little shorter than Alan, balding with curly brown hair and my mother's round nose. Built like a bull, his nickname in high school, Lenny had been the captain and star of the Wildwood High football team, playing fullback and middle linebacker. He was my idol. Lenny wore number 32; years later, I insisted on number 32 on my rec league team as a teenager, even though I was a quarterback and should have worn a number under 20. Lenny threw the hammer at Penn State; I threw the shot put and discus on the track team in high school, even though I was shorter and scrawnier. He followed the Green Bay Packers, even though we lived in New Jersey. I did the same thing. I even memorized how much he could bench press (350 pounds) and dead lift (505 pounds).

And Alan? We shared a bedroom as kids for several years but had less in common. He was always something of a mystery to me. Or maybe he was just smarter. He didn't care that much about sports. He knew how to do things I could only marvel at from a distance. He made a darkroom out of our upstairs bathroom and developed his own black-and-white pictures. He built a mahogany china cabinet in ninth-grade shop class that won statewide honors and a prime spot in our living room. He bought a banana yellow Hobie catamaran and taught himself how to handle wind on the ocean.

Less talkative by nature, he was the inside guy in the partnership with Lenny, the grower overseeing the propagation of poinsettias at Christmas, lilies and hydrangeas at Easter, and a veritable sea of red and pink geraniums for spring and summer. While Lenny was out on the street directing his noisy landscape crews with tractors and power tools, Alan was back in the quiet of the greenhouses, the only sound being the rush of water through hoses, which he could barely hear. He also kept the books and did payroll, solitary tasks that suited his attention to detail.

When he wasn't working at the greenhouse, or helping out after-hours at the campground, he was building his own split-level house in the middle of four wooded acres of pine and oak in Cape May Court House. He bought the land when he was twenty, before he had gotten sick, before he had graduated from college. I was in high school at the time and had no idea where he got the notion, let alone the gumption, to make such adult decisions. Had he not chosen to join Lenny in business, he could have made a fortune as an electrician, plumber, or construction contractor.

"Who's going to live in this big place?" I asked during one of my visits to see the house.

"Me and my family," he said, driving a nail into a roof beam.

"You don't even have a girlfriend."

"Let me worry about that," he said.

It wasn't long before he was seeing someone seriously—Anna Accardi, a local girl, who would indeed become his wife. Anna was as thin as Alan was heavy, with shoulder-length brown hair, an energetic manner, and a penchant for hard work. She was all Italian, just like our family, and had grown up running a family business, too, a motel in North Wildwood that her parents owned. And she loved to cook. Alan couldn't resist her spaghetti and meatballs. She moved into the house he built in the woods, just like he had planned.

But about seven years after his Los Angeles operation, Alan noticed the hearing slipping gradually in his lone good ear. Anna would grow accustomed to visits to ear specialists and learning all about hearing aids. As Alan's hearing grew worse, she started learning about radiation—we all did—and the fact that once it goes in, it never comes out.

It was 1984, the year I married Laurelyn, a year before Alan and Anna's wedding. X-rays and tests at home and in Philly failed to detect anything awry, certainly not another mass in Alan's gradually failing good ear. So he headed back to Los Angeles and the House Clinic. There, burrowing through his medical records, doctors identified what they believed to be the culprit. The radiation he sustained seven years earlier at Jefferson Hospital had been misdirected. Through a technician's error, most of the massive amount of rads meant for his deaf right ear had actually zapped the nerves and area around his good left ear instead. He was suffering from radiation poisoning, a progressive condition affecting the very cells within his ear. The damage was irreversible.

"I'm like a Chernobyl victim," Alan told me, and he was right. But just like his myriad skills and ability to plan for his future, his plight was a mystery to me. He didn't talk about it. "This isn't fun" is the worst I would hear him say.


In May 2004, after being briefed for months on Alan's strange health problems, I traveled up from North Carolina to visit my family in Cape May County. It was my first visit to New Jersey since getting back from Italy less than five months earlier. That winter and into the spring, after Alan finished his work on the new office at the campground, I had gotten frequent telephone calls from my mother and Lenny, which only grew in urgency.

"It's bad, Justin," Lenny told me. "I can see him getting a little worse every day. He's unsteady on his feet. I mean, sometimes it looks like he's going to topple over. And this week he told me he was having trouble swallowing."

"What's going on?"

"Nobody knows. He's been up to Pennsylvania Hospital twice for blood tests and a spinal tap and they can't find anything wrong."

I drove over to Alan's house early that Saturday morning in a red PT Cruiser I had rented at the Philadelphia airport. Alan's daughters, Marsiella and Lisa, seventeen and twelve, came running out of the house to see it, and me. It was a gorgeous spring day, nothing but bright sun and blue sky hovering above this opening in the woods. The house looked great, the flower beds already trimmed precisely with red impatiens below the meticulously cropped hollies and junipers. Ginger, their yellow lab, fat from too many table scraps, waddled out behind the girls, barking and wagging her entire butt.

Alan came out, too. I watched him closely as he made his way from the side of his house across the gravel driveway. He walked with his feet farther apart than normal, planting each foot carefully, as if he were a sailor on the deck of a ship being tossed on stormy seas.

"How are you doing, Alan?" I asked as we shook hands.

"I'm fine, I'm fine," not wanting to say anything else, at least not with Marsiella and Lisa nearby.

Anna joined all of us inside around the kitchen table, which looked out onto a grassy backyard ringed with tall pines. Alan sat on my right, which I made sure of; that way I could speak closer to the hearing aid in his left ear. As I paged through my photo album, regaling Alan and his girls with stories of the *passeggiata* in Reggio and the endless lunch at Pina's, I could feel a knot tightening in my stomach. What was wrong with Alan this time?

My brother kept the conversation focused on Italy. He and his family were set to leave on an Italian adventure of their own in a few weeks. Alan had booked a two-week, high-end tour package of Italy's top destinations, complete with guides, hotels, and meals. He had started planning it soon after I e-mailed him in January about our experiences. In contrast with our budget-conscious sojourn, Alan could afford the best. Jefferson Hospital had refused back in 1988 to settle the lawsuit Alan reluctantly filed regarding the radiation mishap. A jury was quick and generous in its judgment. The jurors wanted to ensure that Alan not only had what he needed to provide for his family, but could also afford whatever technological advance might come along to restore his hearing.

Alan's good ear gave out entirely in 2000, and a year later he was able to pay out of pocket for a cochlear implant at Johns Hopkins Medical Center. The device gave him what he described as a kind of faint, tinny hearing that you might experience at the far end of a tunnel. He was glad for it. The first words he heard after surgery, after a year of stone deafness, were from Lisa. "I love you, Daddy." Alan didn't throw his arms around his daughter or break down in tears, even though Anna and the girls were in puddles. He wasn't like that. He said simply with a half smile beneath his mustache, "I heard that, and you sound like Minnie Mouse."

A lan followed me outside after we all had spent an hour or so with my Italy photographs. He and his family had never been overseas before, and the girls were giddy with excitement.

"I can't wait to see Venice and ride a gondola," Lisa said.

"I can't wait to see Italian boys," Marsiella said.

Anna worried about the right clothes to bring, whether they should have umbrellas, whether the cash machines would work. And Alan, he mostly sat there quietly, staring at my photos, his chin resting in his hand.

As we walked across his gravel drive to my car, I resisted the urge to hold on to his arm to help steady his balance. He would have hated that.

"I started feeling things going wrong last winter, when I was working on the office at the campground, but I really began to notice it about a month ago," he started to tell me.

Ever since he had gotten his cochlear implant, Alan's voice had become more nasally, higher pitched. He talked softly, hearing his words in his head, not in his ears.

"I always treat the lawn with a chemical spray in the beginning of spring. I start at the top near the kitchen, with a sprayer on the hose, and walk backwards. I've been doing this for years, but last month I couldn't."

"Why not?"

"I couldn't walk backwards. I just couldn't do it. I felt like I was going to fall over. And then last week, I went with the girls to Hershey Park for their band trip. They're running around wanting to do everything. And I couldn't keep up. I had to tell them to go on ahead with their friends. I just found a seat and waited for them."

The knot in my stomach was tightening. Alan was never self-pitying. Years of near deafness had made him fiercely independent and more than a little aloof. Enjoying a conversation at a crowded restaurant was impossible. Movies and concerts were out. Talking on the phone was difficult. Television always required closed captions. He loved to watch his daughters march in their bands at the halftime of Middle Township football games and carefully photographed them whizzing through their formations. As for the songs themselves, he could hardly hear them. Anna was happy he wanted to be at the games anyway, whether or not he was taking photos; she knew he could drift away into a world of his own, reading the *Wall Street Journal* or surfing the Internet. Best I could tell, Alan had adapted pretty well to his handicap. He seemed to accept his circumstances and roll along. Not that I really knew. We didn't talk about it.

For the first time, though, I could hear a hint of fear creeping into my older brother's voice. Now *I* felt unsteady. I didn't recognize this emotion in Alan, and his vulnerability surprised me. He needed to talk, to confide in me, something he rarely did. My instinct was to run, like a little brother putting distance between me and trouble. But there was no outrunning what Alan was about to tell me. So I stayed put. And listened.

"I've been online, looking things up. Maybe it's MS, I don't know. Maybe it's something like that."

MS, okay, I know a little bit about MS, I thought. I had written about multiple sclerosis when I covered the medical beat for the daily newspaper in Greensboro. It's awful and can be crippling, but it is different in everyone and the medications are getting better—and it's not fatal. Fatal? I could not believe I had just thought that. I pushed it out of my head. Whatever this is, Alan will handle it somehow. He always has. I wanted to tell him that MS could be managed, or tell him it might be nothing. I wanted to be hopeful and optimistic. But he kept talking.

"I haven't had any X-rays yet, though, so I don't know. And they can't do an MRI of my head because of my implant. The metal in it throws off the machine."

"Can they take it out so you can get an MRI scan?" It was easier just to ask questions.

"I guess. But when am I supposed to do that? We're leaving for Italy in three weeks. I don't know." His voice trailed off and I watched him look away, off into the thickest part of the woods. "I don't know if I'm going to be around much longer."

He turned back and looked me in the eye. He seemed to be saying: *Did you hear me? Do you understand what I'm saying?* I froze. I could see he wasn't exaggerating or being melodramatic. Oh my God, I thought; he's serious. It was my turn to look away.

I can't remember what I said next or how we managed our good-byes. I know we didn't embrace. We didn't do that. But as the tires of my rental car crunched over the long, shaded drive to the road, I caught a glimpse of Alan lumbering back to his house in the rearview mirror. *I don't know if I'm going to be around much longer.* I knew I would never forget him saying that, like remembering where I was when I first heard that a plane had crashed into the World Trade Center. It was clear to me that he believed it and that our neat little healthy world wasn't going to be the same.

I tried to push those thoughts aside as I drove to my parents' house a few miles up Route 9 in Cape May County. I did not want to think that my brother, no matter how many maladies had assailed him already in his life, could actually die sometime soon. It was a perfect time to say a prayer, but it didn't occur to me. Try as I might, I could not sidetrack the darker thoughts coming on. I was too practical and sensible. My work as a journalist had affected my outlook on life far more than any religion. I had shown up on the scene of car accidents where teenagers, no different from my daughters, had been killed in senseless wrecks. I had sat with a young mother of three babies and interviewed her about her chemo treatments for breast cancer, two weeks before she died. I had seen, as most journalists have, bad things happen to people who didn't deserve them.

No, God and Jesus and Gaetano were far from my thoughts. What I was thinking made me dizzy and I knew I wouldn't be telling my parents or even Lenny or Marlene.

I believed Alan.

# 10

# Unanswered Prayers

In that terrible summer of 2004, my mother prayed relentlessly for a miracle. She had good reason. Alan, her forty-eight-year-old son, the child she worried over more than the other three of us combined, had been diagnosed with brain cancer. Inoperable. Day and night, she would ask: How could this happen? But every morning she would rise to the same ritual, working the crystal beads of her rosary as she sat in a wooden armchair next to her bed, still in her nightgown. She would pray the Apostles' Creed, of course, and a host of Hail Marys and Our Fathers. Then she would take a small prayer card in her hands with the smiling face of a priest on it, a humble mission priest from southern Italy. Gaetano Catanoso, our cousin, almost a saint.

My mother would pray to Gaetano with all the hope and conviction her long and unquestioned Catholic faith could sustain. She had known about him for a few years, but he didn't supplant her prayers to St. Jude and St. Therese until Laurelyn and I had returned home from Reggio with our stories of Gaetano's church and nuns and the healing miracle confirmed by the pope. He was real to her now, one of the family. Surely he would listen. So she explained Alan's condition as best she could. She explained that the doctors offered few options and little hope. But she was not giving up, not with her faith, not if Gaetano would hear her prayers.

Then one morning a thought occurred to her and she came out of her bedroom to find me. I spent a lot of time staying with my parents that summer, taking my vacation days and weekends and flying up from North Carolina to New Jersey as often as I could. With Laurelyn and my daughters back home, I stayed in the frilly guest room of my parents' blue ranch-style house just off Route 9 near their campground business. A framed copy of Alan and Anna's wedding invitation hung above the light switch in the room next to a porcelain crucifix. I had been up for a few minutes that morning, reading *The Press of Atlantic City*, standing in the living room with its vaulted ceiling, console television set, and framed photographs of all us kids and our kids on every surface.

"Justin, I've been praying to Gaetano in English," my mother said, walking up to me. Her red-rimmed eyes looked as scared and vulnerable as a child's. "Does Gaetano understand English?"

In any other context, I suppose, the question would have struck me as funny. I would have teased her, as I love to do, and made her laugh. But all I could really think to do was wrap my arms around her as my own eyes began to well up.

"Oh, Mom, I don't know. I bet he can."

She let out a few pained sobs on my shoulder and then calmed herself and stepped back. She lifted her glasses to dry her eyes with a balled-up tissue she had tucked under her sleeve and went back to the armchair next to her bed. She told me later that she searched her memory for some of the Italian her immigrant parents had spoken to her at home as a girl. There was a time when she understood the language clearly, though she learned to speak very little. Finally, a few words came to her, and they were enough.

"*Per favore, Padre Gaetano,*" she prayed aloud, "*aiuta mio figlio.*" Please, Father Gaetano, help my son.

It was early June and Alan's condition continued to deteriorate, his mobility lessening each day. With his Italy trip looming, he began to question whether it was possible for him to go.

"Think about it, Alan," Lenny warned. "You've got all these buses to get in and out of, all this walking and climbing. What if something happens? Who's going to help you?"

For a while, Alan just cracked, "I need to go. Maybe Gaetano has one more trick up his sleeve."

But on June 6, Alan sent me an e-mail. "As you probably know by now, the trip to Italy is off. I've had more than one person tell me we should not be going. I tried to sell Dad and Mom on taking the trip with the girls. I even told them I'd throw in my new underwear but it didn't work. Needless to say, Marsiella and Lisa are more than a little disappointed. I'm going to close now. I've made more than my share of mistakes writing this short letter."

To me, that last line read like a door opening to the truth.

Twenty-four hours later, Alan wobbled into Johns Hopkins Medical Center in Baltimore, carrying a cane, but refusing to use it, Lenny following closely behind. Given Alan's cochlear implant, Hopkins until then had always been a place of hope for Alan. Not this time. Several days after being admitted, the diagnosis finally came. When a doctor walks into the room with a grave look and speaks to a family in measured phrases wrapped in empathy, it's hard to imagine that you are not watching a Hallmark movie of the week. You have seen this before. It is entirely familiar. Almost a cliché. Until you look over and see your brother sitting there in a corner chair, dressed in a hospital gown, his lips pressed together, his eyes filled with fear. That's when you realize that nothing, nothing, prepares you for this moment.

"Well, we got the MRI back and we have a pretty good idea what we're dealing with," said Dr. Aldridge, who took a seat on the long countertop by the window just a few feet from Alan. He was in his early forties and bald, resembling a plainspoken Dr. Charles Winchester of M*A*S*H*, only with unflagging patience. He had delivered countless such speeches and was good at it. As he settled in, he looked us all in the eye, my parents and us four kids, the only ones there that night; Anna had stayed home with their daughters. When the doctor spoke, it was directly to Alan.

"What we think you've got is a grade-three astrocytoma of the brain stem, possibly a grade four. The brain stem controls your motor movements and that's why you're having difficulty with your balance and coordination and even swallowing."

No one said a word. Alan's eyebrows arched a bit and his pressed lips turned to a frown as if he were bracing himself. I tried to imagine what he must be thinking. I couldn't.

"This tumor is aggressive and it's in a bad spot. It's surrounded by this bundle of nerves that come up from the spinal column into the base of the brain. The tumor is tangled up in there. There really is no safe way to operate."

Give us something to latch on to here, Doc, I was thinking, anything.

"What causes something like this? We don't know for sure. But in looking through your medical records, it looks like you got a lot of radiation back in 1977. That was common post-op treatment for astrocytomas back then. So it's possible that this tumor is radiation induced. It's not in the same place as the one you had back then, but it's similar."

That decades-old radiation was resurfacing to attack Alan again. It had stolen his hearing, and now it was set to steal his life. But I was confused. We all were. Was Dr. Aldridge suggesting that Alan had cancer in 1977? We had always thought that the tumor back then was benign. *"They never used the word* cancer," my mother had always insisted. What word had they used?

It turns out, the surgeons at the House Clinic in Los Angeles had used the word astrocytoma then. Did the doctors not explain it any further? Did my parents not ask? Most likely, they were so relieved to have their twenty-one-year-old son safely out of surgery that they let the word, and all its horrible implications, slide right past them. But Dr. Aldridge found it. It was in the medical records.

"Is an astrocytoma cancerous?" I asked.

"Yes, I'm afraid so," Aldridge practically whispered. Then trying to mitigate the blow, he added, "We have a few options. It's possible that you can tolerate a little more radiation, but probably not that much. We'd have to be real precise. And there are some drugs we can get you started on—chemotherapy. There are some experimental drugs we can talk about, too."

There were more questions, but what I remember most—beyond the grim diagnosis—was the shock of having to recalibrate an assumption we had all carried for more than a quarter century. Alan had cancer in 1977 after all. That's why he had been given radiation. To all of us, it was like hearing the diagnosis not once, but twice, like a punch in the gut and a roundhouse to the jaw.

After Dr. Aldridge left, I moved to break the silence. "It sounds like we have some options," I said to Alan, feeling instantly guilty about using the word *we*.

"Do those sound like good options to you?" Alan responded. Now I felt stupid *and* guilty, like I should have kept my mouth shut.

But there was no edge in Alan's voice, in fact, he sounded calm and, in a strange way, serene. My mom was stifling her sobs and my dad had an arm around her, his jaw set. Marlene stood quietly, too, and Lenny tried to say, "We're going to fight this, Alan, we're . . ." but he couldn't get anything else out. We were a picture of the typical family in the early stages of shock and grief, grasping for words as if we were losing our grip while rock climbing. Somehow, Alan was holding on, even reaching back to pull us along.

"Look, I want everyone to just calm down," Alan started to say in a voice far steadier than it had any right to be. We all stared at him, sitting there in the corner, his bare feet crossed at the ankle, his hands folded on his lap. "I've had a lot of time to think. We all have to face this time sooner or later. And maybe this is my time. I don't know. But I do know this. I know I've been lucky. Mom and Dad, twenty-seven years ago, when I was sick the first time, you made sure I got the best care possible. I can't thank you enough for that."

My brother, whose lack of hearing led him to live so much of his life in his head, was inviting us inside. He had just been handed what I figured was a death sentence, and rather than crumbling, he was rising up, even though he could barely stand on his own two legs. For a moment, my sadness was replaced with a couple of other emotions altogether: pride and awe.

"Look what I've gotten to do. I was able to finish college and run a business with Lenny. I was able to marry Anna and have Marsiella and Lisa. I've been able to see them grow up. And you're all here now. I got twenty-seven years that I guess I shouldn't have had. I've been really lucky."

Alan kept talking, kept urging us not to worry, to go home. But it was hard to pay attention. My mind floated up and out of the room. Where was he getting this courage? Where was he getting his wisdom and perspective on what could only have been the darkest, scariest moment of his life?

We rode home in silence, the five of us, Marlene driving us in her Volkswagen SUV with Lenny in the front. I was wedged in the backseat between my mother and father. When we arrived at the campground, my father called us all into his office. His words would be the first words spoken in the three hours since we left Alan's room. He urged us not to tell anyone about what we had just heard, to keep it to ourselves. That's all he said. I found it curious advice at the time. But as I came to understand my father better and understand the context of his upbringing, it made sense: The son of Carmelo was reminding us that crises are to be borne quietly, privately, as a family.

M y mother always intended to put a small photo of Padre Gaetano Catanoso in Alan's hospital room, but she never found the right frame. Instead, she pinned to the wall near his bed a copy of an airline magazine story I had written about our recent trip to Reggio to meet our Italian relatives. The article appeared in June, the month the world changed for us, and it carried a colorful, iconic illustration of Gaetano with his right arm raised, as if giving a blessing. My mother, who has been carrying newspaper clippings of mine in her pocketbook since I first started writing in high school, brought a short stack of copies of the magazine story to Alan's room one day. He made sure that every doctor and nurse who came in took a copy with them. "My brother wrote this," he would say, without any further explanation.

I couldn't help but think that it wasn't the story he wanted them to see as much as the headline: "Miracles Happen."

I was happy with that story, happy to think, as I sat with Alan in his hospital room, that at that very moment countless people flying through the sky were reading about our family and learning about Padre Gaetano Catanoso. Maybe the old priest was even floating somewhere in the clouds. It was a nice distraction. But it didn't last. My agony that summer was feeling like the odd man out, the guy without hope, the one already spinning ahead to the inevitable. Alan needed a miracle. We just happened to have a miracle maker in the family. How convenient.

The language the doctors used was often stark and rarely comforting. I would listen intently, then question them further in the hallway outside Alan's room. I found myself often playing the role of interpreter for my parents, for Anna and her daughters, for Lenny and Marlene. There was something bracing about this responsibility. Catholic author Robert Ellsberg has written: "At least in sorrow, we know we are alive." And there in the throes of death and so much sadness, I had never felt so alive. Every conversation, every medical "translation," every nuanced phrase we spoke reverberated with what felt like epic importance.

But the stress it dumped on us was voluminous. None of us seemed to know how to talk about what we were feeling. We hung together mostly, but it was hard. Marlene, quiet as ever but eager to do something, anything, felt powerless to comfort Alan. My parents, married for more than fifty years, were overwhelmed with the notion that a child of theirs, even an adult child, was so desperately ill. Lenny was the same. We talked, but rarely about what seemed obvious to me: Alan was dying. Maybe they all believed the doctors, or God, or Gaetano, would find a way to rescue Alan. I never believed that. But I had to ask myself: How hard is it to be hopeful? It often felt too hard, like lying. The tension grew.

One morning at my parents' house that summer, I awoke to find my mother in the hallway outside my bedroom. "When are you going to get your daughters baptized?" she demanded angrily.

I couldn't believe it. She had been making this plea since Emilia, my oldest, was born in 1988, so hearing it again wasn't unusual. But the timing to me was suspect, as if she were reverting to something in our lives she might be able to see fixed. I was feeling my own stress those days and was less than sympathetic.

"Mom, of all the things you have to worry about right now, that's not one of them."

What I was worried about was less religious and more practical. Laurelyn helped me sort out my family dynamics in an e-mail she sent from North Carolina while I was up in New Jersey: "Alan is a very sick, probably dying man, and he will deal with that within the context of his life, with his wife and children, with his parents and siblings, and all their complicated relationships. But *you* are his brother. That is pretty uncomplicated. And you get to decide what you want to do with that. You can choose."

What I really wanted to do, I realized, was ask Alan what he was thinking, how he was preparing himself. And on those long, quiet rides from South Jersey to the hospital in Baltimore, I resolved each time that I would tell Alan that he had been a good brother. I would tell him that I loved him. Maybe there was hope in that. Whenever I was talking with my parents or siblings, I would remind myself to simply agree that maybe the doctors would find a way. But with Alan I would be honest.

Except that I couldn't. I would sit right beside him while he lay in bed, forming the words in my head, but I could not get myself to say them aloud. We hadn't learned that language in the past, and I couldn't speak it now. In a way, I needed my own miracle, and it wasn't coming.

It occurred to me that summer that times like these are made for church families. A church family could help me bear this burden; I would not have to walk alone. But I had drifted far from the church, so far that I could not remember if there was actually a reason for disappearing. Had I ever made a conscious decision? I did take some solace in knowing that those whose faith was intact kept Alan in their prayers all the time. Like Anna and his daughters. Like his friend Judi Salasin, who sat with Alan and prayed loud enough for him to hear her. Like his church friends back where he and his family lived in

Cape May Court House. And always, there were the prayers of my mother.

"Justin, do you think Giovanna would mind going to Gaetano's church and lighting a candle for Alan?" she asked one morning.

I offered to send an e-mail to Reggio but warned that it might be weeks before I got a reply from my notoriously fickle correspondent. Yet when I was on the computer two days later, I was surprised to find a note from Giovanna. In four years of periodic communication, I had never heard back from her so quickly. She had visited Gaetano's church as my mother requested. She had lit a candle for Alan. And she had told the nuns about Alan, too.

"They are all praying for him," Giovanna wrote.

My mother was elated. And I was elated to give her some good news for a change. But I wondered: If Gaetano is in heaven, and Gaetano is our cousin, could he, would he, take a special interest in a distant relative he never knew in life?

M y brother Lenny did not have any doubts about his faith. That's because he didn't have any—faith that is. It's not fair to call him an agnostic or an atheist. He was baptized Catholic, as we all were. But he fell so completely and entirely away from the church and religion that neither registered a pulse with him. He would never wrestle with the duality of whether faith without good works is meaningless, or whether good works alone was enough to bolster one's faith.

But that summer, and well into the fall, Lenny did the kinds of things heroes do, instinctively, wholeheartedly. My childhood idol lived up to his billing again in middle age. Mostly, though, he lived a kind of unwavering faith that was spiritual and Christian in the truest, deepest sense. He was channeling Padre Gaetano. I can see that now, even if he still can't.

Alan spent nearly a month at Johns Hopkins, and each day brought nothing but bad news, mostly delivered by Dr. Aldridge. Alan's ability to swallow had diminished to the point that his food now needed to be chopped. He was constantly beset by hiccups. He started getting drowsy earlier and earlier each evening. The tumor in Alan's brain stem was causing these cascading maladies. By the time he was discharged from Hopkins, Alan had lost the ability to walk and his independence was limited to what he could do with his right arm and hand. Dr. Aldridge talked to us about hospice and hinted that Alan might not make it to his forty-ninth birthday on July 21, less than three weeks away. I could see it and kept quiet. But Lenny couldn't, and he let it be known.

"We're not talking about hospice," he insisted. "We're not there yet."

When Alan was prescribed some medication to attack the tumor, a chemotherapy drug called Temodar, the price was staggering—$4,500 for five pills, plus $600 for the antinausea medication to battle the toxicity of the chemo. Lenny didn't hesitate. Finally, he could *do* something. He grabbed the prescription from the oncologist and literally ran to the hospital pharmacy, handing over the script with his credit card.

After several days in a rehab facility in Vineland, New Jersey, Alan returned to the house he built in the woods. His family room, which made up the first floor, was ground level. Alan could be easily wheeled in and out. As a landscaper, Lenny had plenty of friends in construction and the trades. He rallied enough of them to quickly transform that family room into Alan's living space, complete with hospital bed and handicap toilet and shower stall wide enough to roll in a waterproof chair.

While in the rehab facility, Lenny carefully took note of how a nurse half Alan's size was able to get him and his 230-pound frame to sit on the edge of the bed, then crouch low, grab him securely around the waist, and swing him quickly into the adjacent wheelchair. As a track and field athlete, Lenny had mastered the intricate pirouette of twirling a sixteen-pound hammer on a long, steel wire around his head while he kept his center of gravity low and spun three times—heel to toe, heel to toe—before releasing the ball and chain.

"Once I saw how it was done, I realized I could do it, I could transfer him from the bed to the wheelchair," Lenny told me. "I was just the right size to reach around him, grab him by the belt, and pivot him around. I wasn't going to take him home simply to lie in bed."

A lan was home, but it was stressful. Lining up quality nursing care proved difficult. Lenny ended up hiring a neighbor, Diane, a part-time nurse, to be with Alan early in the morning and just before he went to sleep at night. Anna was determined to give Alan as much care as she could, preparing most of his meals, chopping his food, tracking his medications, and simply sitting with him in silence. But she also tried hard to keep things relatively normal for Marsiella and Lisa, which was impossible. Life for them, always so orderly when Alan was at the controls, had veered into unknown territory. Worse still, the chemo Alan took one week a month was brutally toxic and left him weak for days.

Judi Salasin, middle-aged and slender with blond, wispy bangs and warm blue eyes, was a regular visitor. She worked for Lenny at the greenhouse and had always found Alan and his innate gruffness intimidating. Those barriers tumbled with Alan's illness. She saw his physical needs being cared for. But she also saw that none of us was either prepared to or capable of talking with Alan about the obvious. A devout and sturdy Christian, Judi went with Alan where we could not.

How are you with God? she'd ask. What do you believe? Alan's answers, she told me later, were simple declarations at first. He went to church regularly with his wife and daughters, which the rest of us never did. A few years earlier, he even turned a quiet, barren spot next to his church into a lush and colorful prayer garden, designing and landscaping it himself with shrubs, ornamental grasses, and perennials. He didn't know if all that was enough.

"I haven't been that good," he later told her. He confided, too, about the deep anger he sustained about a life full of medical troubles, a complaint none of us in the family ever heard.

Judi kept coming; she kept probing. She would read to him from the Bible, New Testament stories mostly, about the resurrection and Jesus's promise of paradise. She would pray with him, too, leaning in close to make sure he could hear her clearly. "I wanted to take Jesus Christ from his head and put Him in his heart," she said.

Sometimes, Judi remembered, Alan would talk to her about Padre Gaetano. "He's going to be a saint, you know. He's performed miracles." Judi had been a Catholic but eventually came to believe that the religion's preferred conduit of priests and saints merely clogged the path between her and God. She didn't want any filters. Still, she could see that Alan seemed to be finding a certain comfort in the sacred relative whose face smiled from a medal around his neck.

"Do you pray to Gaetano to make you well?" Judi asked one day.

"Sometimes. And my mother does all the time."

The doctors' most pessimistic predictions proved wrong. Alan made it to his birthday. My mother invited Monsignor Jim Mc-Donough of Philadelphia, the priest in our family and cousin of Uncle Charlie's wife, Louise, to say Mass for him at her house. Alan, sitting in his wheelchair, listened as best he could and gratefully took Holy Communion.

Later that summer and fall, Lenny's greenhouse and landscaping operation was operating full throttle. He had more than sixty employees divided into three divisions fanning out six days a week all over Cape May County. Sixteen-hour workdays were the norm through the summer and fall. Now, out of that time, Lenny carved as many hours as he could to be with Alan, relying on his managers to pick up any slack.

"I had to see him first thing in the morning; that was a must. That gave me some reassurance that he was okay. I would get there early and Diane would already be there. He'd see me come in and I'd get the big wave. I just had to make sure he woke up."

There was something else that Lenny would do morning and night. He would take his right hand, thick and calloused from years of planting shrubs, and shake Alan's, which had always been like Lenny's, but was now dry and feeble. It was more than a greeting. For Lenny, it was an effort at a bloodless transfusion of hope and strength, brother to brother.

Antonina Tripodi, the saint's mother, and Antonino Catanoso, the saint's father.

The saint's cousins in Chorio, Italy: Antonino Catanoso and Elisabetta Mangiola, Carmelo Catanoso's parents.

A young immigrant, Carmelo Catanoso in Philadelphia around 1915 as a salesman for Rosa Food Products.

Both Gaetano Catanoso and his cousin Carmelo were born in the village of Chorio in southern Calabria in the late 1800s.

Pentidattilo, a hillside village perched just above the Ionian Sea in Calabria, is where Padre Gaetano led his first parish from 1904 to 1921.

As a young priest in Pentidattilo,
Padre Gaetano, pictured here in
around 1910, fought poverty,
spiritual ignorance, and the Mafia.

The renown of Padre Pio, one of
the most beloved modern saints,
was so strong in 1920 that Padre
Gaetano was lured from Pentidattilo
to Pio's parish in San Giovanni
Rotondo to try to meet him.

The Church of St. Peter and Paul
in Pentidattilo, built in the 1500s.

The first branch of the Catanoso family tree in America, gathered in North Wildwood, New Jersey, in 1936. Caterina and Carmelo Catanoso are seated to the left amid their nine children. Carmelo's parents, his brother Giuseppe, and his niece are to his left.

Justin Catanoso's father, Leonard, was the only one in his family to attend college. He graduated from Penn State in 1943 and was a member of the gymnastics team.

Tony Catanoso driving his father's Ford panel truck, used to deliver groceries in Cape May County, New Jersey, in the 1930s.

While stationed in Sicily during World War II, Tony Catanoso went AWOL in 1944 in search of the only Italian relative he knew of, his aunt Maria Catanoso in Chorio. She can be seen in the window above the door.

Tony, in his military uniform with his smiling aunt, deemed the fact that he was able to find Maria "the first miracle."

Padre Gaetano used the skull
in the background for prayerful
contemplation. The skull is kept
today as a relic in a small museum at
the church in Reggio, Italy.

Padre Gaetano on the phone in
his room at the Mother House
in Reggio.

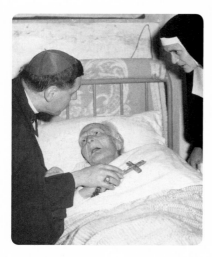

Padre Gaetano on his deathbed,
April 3, 1963. He is pictured with
Sister Anastasia, the first Mother
General of the Veronican sisters,
the order he founded, and Monsignor
Giovanni Ferro, the archbishop
of Reggio Calabria, who later
administered Last Rites.

Padre Gaetano's church in the Santo Spirito section of Reggio was commissioned and planned by him before his death and opened in 1972.

Inside the sanctuary.

St. Gaetano's remains, encased within a lifelike wax vessel, are displayed in a glass tomb in the rear of his church in Reggio. The tomb is a magnet for the faithful—ever more so since the canonization. Here, a group of Veronican sisters, many from the Philippines, gathers at the tomb with Sister Dorotea, the Mother General, far right.

Justin, Alan, Nick (Lenny's son), Leonard, and Lenny Catanoso in 1996 on the campus of Penn State University. They are all alumni.

Justin Catanoso's brother Alan in 2003, prior to the onset of his illness.

Lookalikes: Leonard Catanoso with a flag featuring his cousin the saint.

Manoel da Silveira Cardozo
(1911-1985), Justin's academic
mentor and spiritual instigator.

Homecoming. December 27, 2003, marked the first time American Catanosos
set foot in Calabria in more than thirty years. From left: cousin Daniela
of Reggio; Justin's daughters, Emilia, Rosalie, and Sophia; wife Laurelyn;
Justin; and cousins Giovanna and Pina of Reggio.

Monsignor Aurelio Sorrentino, the archbishop of Reggio Calabria-Bova, greets Pope John Paul II during the beatification ceremony for Padre Gaetano in St. Peter's Square, May 4, 1997.

Pope John Paul II, who approved all levels of Padre Gaetano's rise to sainthood starting in 1980, is seen at the altar at St. Peter's Basilica during the beatification ceremony.

Anna Pangallo, right, recipient of the second Vatican-approved miracle, greets Justin's interpreter, Germaine Sciriha. In late 2002, Anna was stricken with bacterial meningitis and given up for dead. When she arose from her coma and doctors could not explain her recovery, the Vatican deemed her survival a miracle.

Dr. Giuseppe Bolignano, nephew of Padre Gaetano and doctor of Anna Pangallo: "There is a line that is incredible and unexplainable," the doctor said, "and when you cross it, there is nothing else left but faith."

For the canonization on October 23, 2005, the façade of St. Peter's Basilica was hung with the banners of those who would be named saints. It was Pope Benedict XVI's first such ceremony.

Thousands of St. Gaetano faithful traveled from Calabria to Rome for the ceremony. INSET: St. Gaetano's banner.

In St. Peter's Square following the canonization. From left: Rosalie, Emilia, Sophia, Justin, and Laurelyn.

Justin and Laurelyn on the Spanish Steps in Rome.

Rosalie and Emilia gleefully pose beneath a poster of St. Gaetano at a gift shop near the Vatican.

Back in Reggio, June 2006, Justin at dinner with cousins Bruno Calarco, Caterina Catanoso, Vincenzo Infortuna (Caterina's husband), and Daniela Catanoso.

Cousins Tosca, Giulia, and Daniela Catanoso in Rome.

Piero Catanoso, patriarch of the Catanoso family in Reggio, with his wife, Adriana, on the rooftop of their apartment building. Piero died unexpectedly three weeks later.

Family pride: After Justin spoke at the church in Chorio, friends and relatives gathered around for a photograph. The Veronican sisters presented Justin with a huge portrait of St. Gaetano in a hand-carved frame.

The progeny of Carmelo and Caterina, 2003. Since 1957, a Catanoso family reunion has taken place each fall, usually at the Avalon Campground in Clermont, New Jersey.

"I'll see you later," Lenny would always say. He could no more easily tell Alan he loved him than I could. But every day, he managed to say precisely that.

Lenny got good quickly at lifting Alan from his bed to his wheelchair and rolling him outside to enjoy a summer evening. Then he realized he could just as easily lift Alan from the chair to the passenger seat of my father's Lexus sedan.

"Come on, let's go for a ride," Lenny would say. Alan would roll his eyes and smirk. Given the choice, he would stay in bed. "Come on, we're going," Lenny would insist, pushing the wheelchair up next to the bed, pulling back the sheets, leaving Alan no other option.

Together, they would drive all over the county, onto the island of Wildwood to visit Uncle Tony in North Wildwood or Aunt Leona in Wildwood Crest. They would drive across Cape May Court House to see his friends Steve and Marianne Lauriello. They would head up Route 9 to have dinner with my parents, who had a ramp built on their front porch for Alan's wheelchair. The first visits were raw with emotion. Alan, his face puffy from chemo and steroids to fight any internal swelling, did not look much like himself any longer. He would cry when he saw a friend or relative for the first time; they would cry, too. The next visits were easier, and Lenny made sure there were more. Alan eventually grew comfortable with the routine. If Lenny was going to drive him around, fine, he wanted to go to Mass on Saturday nights. Anna and the girls would meet them there and wheel Alan inside. Lenny never stayed.

One weekend in early October when I had flown up for a visit, Anna and I got Alan bundled up, Lenny got him into the Lexus, and we rode together to the Middle Township football field so Alan could catch a glimpse of his daughters in the marching band. Lenny rolled him right up in to the stands, front row, forty-yard line; Anna draped him in blankets. "How did you like it?" we asked him later. "I froze my ass off," he told us, and we were reassured; his familiar grumpiness was still intact.

Lenny didn't care. He was never deterred. You are not going to just lie in bed, he would say. There were days when Lenny would do more than a dozen transfers, bed to chair, chair to car, again and again. Grab

Alan around the waist. Swing him out of bed. Move him. The task got easier as Alan's weight continued to drop.

When he wasn't driving Alan around, Lenny was working the phones. He would keep up with Alan's doctors, he would track down therapists, he would read up on alternative therapies like green tea and macrobiotic diets. He wanted Alan to read Lance Armstrong's best-selling book, *It's Not About the Bike*, which detailed Armstrong's victory over testicular cancer, until he realized that Alan's double vision didn't allow for much reading. Still, he never gave up hope.

"We didn't talk about what he was thinking too much," Lenny recalled. "Even if I wanted to, I just couldn't do it. I was always about tomorrow. What are we going to do tomorrow?"

Lenny's hope and determination could not stop the steady deterioration of Alan's body, weakened as it was from chemotherapy and infections. In late October, Alan developed pneumonia. His lung capacity was limited. He no longer wanted to eat. He now weighed less than me, which had never been the case. He told Lenny emphatically, "Maybe it's time." But Lenny wasn't ready for Alan to give up. "I don't think it's time, Alan." Ever stubborn, but less so in the face of such determination, Alan did not argue. And after a few days in the hospital, with some antibiotics and rehydration, he rallied. For more than a month, all the way through Thanksgiving, his crummy condition seemed to stabilize. He had some good days, relatively speaking. But Alan knew better than any of us that it was temporary. One weekend that fall, as I was sitting with him, he told me something he never had the heart to tell Lenny.

"You did a good job with your story," he said of my magazine article about Padre Gaetano. "He was a miracle worker. That's what you wrote. But I've been thinking about it. I don't know if he has another miracle for me."

I wrote Alan's eulogy in longhand at the Philadelphia airport, a week before Christmas, waiting for Laurelyn and my daughters to arrive on their flight from Greensboro. I sat there with a legal pad in one of those white, wooden rockers in the overhead walkway that connected the terminal to the baggage claim area. I knew that Anna would ask me to write it. It was truly the least I could do. All along, I knew how I wanted the eulogy to start. The line came to me during one of those interminable rides to Baltimore the previous June, a line I didn't share with Lenny, who was driving Alan's Chevy Tahoe, or Anna and her girls, who were in the backseat. What would they think if they knew I was mentally composing a eulogy before Alan had even started chemotherapy? But the line came, and it rang true: Alan always had a plan.

Once I started writing there at the airport, the words came in a rush. And as I brushed away my tears and filled page after page with blue ink, I wondered how I would manage to actually deliver what I was writing. Alan was dead. Just forty-nine years old. Anna was now a widow, her daughters fatherless. There was no miracle, no intercession on the part of a sanctified relative. Just death and loss.

Months earlier, when Lenny and I had tried to assure Alan that we would do what we could to help Anna with the girls, he wailed helplessly, "That's what *I* was going to do!" How could I talk about Alan, knowing what he was missing, knowing that *he* was missing?

Still, I kept writing and crying and writing some more until my own family arrived. The five of us huddled in one tight hug for the longest time right there in Philadelphia's Terminal D.

The morning of the funeral was icy and brittle. Our Lady of Angels near the Garden State Parkway in Cape May Court House was filled with hundreds of people. I handed my cousin Anthony a copy of the eulogy. We have been like brothers since we were in diapers. We had shared the stage during theater productions in high school. Anthony agreed to be in the wings, to step up and finish what I feared I might not be able to do myself. Midway through the service, Monsignor Jim nodded for me to come forward and stand in the pulpit. Before ascending the three steps, I nodded toward the crucifix hanging above the altar, mimicking those who had gone up before me. I then looked out on a sea of sad faces, every one of them connected by their love for my brother, for his family, for our family.

"Alan always had a plan," I began, surprised to hear my voice as it was amplified through the church.

I moved through his early life, his interests, his work, and his years with Anna and the girls. I offered some light stories when I could—like the time when he was eight and bought my dad an Indian head carved out of a coconut for Father's Day after promising my mother he wouldn't "buy any junk." I was relieved to hear laughter.

When I got to his illness and the hard part, I looked out to find Anthony. His shoulders were slumped and his face was wet. So much for our plan, I remember thinking. I took a deep breath.

"Through it all, we learned what's truly important in life—faith, family, friends, and the things we do to support each other. So many people reached out to Alan. So many people wanted to help. With their father at home, Anna and the girls did as much as they could to make Alan comfortable and tend to so many needs. So did Diane and Judi. Larry and Nancy. Anthony coming every week. John and Kevin, his college friends, traveling great distances to visit. Marlene and Joe. My father and mother, who never stopped cooking and never stopped praying. And Lenny.

"Every day, my mother would pray for a miracle, pray for an angel to come to Alan and give him the strength and will to recover. And every day her prayers were answered—when Lenny would come to Alan and lift him from his bed to his chair, from his chair to the car and take Alan out.

"When it was all over, Lenny told me about how he felt going to Alan every day, every day. 'I looked forward to it,' he told me. 'I enjoyed it. I would have done it another ten years.'"

When the service was finished and Alan's casket had been carried out and loaded into the hearse, Monsignor Jim spoke to me on the steps of the church just a short distance from the prayer garden Alan had designed and built.

"Now you have another story to write, and I know what it should be called," he said smiling, his baritone voice rich and soothing. "When Alan Meets Gaetano."

# II

# Soul Searching

Laurelyn and I returned home with our daughters to Greensboro a couple of days before Christmas. Just one year earlier, the five of us were gearing up for the adventure of a lifetime, our first trip to Italy together. It now seemed like ages ago, or as if it had happened to someone else. All the color felt as if it had been washed out of the world. When I was able to look up, I saw only the heaviest shades of gray.

An e-mail from Giovanna in Reggio, offering her condolences, helped me remember that the loving embrace of the Catanoso family had gotten so much bigger in the past twelve months. I wished I could have seen her right then. I wished I knew her better. I wished I spoke Italian so that I could. I wrote back and told her that.

Returning to work, I had a phone message from a producer at National Public Radio. During the previous summer, I had submitted a commentary that condensed my magazine story on returning to Reggio and having a near-saint in the family. The hook, if there was one, was that I felt blessed to have these Italian Catanosos in my life, but that my Catholic soul remained dormant, even with the sudden inclusion of a sacred relative. It didn't feel honest when I wrote it; I hadn't wrestled with my religion, or lack thereof, enough to draw any conclusions. But I needed an ending. Laurelyn urged me to simply write what I know and tell the truth.

"You need to write about Alan," she said.

"I can't," I told her, having just returned from another grim weekend in New Jersey. "It's too hard."

The NPR producer accepted the draft I submitted in August 2004, but said I would need to rework the ending. She knew nothing about Alan or his ordeal that summer, but she could tell the conclusion sounded hollow. After months of hearing nothing about the status of the commentary and when it might air, she left a message on December 17 requesting a rewrite. On that day, of all days, I was in New Jersey with my parents, with Lenny, Marlene, and her husband, Joe, and with Anna, Marsiella, and Lisa. Monsignor Jim was there, too. We were all crowded around Alan's bedside in a curtained intensive-care bay at Cooper Hospital in Camden as he died. I stared at my phone as if it were bringing a message from another world. Was the timing of the producer's call merely a coincidence? It seemed more like a partial pathway to healing. In the cold, gloomy fog of grief, I felt my commentary come perfectly into view. I turned to my computer and out came an entirely new opening.

"When my brother was diagnosed with inoperable brain cancer, my mother prayed relentlessly for a miracle."

I went through the motions that winter of 2005. I helped put out the weekly business newspaper where I work as an editor. I taught my journalism classes at Wake Forest University. I had dinner with my family and talked with Laurelyn and the girls about what they were doing. And I felt awful, depleted, bereft. All the time. And if I felt that bad, I could only imagine how Anna felt, and her daughters, my parents, and my sister. Lenny and I talked a lot on the phone.

All through the previous summer and fall, I figured the best thing I could do for Alan was be as supportive as possible to Lenny. Now I kept it up as Lenny kept going back to things he could have done differently. Time lost before treatment started. Doctors who seemed to give up too soon. He was still fighting for Alan, which was his way of recovering. Laurelyn urged me to see a counselor, and I told her I would. But she's trained as a counselor, and no one listens better than she does. I didn't think it would help.

David Talbot, a close friend in Greensboro, an internal medicine doctor, came to visit one afternoon. We have often traveled together and have gone on camping and kayaking adventures to Montana, Maine, and the Outer Banks. We know each other well.

"Of course you feel bad," David told me as we sat in my dining room across the oval oak table from each other. "How could you not? You lost one of your tribe. You're out of balance."

Something about that small insight helped crystallize so many scattered thoughts. Death in the immediate family was new to all of us. What am I supposed to say when someone asks how many brothers and sisters I have? Should Lenny, Marlene and I ever bother to pose with our parents for a family photo again? Oh, and by the way, where exactly did Alan *go*?

"You won't always feel this way," David said, and I remember thinking that this doctor friend of mine had a nice bedside manner. "But it's pretty normal that you feel this way now."


A light started to flicker near the end of February. I was driving west to Boone, North Carolina, to Appalachian State University, to speak to students at a career fair. It was a drizzly day, and the Blue Ridge Mountains were banked in clouds. I was practically driving blind when my cell phone rang. It was my best pal and cousin, Anthony, calling from New Jersey.

"Jus, we've got a date!" he yelled excitedly, his voice hanging barely on one and two bars. "October twenty-third."

"What are you talking about?"

"The pope approved five blesseds for canonization. Gaetano's in the group. Monsignor Jim just got the word from a friend of his at the Vatican. They set the date. We're all going to Rome, brother!"

Driving through the clouds as I was, it felt like I was getting this news in heaven. A Catanoso is going to be made a saint. Pope John Paul II, in the last weeks of his own life, had seen to it. I laughed and shouted with joy for the first time in what seemed like months.

"We'll see you there, Anth."

As I drove on, I found myself looking ahead. There would be plane reservations to make, and hotel reservations, too. My parents would surely go, and so would Lenny and Marlene. There would be lots of cousins going, and aunts and uncles. Most of these relatives had never been to Italy before. Amazing. Would Anna and the girls go? Alan had always handled every detail of their travels; could Anna pull it off? I hoped so.

As I ran through the planning I would need to do, it hit me: Gaetano may not have seen fit to rescue Alan from his cancer, but he was surely rescuing me and my entire family from our dark funk of mournful depression. He was drawing us all to Rome, to the Vatican, to St. Peter's Square for one of the most sacred ceremonies the Catholic Church performs—the elevation of its most heroic sons and daughters to sainthood.

The historical nature of that simple fact warmed my heart; what an incredible thing to be a part of and to claim a connection to. But the spiritual nature? It bounced off my soul like a rubber arrow. And it got me wondering. I had this relative, this contemporary of my grandfather, who devoted his whole life to the church and modeled his every action after Jesus Christ. At that time, that's about as much as I knew. And that little bit of knowledge, which I had brought home from Italy a year ago, glowed in the distance for my family—particularly my mother and Alan—like a glimpse of salvation itself. During Alan's illness, Gaetano's holiness had floated across the Atlantic at long last and become a tangible part of our lives. My mother prayed to Gaetano. Alan prayed to Gaetano, and both of them, I believe, found some measure of comfort in thinking that this lovely relative was waiting on the other side, ready with a smile and a helping hand.

I was happy knowing that. But I was sad, too. Ever the journalist, I was merely an observer of this powerful, mystical act of faith. I could see it, admire it, even write about it. But I couldn't feel it. I was born a Catholic, baptized and confirmed. I was still a Catholic, but in name only. Like so many others, I was in early, immersed in the doctrine before I was mature enough to grab hold of any of it, and then fell away easily, entirely, though never coming fully untethered.

Alan's death got me thinking about my faith again. But so did Gaetano's life. And as I emerged from the Blue Ridge Mountain clouds on the downhill drive into Boone, one question kept bouncing around inside: What had happened to my soul?

I grew up on the same five-mile island as my father—on Central Avenue in North Wildwood, New Jersey, several blocks from where Carmelo Catanoso's Italian-American grocery had been on New York Avenue. My best friends as a child lived just a few houses down on Twenty-fourth Street closer to the ocean: Janine Sicilia, whose father was a beer distributor, and Billy Dietrich, whose father ran the paper wholesaler in town. When I got a little older, I marked the seasons by the sports I played with my cousins and friends. Football in the fall, mostly pick-up games after school played on any empty lot we could find. Basketball in the winter, played on Anthony's backyard half-court with Aunt Louise holding a floodlight from a second-floor window so we could keep going after dark; baseball in spring, where I donned the blue flannel Little League uniform of the Optimist Club and pictured myself making plays at third base like Brooks Robinson. Those nine months were as sleepy and idyllic as any in small-town America.

But summer? Sports took a rest as Wildwood lived up to its name. Summer was for raising hell. That's when the island and the summer season—bookended by Memorial Day and Labor Day—made a schizophrenic turn and ballooned from fifteen thousand year-round residents to nearly a quarter million when all the motels, condos, and cheap rooming houses were full. Back then the drinking age in New Jersey was eighteen. Thus, kids as young as fourteen only needed the flimsiest of fake IDs to get served in most bars in town (a friend and I once secured a pint of MD 20/20 with an ID that claimed he was thirty-two—we were, with our ages combined). Indeed the working-class resort town of my youth was the destination of choice for alcohol-crazed high schoolers from across the Delaware Valley. Sure, it had a two-mile boardwalk and six monstrous amusement piers reaching toward the ocean, packed with roller coasters, giant slides, and bumper cars for family fun. Mostly, though, the town was crawling with bars and night clubs.

If Frank Capra would have selected Wildwood as a quaint, bucolic movie set in the 1930s for a sweet tale of first-generation Americans, Quentin Tarantino would have picked it in the 1970s for a violent film starring teenagers having sex under the boardwalk, Hells Angels screeching on choppers down Pacific Avenue, and loud rock bands playing Led Zeppelin covers at the Rendezvous and the Penalty Box.

Like Chorio in the late 1800s, Wildwood a century later was an unholy place.

Not surprisingly, my memories of growing up Catholic aren't the first things to spring to mind when I consider my upbringing. I didn't attend St. Ann's elementary school, so I missed the drill of nuns telling Bible stories, teaching grammar rules, and rapping knuckles with a ruler. I was never an altar boy. The forced march to Mass each Sunday as a little boy baffled me more than anything. All those candles. That gold container on a chain that sent out smoke rings. Men in colorful robes droning endlessly. What was going on? It was never explained, not at home nor at church. The life-size statue of Jesus hanging from the cross didn't make much of an impression either. It became a common sight after a while; we had smaller ones hanging in our house. And the steel-gray drape that hung tall and wide behind the altar? Now that got my attention. I was certain that drape was the Iron Curtain I heard mentioned on the evening news my father watched nightly. I daydreamed about peeking behind it and glimpsing the Soviet Union. I didn't dare.

Then there was confession. I can remember pedaling my Schwinn bike with its fat tires and banana seat down Atlantic Avenue on Wednesdays after school, the salt air of the resort island blowing in my face. My destination: the barnlike, block-long brick edifice that was St. Ann's Church, just three blocks from the beach and boardwalk. My mother reminded me when to go.

"Bless me, father, for I have sinned."

There wasn't anything scarier or creepier in my childhood than entering a small, darkened closet in the cavernous St. Ann's, closing the curtain behind me, then kneeling in there before an opaque screen to spill out the imperfections of my life as a ten-year-old.

"It's been three weeks since my last confession."

Why did my mom make me do this? It's not like I knocked over the Marine Bank, or even stole a pack of football cards from the gum rack at Newberry's. So my room was a mess, I sassed her a few times, and Anthony and I nearly burned down the garage playing with my chemistry kit. Big deal.

"Father, I've lied seven times. I disobeyed my mom four times. I've cursed, umm, a lot, I think ten times, maybe. And I had no idea that that smelly stuff me and Anthony mixed together would blow up if you lit it. They were Anthony's matches."

I awaited my fate in the dark, bracing for more Hail Marys and Our Fathers than I could say in an hour. I couldn't see the priest. He was on the other side of the screen. I could hear him breathing, though. Is that what God sounded like? And if this priest was working for God, he surely knew that I had lied more than seven times. Cripes, I hadn't even mentioned the dreaded meatloaf I had snuck off my plate, into my napkin, and into the bathroom bound for the toilet just a few nights ago. That's got to be some kind of sin.

"Um, Father, can I add something? I think I lied eight times."

On my knees in a pew in front of that huge crucifix, I rushed through my sentence of prayers and got back on my Schwinn as fast as I could. I did feel lighter on the way home, ready to sin again. As much as I hated going to confession, I can't say that it undermined my connection to Catholicism. All the priests I knew as a boy behaved like mature adults, only more distant and strange, a world apart. I was a witness to all the rites they performed, all the sacraments they dispensed. They just didn't take.

Looking back, it seems I had slipped beyond the grasp of the church by the time I reached Wildwood Catholic High School for ninth grade, after attending public school since kindergarten. There was one person, though, who tried valiantly to reel me in.

"Who do you think you are?" Father William Hodge would ask as I ran to track practice or play practice or ducked into the small office of the school newspaper next to the cafeteria. Father Hodge was a young priest in the late 1970s, the religion teacher at Wildwood Catholic. He stood about my height with thinning, brown hair and a dimpled smile. He preferred wearing a long, black cassock at school instead of the standard-issue black slacks, black shirt, and black suit coat worn by most priests. He liked to sing with an Irish brogue when he played his accordion.

The nuns at Wildwood Catholic? Many of them struck me as old and bitter, gossipy, and judgmental. As Sisters of St. Joseph, they wore the high, flat-topped habits that concealed their hair. Dressed all in black with white trim, they resembled penguins and that's what we called them under our breath. Their holiness escaped me; they didn't seem real. But Father Hodge radiated a kind of goodness that felt genuine. And he could get me to slow down and even think about God once in a while, though not often. "And where do you think you're going?" he would ask.

Easy questions. I was an athlete and an aspiring journalist, on my way to practice or the school newspaper office. But that's not really what Father Hodge was asking.

Maybe if I had known that we had someone as holy as Padre Gaetano Catanoso in the family tree, I might have paid a bit more attention. I might have put my discus aside or reporter's notebook down long enough to think about something bigger, more glorious than tallying the winning points at the end of a track meet, or writing the perfect lead. But I knew nothing of Gaetano, none of us Catanosos in America did. Not back then. Honestly, I don't know that it would have made a difference. I was drifting away.

In his memoir *Turbulent Souls*, Stephen Dubner writes of spending years grilling his mother about her adult conversion from Judaism to Catholicism. She embraced her new religion completely and profoundly, everything from the virgin birth to the resurrection. She studied the Scriptures. She studied the life of Jesus. Coming to it late as she did, she didn't just live her religion and all its many rituals, she could clearly articulate the wellspring of her faith. I read that book after Alan died, imagining myself searching for my faith as Dubner did. Mostly, though, I marveled at the clarity of his mother's convictions.

Taking Dubner's lead, I asked my mother to help me understand her faith, as a way, I realize, of trying to understand where and when mine disappeared. She tried. But it was like lighting a candle in a huge, darkened cave. I couldn't see much and I wanted a floodlight.

"I guess we just had it built into us," Mom said, referring to growing up in an Italian immigrant household in South Philly, one of two children of Giustino and Gioconda Giandomenico. "When I was a little girl, you had to go to confession every Saturday, you had to go to church every Sunday. That's how it was. And it became a part of my life. I don't know much about the religion, but I like my religion. I like saying my prayers, praying the rosary. I like going to church. What else can I tell you?"

Connie Catanoso, my mother, got her Catholicism at birth, in her genes. It is strong and mystical and real. She believes in God and prayer and the healing power of saints, just like her mother, who gave her the middle name Rita because St. Rita was her favorite saint. Connie didn't need to study the life of Jesus or the foundations of her beliefs; her faith comes as naturally to her as her love for her children, and she doesn't question it. She tried to build religion into me and my siblings in the same way it was built into her, the only way she knew how. We are Italian, we are Catholic, and because of that, there are certain things you just do, without question. It worked for her.

It didn't work for me. Yes, I went to Mass for a time and I went to confession until well into my teens. I took Holy Communion. I got confirmed. I said prayers in the dark of night and went to a Catholic high school. I moved through my childhood and teen years surrounded by a religion I was expected to absorb unflinchingly—forever, but which was actually speeding past me, like signposts on the Garden State Parkway. Catholicism in my family meant believing because my parents believed, and doing what the priests told us, no questions asked. It was never a topic of discussion.

But I decided when I was thirteen years old to become a journalist. My entire life would be about asking questions and gathering details: evidence. As a teenage sportswriter for the *Wildwood Leader*, I could go into the locker room after a football game and ask the coach why he called a certain play or made a certain substitution. Yet I wasn't encouraged by either my parents or my Catholic school teachers to inquire about the very things that were essential to my spiritual development. Why should I go to confession? Why should I go to church? Why should I believe?

As I got older, the questions multiplied. What is this preoccupation with sin? Original sin. Venial sin. Mortal sin. Am I really so flawed that the slightest misstep, the most unpreventable, impure thought requires a bike ride to the confessional? Is it all really the fault of that easily tempted pair Adam and Eve? And what about all the awful places you can tumble into if you happen to expire with a blemish of sin on your soul—limbo, purgatory, and hot, fiery hell? I need a reason to fear those places. I need details, evidence.

In the summer before I graduated from high school, my mother often invited Father Hodge out to our campground to say Mass for the campers. I would help him arrange an altar out of the Ping-Pong table in the game room. But I didn't stay, which my mother always lamented.

"My Justin doesn't go to church, Father," she would tell him. "He says he doesn't get anything out of it."

"He'll grow up, Connie," I remember Father Hodge telling her. "You wait and see."

# 12

# The Professor and Laurelyn

My process of maturing—intellectually, and in fits and starts, spiritually—was assisted in no small measure by an unusual man I met by chance during my sophomore year at Penn State. Given his advanced age and the distance he lived from central Pennsylvania, Manoel Cardozo was an unlikely mentor. But our paths crossed at a time when my world was starting to look bigger than the five-mile island I had grown up on. Whether I knew it or not, I was looking for people who could point me in a new direction—away from home. Lenny and Alan had both followed in our father's steps in attending Penn State, and I did, too. But unlike them, I had no intention of returning to Cape May County to work in either family business—the greenhouse or the campground. I wanted to work with my head, not my hands and my back. I wanted to think big ideas and write graceful stories. In a place as large as Penn State, especially for underclassmen in enormous, impersonal lecture halls, academic mentors were hard to come by. So I hung around the seasoned juniors and seniors in the newsroom of *The Daily Collegian.* I made a couple of good friends in the dorms and followed them closely. And I studied the neatly typed letters sent to me by Professor Manoel Cardozo. Years later, when I reread those letters, the answer to my now pressing question—what happened to my soul?—became apparent in ways I had not realized.

We met in the Benjamin Franklin room of the U.S. State Department in Washington, D.C. It was January 1980 and a two-day, foreign policy press briefing put on by high-level officials in the Carter Administration had just concluded. The *Collegian* had been one of a handful of college newspapers invited to the briefing, and as the newspaper's political reporter, I got to attend. At the reception afterward, I stood with a horde of journalists, guests, and politicos gathered in the Benjamin Franklin room on the State Department's eighth floor as we picked over fancy hors d'oeuvres piled high beneath immense crystal chandeliers. Ordering a drink, I found myself standing next to an elegant older man dressed in a prim, tweed sports jacket and wool vest with a sharply knotted tie. He teased me about the Bloody Mary in my hand, noting that the vodka was from the Soviet Union; the Carter administration officials hosting this reception, he pointed out, were none too happy with the Soviets and their recent menacing push into Afghanistan. He introduced himself with a smile and a slight bow, telling me his name was Manoel da Silveira Cardozo. He wasn't a journalist, but rather a guest at the reception. His hair was nearly silver and his white mustache was neatly trimmed. He asked me if I were Italian and told me he was Portuguese, born in the Azores but raised in California. He was, he told me, a retired professor of history from the Catholic University here in Washington; he lived nearby.

I don't recall much of what we talked about, but I remember vividly being charmed by his wit and intelligence. The room was crawling with big-city newspaper editors I should have been schmoozing. But I was content to chat amiably with the professor, as he suggested I call him. The past two days had been terribly exciting, with administration insiders such as Warren Christopher and Hodding Carter speaking gravely about the hostage situation in Iran and the White House's emerging plan to boycott the Summer Olympic Games in Moscow. For me, a budding newsman, it was thrilling to get such information directly from Washington's primary sources. The professor, nearly seventy, seemed happy to listen to the unbridled exuberance of a college reporter bearing an uncanny resemblance to a twenty-year-old Gabe Kotter, bushy hair, mustache, and all.

Surely he would have forgotten about me had I not written to him once I got back to my dorm room a few days later. My letter was a simple note of thanks and praise for the wisdom he shared. His response was an appeal to a young, malleable mind disguised as a treatise on the nature of modern education. It was one page and single-spaced, composed on a manual typewriter. That letter, or rather the discourse it launched, changed my life:

> What society and the schools did to you and young people who are less sensitive and sensible than you is a crime against humanity and a danger for the ultimate survival of the nation. My generation escaped much of the damage caused by the so-called educationalists. I still was subjected to a bit of formal logic, to some philosophy, to precise thinking in the classroom (rather than "precise" feeling). Still, I grew up without a theological dimension to reality, and what saved me in this respect was The Catholic University of America. Not Stanford, which awarded me the three degrees that I have. Your generation has generally been deprived of the Art and Discipline of Thinking and instead you've been taught to hold that "feeling" is more important.

I could not be certain of exactly what he was talking about, no matter how many times I read it over. I felt way out of my depth. But I loved the sound of those sentences, and I wanted in on that kind of thinking. College, even a big state school like Penn State, had taught me how poorly my small-town, Catholic high school education had prepared me for anything resembling intellectual rigor. I thought I was pretty smart, until I met plenty of students from Philadelphia and Pittsburgh who were just plain smarter than me. I wanted to get that way, as fast as I could. I wanted to speak in syllogisms and quote parables and engage in spirited, far-ranging theoretical debates that dragged on into the small hours of the morning.

"That's so fallacious!" a pal would yell at me, and I would laugh, while making a mental note to look up "fallacious" as soon as I got back to my dorm room.

The friends I was drawn to talked like that for sport, even before they fired up their bongs. I loved it, and watched their back-and-forth banter as if it were a tennis match. But my brain wouldn't play along. I took a logic class and dropped it early. I just couldn't read Plato. But I didn't want to give up. Now it seemed, my own philosopher–tutor, in tweed and corduroy, had materialized from my mail slot. I was ecstatic. I kept reading. The latter part of the letter rumbled into my head with the force and clarity of a perfectly struck church bell:

> As to the wisdom that you admire, the secret (if there is one) is to prepare yourself NOW, while there is still time. With a good theoretical basis at this stage of the game, you'll be able to build upon it with the experience that life regularly furnishes us. Wisdom does not require keen intelligence, for there are intelligent people who are not wise. Intelligence is to be cherished, provided you use it properly. Wisdom is a matter of GROWING with life. Age helps, naturally. (The youth culture is for the birds.) You, dear Justin, cannot be truly wise at your age, only attractive, physical, euphoric, dynamic, fascinated. God has judiciously arranged it that way. Wisdom takes the passage of time. Wisdom is a kind of fruit cake; when laced with a fine rum and properly aged, it is a superb thing to enjoy.

I had grown up in a working-class household, not an intellectual one. Academically, I had fairly squandered my freshman year at Penn State. What I heard the professor telling me was simple: Stop wasting time, stop wasting your brain. No one had ever spoken to me like that before. No one of his smarts and stature (the books he wrote were listed in the card catalog at Penn State's main library; I checked) had ever taken the time to smooth out the map and explain that this is how you get from here to there. I couldn't believe my good fortune. And it scared the hell out of me. What happens when the professor realizes I'm just an idiot from South Jersey, no deeper than a cup of coffee, no more insightful than the last news analysis I had read in the *New York Times*? Tim Beidel, my best friend at Penn State, one of those guys singled out for honors classes without ever trying, assured me I had nothing to worry about.

"The guy's gay, Justin," Tim insisted. "He doesn't give a shit if you're smart or not. Can't you see that? Look, it's fine to be enamored with him, but let me tell you, if you ever get together with him again, you better watch your back."

Tim may have been right, but I never knew for certain, and it was never an issue, not then or later. Mostly, it was immaterial to me. I was captivated, like any eager student is by an exciting new teacher. The problem was, I didn't know how to respond to his letter to keep the conversation going. I was afraid of blowing my cover. My confidence shrank. Nearly a year passed. Then in December 1980, well into my junior year, I sent him an innocuous note telling him about some campus reporting experiences and wishing him a happy holiday.

I got a letter back in a week, dated December 17:

Dear Justin, Our beginnings never know our ends, as T. S. Eliot says. I thought that I would never again see the sunshine in your face and lo and behold! It's coming right through the house. What a grand surprise at this joyous time of the year, to be reminded of a chance encounter that began to grow roots and that now promises to blossom into a full-fledged friendship.

To my great surprise, this glorious bloom of finely crafted words, careful allusions, and gentle advice unfolded over the next several years, critical years in my adult formation. I would learn only later of his intellectual credentials—his half century of scholarship and teaching devoted to Brazilian and Portuguese history, his leadership of international historical associations and library archives, his Benemerenti Medal from the Vatican honoring his service to the church. At the time, I knew him only through the words he sent in the mail.

"Do hurry back to Washington," he wrote early on. "Not to repeat the electricity of our brief encounter in the Benjamin Franklin room—because nothing is ever automatically repeated or re-created—but to try to generate another bolt of lightning, to acquire new insights, to enjoy new feelings."

I have copies of only a couple of the letters that I wrote him, but I carefully preserved all twenty-one that he wrote to me. His letters, each one typed on his white, monogrammed stationery, often began as travelogues of his adventures in Brazil or Spain or California. Sometimes he would comment on the politics of the day or world events, usually with a conservative slant. And always there were a few sentences that to me, an aspiring writer, seemed like gifts of language.

"It is refreshing to know that the sun will rise tomorrow to light up the world and give us warmth," he wrote on March 13, 1981. "Some live as others die, but death fructifies the earth and assures a place for the living. The cycle is endless, but our minds and hearts give it meaning, and an awareness of the moments that pass by."

Literary preening? Perhaps. But it didn't seem that way to this twenty-one-year-old. I would read lines like that over and over. To my roommate, Mark Waldman, I would say, "Hey, listen to this," and read them out loud. The professor may have been reveling in his own winsome thoughts, but to me, it seemed like he had a plan, like any good teacher, to prepare the seedbed carefully so that the roots of my thinking could take hold and sink in. This strategy, this intellectual appeal, actually worked.

Through the professor's encouragement, I came to view my previous attempts at course selection at Penn State largely as a dodge whereby I avoided small classes with tough professors so I would have more time and energy to devote to my story chasing for *The Daily Collegian.* You have a lifetime to do that, the professor reminded me. You're in college now, he would say, make the most of it. The message got through.

In my junior year and throughout my senior year, I vowed to do things differently. I vowed to learn, taking Shakespeare and Italian Renaissance Art History, memorable courses I would not have considered without the professor's influence. Moreover, I vowed to learn how to think. I wrote the professor and told him so. He was glad to hear it. "There is no better way of sympathizing with the human condition," he wrote.

And then he reached for more. Just a little at first.

In commenting on a newspaper column of mine I had sent, he buried this one line in a letter on December 4, 1981: "Don't overlook the theological dimension of life. Without it we fail to contemplate life's glory fully, or understand its failures."

By spring of 1982, my senior year, I made it clear in my letters that I was scared to death about graduating. The job market for journalists was terrible and the notion of returning home to work at the family campground, cleaning restrooms and collecting trash, was too horrible to contemplate. The professor, who for more than two years had been appealing to my head, decided to take square aim at my soul—a place he sized up as confused if not hollow. On April 13, 1982, he wrote:

> I don't know what I can say or do to encourage you to celebrate life, to see it as it is—the tones as varied as the visions—glorify it, appreciate it as the precious gift that it is, savor it, be joyful in it as the years recede from the blossomtime of our beginnings.
>
> You are still nervously in search of something, believing that what you seek is within reach, that tomorrow, by dint of hard work, you may find it. What if you never do? What if there is no pot for you at the end of the rainbow? I am not saying that you should not look for it. My concern is that you may not know that along some paths there is (as Gertrude Stein said in some other connection) no there there.
>
> When that glorious "failure" dawns upon you, will you have the resources to be at peace with yourself, and keeping moving? Now I am not suggesting that you are on the road that must inevitably lead to failure. What I must point out is that you cannot begin any journey of life without alternatives within yourself that will support you in times of disappointment and despair. The trouble with so many journalists is that they have no theological dimension to their lives.

My response, which I still have, suggests I was open to just this sort of plea. What my Catholic upbringing had not done, what my mother and Father Hodge could not accomplish, the professor caught some traction. "I've never really had a decent understanding of my own spirituality," I responded, being more candid with him on such a matter than anyone else. "And I've always questioned the depth of my faith. I believe in God. I believe in God, and that's as far as I take it. Yet at this stage in my life, that basic belief is easily shaken and doubted. All of this together has never really bothered me much. It has always been too easy to ignore."

No longer, not with the professor's persistent knocking on the door to my soul. It got me thinking that maybe I could reason and study my way through the challenge he was laying out, a challenge that began to seem fairly appealing. Maybe I could start gathering some facts. I signed up for a course on Christianity's major reformations. We studied Erasmus and Luther, Kierkegaard and Tillich, Edwards and Calvin. The readings were hard for me, and I struggled with them. But I found this sweaty, passionate grappling with spirituality—Catholic and Protestant—fascinating, even romantic. I felt like I was rising from a coma. It felt good, bracing. Or maybe it was just Alyson Rice, a blond, fresh-faced woman in my class. She wore powder-blue sweaters to match her eyes and a smile of pure joy. She was a born-again Christian, a being as alien to me as a creature from another planet. A swarthy, lapsed Catholic, I must have been just as alien to her. That's probably what sparked our brief crush and a few dates, including one to her evangelical Baptist Church in State College. We sat on folding chairs in what looked to me like a metal-walled warehouse; no stained glass, no Jesus hanging from the cross, no thin, white wafers dispensed by a robed holy man as Communion. As a journalist, I was curious, though not enough to consider going back. What really struck me about Alyson was the way her eyes blazed when she talked about her beliefs. They became luminous. One late night, she breathlessly described Luther's courage in breaking from the Catholic Church and nailing those ninety-nine theses to the door of the church. I could tell it was real to her, as if it happened yesterday. I listened mesmerized, captivated not by Luther's historic actions so much as by the force of Alyson's faith. Like the professor's wisdom, I wanted some of what Alyson had, too.

I knew something important was missing and I wrote the professor and told him. I told him I was cynical about religion and skeptical about my faith. I told him, too, just as Father Hodge predicted as I was finishing high school, that I was growing up enough to know that maybe I needed to do something about all this. I wrote to him:

You've encouraged me not to overlook the theological aspect of life. Your encouragement has intrigued me, but I'm afraid I hardly knew where to start. Today, I see myself closer to that starting point, but out of curiosity, not conviction. Alyson, the friend who helped me understand your last letter, fascinates me because of her firm grasp of theology and understanding her own spirituality. I find her confidence enviable. If, like you wrote, she were to find no pot at the end of her rainbow, I'm led to believe she would remain undaunted, smiling, content. As we both prepare for graduation, I feel she has an incredible advantage over me.

I'm fully aware of my spiritual shortcomings. And because of you and other people close to me, I can no longer ignore them.

I had flung the door open, and the professor came charging through, triumphantly. I'm certain he heard the horns of archangels when he wrote to me again that summer after my graduation. "I liked the way you expressed yourself in your letter, and all the doubts that you bring into play are normal for the course and indeed indispensable," he wrote on August 24, 1982. "At your stage of the game, you're bound to proceed from doubt."

What followed was a precise, exhaustive reading list that surely would have prepared me quite well for the seminary had I the slightest inclination to strap on a white collar. He started with the Bible, an approved Catholic Church version, not King James ("unless you're only interested in the Bible as literature"). Stick with the New Testament and Jesus; don't waste time with the Old Testament like so many Protestants. Avoid the "pagan sages of the Orient," he advised without explanation. Then he ticked off a lineup of heavy hitters who would have made any decent theologian's all-star team: Aristotle, St. Thomas Aquinas, St. Augustine, St. Ignatius Loyola, St. Teresa of Ávila, not to mention Gilbert Chesterton, Thomas Merton, Hilaire Belloc, and on and on.

"Accept as many as you can, remembering what happened to Ford Madox in Paris," the professor wrote, with obvious glee. "One day, when he went to confession at St. Sulpice, he told the priest that he couldn't believe everything that the Church taught. 'My son,' the wise confessor said, 'believe what you can.'"

I really did imagine charging out and buying every book. But I didn't. I was out of school. I had just gotten my first job as a borough hall reporter for the *Centre Daily Times*, a small paper in State College. I was making a scant $200 a week, half what my father paid me to clean toilets and collect trash at his campground. Now I had rent and food and electric bills to pay, not to mention meetings to cover and deadlines to make. I didn't want to disappoint the professor. I was grateful for his guidance. But the urgency I felt to find my soul on the campus side of College Avenue a few months earlier had lessened considerably, predictably. I liked the idea of becoming spiritually literate, but I couldn't get myself to do the work after working all day. I tried reading the Bible, the Gospels, but the stories, however fanciful, seemed less real to me than the life of Martin Luther. I even went to Mass a few times and found myself acting precisely as I did when my mother made me go as a kid—daydreaming for an entire hour, not hearing a thing. Was my spiritual quest dead already? I was ashamed. I stopped answering the professor's faithful, increasingly insistent missives.

"The silence has been so profound that I am at a loss to know what may have happened to you," he wrote on May 8, 1983.

At that time in my life, what I was really, truly, honest-to-Jesus looking for was no longer God, but love. And on a swelteringhot Central Pennsylvania day in mid-July that year, love bounced out of a brown Dodge Colt wagon and walked up onto the front porch of a friend's house wearing cut-off shorts, a faded blue tank top, and $1.99 wraparound sunglasses she had just bought at Kmart. Her long, straight hair was silky blond and her shoulders were bronzed. The sudden bass-drum thrumming of my heart was like an early detection signal. She was trailed by a handsome teenage boy who stood a head taller than her and had hair just as blond. I had been hanging out on the porch talking with my friend John Allison when they arrived. Now I was staring.

"Hey, John, we're having a party tonight at our apartment, a pool party. It's so hot we figured we had to do it," said Laurelyn Dossett, coming up the steps. "Tell everyone in the house to come over."

"That sounds great, but—you guys don't have a pool at your apartment, do you?" John said.

"The pool's in the car. We just got back from Kmart," she laughed, then said. "This is my brother, Bill. He's in high school. He drove up from Hershey for the party. Who's your friend?"

"That's Justin." I let John do the talking. I smiled and gave a little wave.

"Justin Catanoso? Didn't you write for *The Daily Collegian*? We studied one of your columns in English class. The one about Wildwood."

Fortunately, before I could say anything, anything stupid, that is, she turned back to John and said, "Gotta run. We need to get some floats. Bring your friend to the party."

That night, on the crowded lawn outside her redbrick duplex apartment on East Beaver Avenue, I talked to everyone but Laurelyn. I even dipped my feet occasionally in the plastic wading pool. But I kept an eye out for her, watching her talk and laugh and welcome newly arriving friends. She seemed to float on a cloud of her own enthusiasm. As the evening wound down, several people drifted inside to the living room. I followed and found a seat as a couple of guys got out acoustic guitars and started to play. Laurelyn was lying on her back on the hardwood floor, her knees up, holding hands with her brother, who was sitting next to her. She started to sing a jazzy Joni Mitchell song, "The Hissing of Summer Lawns." Her eyes were closed and her voice, ranging effortlessly, sailed clear and high. I was transfixed.

I contrived a reason to see her a couple of days later. I had just gotten a new car, a metallic brown Toyota Celica GT coupe. With all my college friends gone, I had no one to show it to. So I drove over to Laurelyn's apartment. She and her roommate, Robin Urda, came out and jumped up and down beside the car, shouting, "Oh what a feeling!" just like in the TV commercials. It was silly. And adorable. I asked Laurelyn if she wanted to go to Hi-Way Pizza for dinner, but she was leaving to practice with a band she had just put together. I took Robin instead. We talked about Laurelyn the whole time.

Later that same week, Laurelyn and I had our first date, mostly by accident. I was in my apartment after work when she phoned. She was terribly upset. She had just hung up on an obscene caller who had fooled her into giving away where she lived before revealing his intentions. She was home alone and her hound puppy needed to go out. She didn't want to go by herself, thinking the creepy caller might be lurking. When she failed to reach a half dozen friends, she opted for me. Her tone was both angry and annoyed. My reaction, I knew, would be critical. Tell her you're concerned, I quietly counseled myself, not what you're really thinking—man, she *called*!

"I'll be right over," I told her, but not before taking a quick shower and brushing my teeth.

I was twenty-three at the time; she was a year younger, a few credits shy of graduation. Later that night, after my gallant rescue of her and her puppy, we sat outside a record store on College Avenue and she told me about her family. Her father, John Dossett, was a pediatrician, a specialist in infectious diseases and a professor at Hershey Medical Center, Penn State's medical school. Her mother, Weldine, stayed at home with Laurelyn's three younger brothers and sometimes sold antiques. They were southerners, her father from Mobile, Alabama, and her mother from Lubbock, Texas. She told me about her favorite aunts in Birmingham, and her Baptist minister grandfather who lived outside Mobile. She told me about the house she grew up in, in Campbelltown, near Hershey, built in 1848, and how her parents had completely restored it. It was on the National Register for Historic Places. She talked and talked, and I listened in a blissful fog. I was already in love, so I just sat there smiling and nodding, trying to figure out if her eyes were blue or green. She stopped for a moment. I leaned over. "You're going to kiss me now, aren't you?" she said and then covered her face in her hands. When she looked up, I did.

One weekend, I took her to South Jersey to meet my parents. Soon after, I met her parents and brothers in Campbelltown. The real test came when we went to Philadelphia for a Jackson Browne concert at the Spectrum. We picked up Tim Beidel, my best friend all through college, on the way. His opinion mattered. She was a match for Tim's brains and wit. He liked her right away. "As soon as you started spelling her name right," Tim said of my letters that posted him weekly on the progress of this relationship, "I knew you were serious."

Things were moving fast. I wasn't thinking about marriage, but I wanted to spend every spare minute I had with Laurelyn. After about five weeks, she wanted a little space. She broke a date. I panicked. Rather than back off, I went for broke. I showed up at her duplex the following morning. It was a Saturday, August 28, 1983. "Today's the twentieth anniversary of the March on Washington," I told her. "There's a huge civil rights rally on the mall. Let's go to D.C. I know where we can stay."

I don't know what I would have done had she said no. But the idea appealed to her sense of adventure, which I was slowly coming to discern. By noon, we were on our way from Central Pennsylvania to the nation's capital. Laurelyn wore a long peasant skirt and a sleeveless top. The wind from the open sunroof of my Celica blew her hair back. We turned the volume all the way up for my Prince and Talking Heads cassettes. I let go of her hand only to shift gears.

Following country roads and highways, the ride took four hours, and we missed the rally entirely. When we finally parked and made our way to the west side of the United States Capitol, we found the mall, stretching past the Reflective Pool to the Lincoln Memorial, practically empty except for piles of litter. There was someone left, though. An old black man was sitting on a folding chair beneath the shade of a nearby elm tree. He had a saxophone and he was playing ever so slowly, ever so soulfully "We Shall Overcome." It was almost as if he had been waiting for us. Laurelyn put her arm around me and asked if I had arranged for him to be there. No, but I did have a copy of Martin Luther King's "I Have a Dream" speech printed in that morning's *Washington Post*. I read it to her on the marble steps of the Capitol as she lay back with her hands behind her head, looking up at the sky.

A little over a year later, we were married. People say opposites attract. But in many ways, we were the same. Outgoing, enthusiastic, full of dreams. Our differences even meshed. She was the oldest in her family, and as a result, she was decisive, a natural leader. I was the youngest in my family, always open to mentors, willing to follow her lead. It was actually Laurelyn who proposed. Let's get on with this, she said. That was fine with me. It was her idea, too, for me to quit my newspaper job so we could take a two-month honeymoon tour of

Western Europe. That was harder to embrace; a career break at age twenty-four? But she was right about that as well.

Religion was another story. There were vast differences. Laurelyn was raised by Southern Baptists who were born-again Christians. Her parents had helped found an evangelical church that started in the living room of their home. They took their children, when they were young, to all-night prayer meetings. When those meetings were held at her house, Laurelyn would sit at the top of the steps when she should have been in bed and would hear people speaking in tongues downstairs. This led her as a teenager to dive in deep, eager at first to be as spiritual as her parents. When she surfaced in college and looked around, she found the extreme nature of such beliefs too difficult to sustain. She had no intention of becoming exclusionary and judgmental. She backed away, but not from faith. The God she envisioned was far more tolerant and rational.

What about you? she asked. What about Catholicism?

Good question. Exclusionary and judgmental did not jump readily to mind. I was oblivious to those elements of the church, the history of which predated Laurelyn's church by a good two thousand years. I told her, truthfully, that I was a lousy Catholic. I told her that I had thought hard about my faith and my place in it and was still pretty confused. I told her it would not stand in the way of our relationship.

The professor was not going to let me off quite so easily. When I look back from the vantage point of a quarter century of hindsight, it becomes clear to me that the person who had the greatest influence in getting me to peer deep inside, ponder religion and theology, and walk right up to the front steps of the Catholic Church also played the most decisive role in driving me away.

The morning after the March on Washington, I took Laurelyn to visit the professor at his home on Sigsbee Place in the northeast section of the city. I had been there once before and liked its stuffy elegance, the Victorian furniture, the oil paintings in gilded frames, the collected treasures from his world travels. (On the previous visit, he proudly showed me an ancient fish fossil, saying with a laugh, "I'm not a creationist when it comes to things like this!") The night before, during dinner in Georgetown, I told Laurelyn all about the professor, his charm and flair and how fortunate I felt to have him as an academic mentor. That morning, though, he was not charming. He had a house guest and was distracted. He said rude things about the civil rights march and made racist cracks about the welfare mothers who lived in his neighborhood. Laurelyn was puzzled, if not aghast. This guy is your hero?

She argued with him, not letting his points go unchallenged. I had never done that before and found myself jumping in, arguing her side as well. I felt emboldened, like I was growing up right on the spot. The professor backed down and lightened up. He was laughing by the time we left, walking us out to my car. It all felt like good fun to me. Laurelyn left with another impression. And it wasn't good.

The next day, the professor wrote me saying, "What a pretty girl Laura Lynn is but of course I say this without the slightest hint of sexism." Then he went off on an ugly sexist screed, the likes of which he had never revealed to me before. "The American female is in for a lot of disappointments because they are purposely shattering their more sheltered lives and moving into the arena where punches are not held back." After writing that men would surely put such women in their rightful place and return them to the baby factories they were meant to be, he closed on more familiar ground. "Keep your mind and heart open to the world, always remembering that reality is many faceted and that man will find more comfortable the trajectory if he has a theological dimension to help him shoulder the burden of The Unfathomable Mystery."

But the spell was broken. His words, once glorious to me, suddenly sounded hollow, contrived, especially when I considered our recent visit. Beneath the surface of my sage stirred sentiments I did not want to know. I backed away for months, not writing again until late March 1984. That's when I told him that Laurelyn and I were engaged and that he would be invited to the September wedding. In a naïve attempt to assure the professor that my fiancée was a woman of genuine faith, I told him about her Christian upbringing and the devoutness of her parents, who were unfailingly warm and accepting of me in every way. Then I told him they were Baptists as heedlessly as telling him what state they lived in. That's how oblivious I was. I actually thought he would be impressed. He wasn't.

"Your relationship with Laurelyn [*he spelled it right this time*] has obviously blossomed into the kind of firm friendship that must inevitably move upward. She is a lovely girl, as I fondly remember from your quick visit, and you're a good man. I've realized it all these many years, otherwise I would've dropped you! Marriage is ultimately a matter of reproducing ourselves and its purpose, as St. Thomas Aquinas said, is to raise children. You are facing up to it."

He moved on to his favorite topic, the spiritual dimension. He reminded me that of all the Protestant sects, the least ecumenical "and the most profoundly anti-Catholic" are the Baptists. You don't want to "trade good money for bad," he warned. You don't want to be insulted by the narrowness of the Baptist faith and the weak emotionalism of its spirituality, he added. Then he got really personal.

"When the spiritual education of children is concerned, the problem is one of history: do we saddle them with the very lightweight cultural baggage, which is the reality of the Baptist faith, or do we open their minds and hearts with the richness of the Catholic heritage. Do we saddle them with the Old Testament of the Chosen People, which Baptists have, and which will explain their racism, or do we open wide the world in the spirit of the New Testament?"

It was devastating. It was hateful in its own high-minded way. It was exclusionary and judgmental. And more than anything, it was demanding that I choose sides. Catholicism or Protestantism? Serious or superficial? Good or evil? Him or Laurelyn?

*What's it going to be, young man? Your soul, and the future souls of your children, hang in the balance.*

I wondered: Was this really the kind of God I was looking at? It certainly wasn't the kind I was looking for.

One look at Laurelyn after she read the letter told me all I needed to know. She could not have been more wounded than had the professor plunged a knife in her back. "Lightweight cultural baggage," she raged. "What does he *know* about me?" She started to write an angry reply of her own but set it aside once her fury ebbed.

"He's been important to you for a long time," she said. "I can respect that and don't want to be the one to ruin your relationship. But I can't respect him."

Faith and religion were still a confusing mess to me, though now, the meaning of Catholicism being "the one true religion" was becoming clear. There was an either/or cost connected with being Catholic and I wasn't prepared to pay. I had found a good woman with a pure heart, a strong mind, and a quiet, accepting faith. And she had found me. I could not imagine anything more important and believed in us far more than I believed in the Catholic Church. For the first time, religion felt like a wedge. However unintentionally, the professor led me to that realization, and in a way, I suppose I was lucky. I made a decision, and Laurelyn did, too. Religious differences would not complicate our life together.

We were married on September 22, 1984, at the Evangelical Free Church in Hershey. My mother was disappointed that a priest wasn't there to officiate. The pastor, Dave Martin, was willing to share the altar, but no priest in the diocese agreed to participate without Laurelyn and me agreeing to make promises we were not prepared to keep. It was still a sacred ceremony, made more so by the words of Frank Wilkinson, a close friend from Wildwood Catholic who introduced a Shakespeare sonnet with his own words: "I propose that the love Christ presented 2,000 years ago is the very same love that Laurelyn and Justin present today. I do not mean the same type of love, but rather that it is, in essence, the exact same love. That the same love that flowed through and from Christ, has traveled whole and intact, through the ages, through a Michelangelo, through an Elizabeth Barrett Browning, through a Mahatma Gandhi, and that this same love is now here before us, preserved and protected, glorious and eternal, in Laurelyn and Justin."

I wished the professor had been there to witness our marriage and celebrate with us afterward. He had been such a valuable mentor in so many ways. His influence had been indelible, just not infallible. I was grateful. But he wasn't there. He had written earlier to say he would be in Brazil. We exchanged another letter or two, then nothing. A couple of years later, I received a card from Washington that included a poem and a black-and-white photo of the professor, smiling winningly and wearing the kind of tweed sport jacket and wool vest that he had on when I first met him at the State Department. Beneath the photo, it read: Manoel da Silveira Cardozo—1911–1985.

# 13

# A Pope's Blessing

If we didn't get a blessing from the professor for our marriage, we did get one from the pope.

On November 14, 1984, six weeks into our backpacking honeymoon through Europe, Laurelyn and I left early from our *pensione* on Via Nazionale in Rome and headed for the Vatican. It was a Wednesday morning, the day of Pope John Paul II's weekly audience in the modern auditorium on the far side of St. Peter's Square. We learned earlier that newlyweds were entitled to special tickets for this event and showed up at the Vatican the day before to request them. In a second-floor office near the basilica, I took the gold band off my ring finger to show the priest behind the counter the date of my wedding; it was inscribed on the inside. He didn't ask if we were both Catholic and I didn't tell him. The priest just handed over two white tickets, along with two gifts in brown plastic pouches—a rosary made of faux pearl beads and a gold-plated key chain with a medallion of the pope's profile.

It was gray and drizzly that Wednesday morning. Laurelyn and I ran across St. Peter's Square and through the arching colonnade. Swiss guards directed us to the entrance of the auditorium named for Pope Paul VI. Our white tickets got us sent straight down to the front of the clamshell-shaped space, which had seating for eight thousand. We settled into the tenth row with scores of other newlyweds, mostly young Italian couples. Looking at the handsome young husbands in their stylish dark suits and white socks, I felt a kind of welling pride that had started to bubble up ever since we arrived in Italy a week earlier. As a second-generation Italian American growing up in a small town, I harbored more than a little uneasiness about my ethnic roots, just like my parents had. Enough Mafia jokes and "greasy dago" cracks will do that. But having immersed myself in the Italian Renaissance in Venice and Florence, having witnessed so much beauty in art and architecture, having been treated so kindly by so many Italian strangers right here in Rome, well, I was beginning to feel an Italian renaissance of my own.

There was plenty of time for such thoughts. We had arrived two hours early and waited anxiously. In front of us sat nine rows of nuns from Spain, nervous and giggly as schoolgirls anticipating the start of a pop concert. Laurelyn kept asking me questions about the church, about Catholicism, about the authority of the pope. This is the big difference between the Christian faiths, she reminded me. Protestants don't put anyone between man and God, not saints, not priests, and certainly not the pope. However foreign all this was to her, she was fascinated by the enveloping aura of history and holiness. I told her what I could about Catholicism, but it wasn't much. Even in the capital of this ancient religion, the gulf between faith and me was wide.

Then John Paul II entered from the wings on the left side of the long stage, trailed by ten cardinals. We leapt to our feet along with everyone else as a huge ovation filled the hall. Dressed all in white, the sixty-four-year-old pontiff looked in robust health, fully recovered from the attempt on his life three years earlier. His presence was astonishing. I had never seen or felt someone exude so much charisma with merely a nod or a wave. His every movement seemed to ripple through us like an electrical current. "He is so *cool*," I said to Laurelyn, meaning it as the highest possible praise.

Whether by fate or coincidence, John Paul's address was on the sanctity of marriage as a blessed sacrament. His message, steeped in Catholic theology and grounded in the notion that marriage is "a gift of the Holy Spirit," sailed mostly over our heads. We were too star struck. He sat before us like a king in a high-backed, thronelike chair at the center of the stage, flanked by black-robed cardinals. Behind him was a massive, bronze statue of Jesus ascending. He delivered his address in eight languages. Raising his right hand and waving it slowly, dramatically in the sign of the cross, the pope gave his blessing to all the newlyweds in the audience.

Then an amazing thing happened. John Paul spoke last in his native tongue, Polish, and looking up from his notes, he seemed to depart from his text. Several rows behind us sat a cluster of Poles who took every chance they could to cheer wildly for their local hero. The pope basked in that outpouring earlier, but now he was solemn, speaking in a low, steady voice charged with emotion. He seemed to be exhorting them to something, calling on the considerable power in his heart and soul to lift them up. We knew from following the news in the *International Herald Tribune* that a month earlier, the pope's close friend, Father Jerzy Popieluszko, had been murdered by Communist thugs, silenced because of his involvement in the Solidarity movement and his vocal opposition to the government. His body had been dumped in a ravine. Beyond such reading, I knew nothing about political oppression and its frightening implications. But through the tenor of the pope's words in a language I couldn't understand, I imagined what it might feel like. When John Paul finished speaking, the Poles behind us stood in unison. They unfurled a red-and-white Solidarity banner, stretched it wide, and held it aloft. Others held up crucifixes or merely their hands with fingers raised in a V-sign. In 1984 in Poland, an Orwellian nightmare of a society if ever there was one, such simple gestures would have landed them in jail, or worse. Now these people were emboldened. Defiant. All eyes in the auditorium were fixed on them as they began to sing a gorgeous, hymnlike song in Polish. Their voices rang out, but their faces remained stoic masks of determination. As they sang, John Paul leaned over on the arm of his chair and put his head in his hand. The symbolism was unmistakable: *Your pain is my pain; your struggle is my struggle.* I looked at Laurelyn. Tears were streaming down her face.

Though we hardly understood it at the time, we were witnessing the extraordinary influence of a remarkable man. The Polish pope clearly understood the power of symbolism—his own. By virtue of his unparalleled spiritual force, he was bestowing courage to an entire people right before our eyes. That force helped bring about the eventual collapse of Communism in Poland and beyond. And, I believe, it was the same force that led John Paul a year earlier to approve the most dramatic and far-reaching changes to the Vatican's rules for saint-making in nearly four hundred years. Out went the office of "the devil's advocate," which for centuries had slowed canonizations to a crawl. Diocesan bishops were granted more authority to initiate the causes of worthy local candidates for sainthood. And the necessity of four miracles—two for beatification and two for canonization—was reduced to one each.

For John Paul II, who would become the Vatican's most prodigious saint-maker in half a millennium, there was a clear purpose behind it all. In time, his critics would howl that he named too many saints, thus diluting and diminishing the value of those already listed in the canon. But he believed otherwise. He believed, as we had witnessed, that he could not defeat godless Communism on his own. It would take legions of inspired faithful to do so. Where he could not offer his own inspiration, newly named saints—devout Catholics who had lived lives of heroic virtue—would offer inspiration in his stead. Their courage and faith in the face of adversity would be held up as symbols and models for the others to emulate. If the church was going to be invigorated to respond to so much oppression, hopelessness, or simply spiritual listlessness around the world, it would need new saints everywhere—not just in Warsaw but in San Juan; not just in Berlin but in Dar es Salaam; not just in Santiago but in Reggio Calabria.

Laurelyn and I did not return to Rome for nearly twenty years. Over time, we tussled with the spiritual baggage we had both been carrying, which was anything but lightweight. Periodically, we would pick a church to attend. We would try it for a while, always bringing our girls along, but we would fall away. None of the churches was Catholic; I didn't press for that.

No, I would return to church much later—on my own, and on my own terms, drawn entirely by a new pope naming a Catanoso cousin to the communion of saints.

Yet on that rainy November day in 1984, I had no idea that the process for that cousin's canonization was under way. A *positio*, a voluminous summary of the life of Padre Gaetano Catanoso, was being prepared right then at the Congregation for the Causes of Saints. Laurelyn and I thought during our honeymoon that we would have to travel all the way south to Reggio to meet Catanoso relatives and weren't brave enough to do so. We didn't know that we could learn about the most exalted of my Italian relatives by simply walking a few steps across St. Peter's Square. Pope John Paul II had already given his approval for the canonical process to begin. That approval had come three years earlier on October 15, 1981.

You could argue, though, that the cause started long before that, like the day before the Calabrian priest died.

On the morning of April 3, 1963, Monsignor Aurelio Sorrentino heard that his dear friend and mentor was gravely ill. He went to visit Padre Gaetano in the Santo Spirito neighborhood of Reggio Calabria. The old priest lived there in a ground-floor bedroom next to the Mother House for the sisters of St. Veronica of the Holy Face. The three-story house accommodated dozens of nuns and included a nursery school. Like an answer to a prayer, it had been completed two years earlier.

Monsignor Sorrentino came to the bedside and bent over to kiss the forehead of the eighty-four-year-old priest, whose face was pale and gaunt, his eyes nearly blind from diabetes. The monsignor heard only shallow, labored breathing and knew the end was near. He told Padre Gaetano that he had come to Reggio the day before to celebrate Mass at the seminary where the two had met twenty years earlier for the first time as seminarian and confessor. Monsignor Sorrentino said he spoke with the students about the life of St. Francis of Paola, who had been named a saint more than four centuries earlier, the last saint from Calabria. Padre Gaetano turned his head to the monsignor, his hands trembling as they clutched his rosary. In a weak voice, he spoke of his great love for St. Francis of Paola, as well as the need for reparation and continued devotion to the Holy Face. *"In Domino, semper in Domino. Deo gratias,"* he said. In Christ, always in Christ. Thanks be to God.

Mother Anastasia, the mother superior of the Veronican sisters, was sitting nearby. "Calabria needs saints," she whispered to Monsignor Sorrentino.

"Yes, Calabria needs saints," he agreed, lodging the idea in his head.

Much of Reggio, it seemed, knew the holy priest was dying. People came from all over to be near the scene. The mother superior had put the word out to the eighteen communities in Calabria where the Veronican sisters were living and working. About a hundred of them returned to Reggio that afternoon and evening, filling the bedroom and spilling out into the hallway. Their constant prayers made a steady murmur. One nun begged Padre Gaetano to "pray to the Holy Face to heal you because we still need you." He smiled. God was waiting for him, he said.

Catanoso relatives came as well, including nephews, cousins, and three of his eight living siblings (sadly, Pasqualino, his younger brother the priest, had died two years earlier). To the extent that he could, Padre Gaetano offered each relative a blessing. He urged them to always be kind, to remain faithful to Jesus and the Virgin Mother, and to pray for him. He promised to pray for them from heaven.

Late that evening, Monsignor Giovanni Ferro, the archbishop of Reggio Calabria, the last of a half dozen archbishops Padre Gaetano would serve during his sixty-one years as a priest, squeezed into the room and made his way to the bedside. He prayed silently for an hour and then after midnight, he anointed the dying priest with the holy oil of Last Rites.

At around one in the morning, Sister Dorotea Palamara was close enough to Padre Gaetano to hear him say, "In you Lord, I hope never to be confused in eternity." A moment later, the lights in the room flickered, then went dark. There wasn't a storm outside, nor was it windy. The power had simply failed. Several nuns hurried off to gather candles. By the time they returned to toss a soft glow over the priest, he had passed on.

"That day a light went out, a light that had illuminated the road to the Lord for so many men and women," recalled Don Basilio Guzzo, a Franciscan priest who stayed close to Padre Gaetano in his final days, right to the end on April 4, 1963. "A star had gone out, too, a star that had shown holiness for years and years."

A few hours later, Sister Paolina Ligato, stifling the coughs from her chronic asthma, prayed over her late mentor for a healing miracle. She did not have to wait long for her answer.

Those closest to Padre Gaetano never doubted that he ascended directly to heaven and was immediately recognized by God as a genuine saint. But official veneration is more involved than that. It requires an infallible proclamation of the Supreme Pontiff of the Roman Catholic Church. And that only comes after a lengthy and meticulous process that for some candidates takes centuries and for a few others, like Padre Gaetano Catanoso, takes decades. For countless other nominated candidates, however holy they may be, it never comes at all.

On April 4, 1978, the fifteenth anniversary of Padre Gaetano's death, Monsignor Aurelio Sorrentino, now the archbishop of Reggio Calabria-Bova, organized a commission to begin collecting information on the long life of the priest and all his many sacred accomplishments. This fact-finding was informal at first, merely satisfying the idea that had come to the archbishop when he sat at his mentor's deathbed. The idea gathered momentum and urgency later that fall when Monsignor Sorrentino traveled to Rome, where the clergy from Calabria had been invited to meet with the newly elected pope. Bring me saints to consider from your region, John Paul II implored Sorrentino and his Calabrian friend Monsignor Giuseppe D'Ascola, a member of the Congregation for the Causes of Saints. They both knew who to bring first.

In Reggio, the faithful in and around Santo Spirito had never stopped praying to Padre Gaetano. In 1972, when his church was finally completed next to the Mother House, his casket was moved from a vault at the city cemetery to the basement of the church, where it stood as a shrine. Pilgrims came regularly to touch the casket, bow their heads, and ask for favors, blessings, and miracles. Meanwhile, priests and bishops throughout Calabria, those who revered Padre Gaetano as a spiritual mentor from their seminary days, never stopped invoking his name during Mass or emulating his compassionate style in the confessional. This "renown of sanctity" long after death was key to what happened next.

On December 5, 1980, Monsignor Sorrentino filed a *"nihil obstat"* petition with the Congregation for the Causes of Saints at the Vatican to introduce the cause for canonization of Padre Gaetano Catanoso. "He was a man of a deep interior life, always united to God by prayer," Sorrentino wrote. "He left a testimony of heroic virtue wherever he went." The petition carried forty-seven letters from bishops, priests, and former parishioners, which initiated a long paper trail of testimony that began bringing to life the words and deeds of a man who aspired to be little more than an always-compassionate parish priest.

"Padre Catanoso was an old-fashioned clergyman, but still modern, and who still has a lot to teach today's shepherd of souls," Father Luigi Carusone of Calabria wrote for the petition. "His pastoral commitments, his spirit of prayer, his unquestioned obedience to his bishop are valid examples even for today's clergy."

Added Monsignor Vincenzo Lembo: "He was a spiritual force where the voice of man could be heard, and sometimes very clearly, the voice of God."

The petition also included this appeal from the Calabrian Episcopal Conference: "Calabria needs Saints who with their life testimony will call the faithful to a more Christian life, more worthy of the fathers who, in the past centuries, gave the Church notable Saints, the last of whom was St. Francis of Paola."

Nearly a year later, on October 2, 1981, the petition was examined by the Promoter of the Faith and postulator-general of the Congregation for the Causes of Saints. The petition was then taken to the Ordinary Congress of the congregation, where the voters—a panel of bishops and cardinals—recognized the existence of the reputation of holiness, the absence of any objectionable obstacles, and the spirited support of the cause back in Calabria. The panel unanimously recommended that the cause proceed, and two weeks later, Pope John Paul II made it official with his own approval.

The last earthly journey for the "little donkey of Christ" was under way.

On February 9, 1982, back in Reggio Calabria, Monsignor Sorrentino opened what's known as the Cognizance Process, an inquiry into the life and virtues of Gaetano Catanoso, who was now being called "servant of God." With the assistance of a five-person commission of local clergy, Monsignor Sorrentino drafted three hundred and twenty questions that ranged from biographical to spiritual. Over the next five and a half years, forty-two witnesses were called before the commission in one hundred and thirty-two separate sessions. The witnesses—mostly clergy and parishioners who knew Padre Gaetano from various stages in his life—answered every question. All answers were recorded and compiled. Meanwhile, the commission drew assistance from the Veronican sisters and local historians in gathering everything Padre Gaetano had written during his long life, including personal letters, sermons, and copies of *Il Volto Santo,* the newsletter he began publishing in 1920 in Pentidattilo. No detail was too small, nothing was left unexamined—good, bad, or indifferent. With the exception of Gaetano's short temper from time to time, and his crushed feelings after being separated from his nuns for five years, the commission found nothing in the life of the priest that shook its confidence that "the servant of God" was worthy of being named a saint.

On November 21, 1987, in a high Mass celebrated at the cathedral in Reggio with all the bishops of Calabria attending, Monsignor Sorrentino drew to a close the Cognizance Process. All the information that had been gathered was published in multiple hardback volumes and shipped to the Vatican, to the Congregation for the Causes of Saints. There, a relator was named—Father Francesco Moccia. His role in the Vatican process was critical. He reviewed all the biographical documentation from Reggio and added whatever historic context he believed was necessary. If there were any red flags in the testimony or gaps in the history, Father Moccia pursued the answers until they met with his satisfaction. There were very few concerns. The process kept moving steadily forward.

Two years later, on September 26, 1989, a Special Congress of theological consultants met at the Vatican on behalf of the Congregation for the Causes of Saints. The case before them: Gaetano Catanoso, servant of God. The question: Had he lived a life of heroic virtue, as defined by the congregation in its authority to recommend saints? Their vote was unanimous. Yes, he had. A few days later, a panel of cardinals and bishops voted similarly.

On March 3, 1990, less than ten years after the process started in earnest, Padre Gaetano reached the first level of official Catholic sanctity. In an elaborate ceremony at the Vatican attended by cardinals and bishops in full regalia, Cardinal Angelo Felici, prefect of the Congregation for the Causes of Saints, summarized for Pope John Paul II the findings and decisions of the theologians and high clergy. The pope thus ordered the preparation of a Decree of Heroic Virtues. From that day forward, the pope declared, Padre Gaetano Catanoso should be called "venerable."

The news touched off a round of celebrations back in Reggio. Medals were struck and prayer cards were printed with the image of Venerable Gaetano Catanoso. They were given out by the hundreds during Mass at churches throughout the city. Newspaper stories were written. The late priest's "renown of sanctity," so crucial to launching the cause in 1980, was now spreading. Monsignor Sorrentino was well pleased.

Many causes for canonization stop at this point; exactly how many is something Vatican officials aren't willing to share. But a venerable cannot proceed to beatification—to being named a "blessed" by the pope in the last step before canonization—without being credited as an intercessor for a healing miracle. That miracle must meet the scrupulous criteria established by the Congregation for the Causes of Saints and be approved by both a panel of doctors, called the *Consulta Medica*, and a panel of theologians. From this point forward, the relator steps aside and the cause is led by a postulator, who shepherds the process on through to sainthood, if it makes it that far. Monsignor Giuseppe D'Ascola, a native of Calabria, was named postulator for the cause of Venerable Gaetano Catanoso.

Sister Paolina Ligato's cure of severe bronchial asthma, coming as it did in the hours after Padre Gaetano's death in 1963, was precisely what both Monsignor Sorrentino and his friend Monsignor D'Ascola needed next. The case was clear and uncomplicated. Her prayers for a miracle went to one heavenly person, and one person alone. Her cure was immediate and lasting. The medical records provided all the documentation the physician consultants to the Vatican could want to render their technical judgment. Sister Paolina, still alive and well, was even available to testify. All the records and testimony were reviewed and approved between 1993 and 1996, from the postulator to the *Consulta Medica* to the pope. There would be no suspense, no last-minute surprises, no doubts. The first miracle was secured.

On May 4, 1997, tens of thousands of people crowded into St. Peter's Square for the beatification of five Catholic heroes. Their banners hung between the tall columns of St. Peter's Basilica and were covered by beige drapes. At the dramatic moment when John Paul consecrated them as blesseds, assuring the faithful that these heroes were indeed in heaven and working on God's behalf, the drapes were raised. Blessed Gaetano Catanoso's banner hung second from the right. Of the five, he was the most contemporary, the others having all died before 1938. The lone female in the group, Mother Maria Encarnacion Rosal of Guatemala, had died more than a century ago, in 1886.

That warm, sunny day was marked with unimaginable pride and joy for the Catanoso family of Italy. Scores of them, spanning three generations, traveled by bus and train from Reggio. They were joined in the square by the Veronican sisters, by the clergy of Calabria, and by hundreds of others from Reggio, Chorio, and beyond. They cheered and hugged, prayed and cried. They basked in the reflected glory of one of their own.

That same day passed as any other for the Catanoso family in America. I couldn't tell you where I was or what I was doing. We knew precious little about our Italian relatives and absolutely nothing about the man whose extraordinary life of faith and service was hailed that day by one of the most extraordinary popes in the history of the Catholic Church.

"Father Gaetano Catanoso followed Christ on the way to the cross, becoming with Him a victim of expiation for sins," Pope John Paul II intoned from a huge altar set up on the marble steps of St. Peter's Basilica. "He often repeated that he wanted to be the Cyrenaean who helped Christ carry the cross, heavy more from sin than from the weight of the wood.

"A true image of the Good Shepherd, he worked tirelessly for the good of the flock entrusted to him by the Lord, in parish life and in assistance to orphans and the sick, in spiritual support to seminarians and young priests, and in directing the Veronicas of the Holy Face, which he had founded.

"He fostered and spread a great devotion to the bloodstained and disfigured face of Christ, which he saw reflected in the face of every suffering person. All those who met him recognized in this person the good fragrance of Christ; and for this reason they loved to call him 'father,' and this they really felt he was, since he was an eloquent sign of the fatherhood of God."

In America, we missed it all, as if it had not happened. That was before Giovanna's e-mail found me at work, before I took my wife and daughters to Reggio Calabria to embrace so many Italian Catanosos, before Alan died amid prayers to Padre Gaetano.

When the second miracle was accepted and the canonization was set for October 23, 2005, we knew about it. And we knew we had to be there.

# PART III

---

# *Miracles*

## MIRACLE STORY—DANIELA

Daniela Catanoso had a story to share. She was seated in the living room of her small apartment in a residential section of Rome. An Italian interpreter was on her left; an American relative she barely knew was on her right.

"My mother has never told this to anyone—just to me and her mother. Of course my father knew it for himself," Daniela said. "But Mother gave me her permission to tell you."

*Grazie, grazie mille*, I said.

Daniela was in her early forties, a few years younger than me, the mother of two small children. She had thick, wavy brown hair and dark eyes the exact shape and color as my cousin Giovanna, and my own, for that matter. She was born and raised in Rome and worked as an architect specializing in historic restoration. She has many relatives in Reggio Calabria whom she saw occasionally. But the relative there she felt the closest to died in 1963, her great-uncle, Padre Gaetano Catanoso. She thinks about him always and prays to him often. She wanted me to understand why.

Her parents, Pierangelo and Tosca Catanoso, had been married for several years and wanted desperately to have a family, Daniela explained.

But they could not. This saddened Tosca tremendously, and it was weighing on her mind in April 1963 when her husband said they must take the train to Reggio from their home in Rome as soon as possible. Uncle Gaetano was very sick. Pierangelo was especially devoted to the priest, as his father was before him. Whenever he traveled for family visits to Reggio, Pierangelo's first stop was always to Santo Spirito to see his uncle and ask for his blessing.

When the couple arrived in Reggio this time, they found Padre Gaetano in bed in his small room adjacent to the Mother House of the Veronican sisters. They came close, Pierangelo offering his greeting. Tosca said little, and the old priest, frail as he was, sensed her uneasiness. He spoke to her as he had for decades to the peasants of Pentidattilo and the parishioners of Reggio.

"Something is troubling you, my child," he said, his voice just above a whisper. "Tell me; tell me what it is."

Tosca was embarrassed, reluctant, but she did as she was told. She and Pierangelo wanted to become parents, she confided, but they feared they could not produce a family of their own. She never forgot the priest's simple response:

"My child, for a baby to be born, someone must die."

As Daniela got to that part of the story, I was startled to see her cheeks flush and her eyes well up. She reached across the table and took my hand. She was on the verge of tears.

"Padre Gaetano died the next day. And I was born nine months later," she said through short gasps, brushing the tears off her face. "I am *alive* thanks to this miracle."

All right, all right, I said slowly, taking a deep breath. Can we back up a bit? I'm not sure I understand. How is that a miracle? Daniela nodded as she listened to my words being translated.

"This problem was related to my father," she explained calmly, offering answers to questions she obviously had asked herself. "He was infertile. That was the problem. But my parents didn't learn this until after I was born and after they tried to have another child. My father went to the doctor, who told him the problem was with his sperm. It died immediately. This was related to an infectious disease my father had when he was young."

The doctor told Pierangelo he could never have children, which made him laugh. He reached for his wallet and pulled out a photo he kept of baby Daniela. You're very lucky, the doctor said. That never should have happened.

Pierangelo knew then that Daniela, the only child he and Tosca would ever have, was more than luck.

"You cannot *not* believe in God when you have something as special as this; you cannot *not* believe in the powers of this saint," Daniela told me, her face a radiant reflection of her certainty. "It makes you want to be a better person and live a better life. You feel responsible. It is part of what it means to be a Catanoso, to have this saint in our lives. Do you understand now?"

# 14

## Our Saint

Every fall without fail, the American children of Carmelo and Caterina Catanoso come together for a family reunion. The tradition began in 1957, a gathering of five brothers and four sisters, their spouses and their toddling and school-age children. Each sibling would take a turn hosting the annual event. Tony, the eldest son whose early adulthood was defined by the year he had spent in Sicily during World War II, had long outgrown the wild ways of his youth. He was a member of the North Wildwood town council and would be elected mayor in 1958, an office he would occupy for twenty-seven years. He and his wife, Phyllis, owned a general store on Seventeenth and Central called the Central Shop, which sold over-the-counter medications and had a soda fountain in the back. It was located just three blocks away from his father's Italian-American grocery. For a quarter century, Tony and Phyllis were the town's leading citizens. They hosted the first Catanoso family reunion in the backyard of their Twelfth Street home. It was two years before I was born.

As the family grew to include twenty-two first cousins, their spouses, and the next generation of Catanoso offspring, the backyard reunions got too cramped. With attendance topping more than a hundred relatives and family friends, it moved to my parents' campground on U.S. Route 9 outside of Avalon, New Jersey. There is plenty of room to get together there, the sprawling, potluck lunch of lasagna, meatballs, fried chicken, salads, and hoagies spread out over several picnic tables. One table is always reserved for the burgeoning scrapbook kept religiously by Aunt Phyllis, the family historian. The book lies open to a blank page for the signatures of reunion attendees, while the rest is stuffed with year-by-year newspaper clippings, cards, and photos of family milestones: births, graduations, awards, weddings, and lately, deaths. By all appearances, the history of the Catanoso family in America began in 1957 with the first reunion.

Before and after lunch, the youngest children clamor on the playground monkey bars and swings. Later, the sack races and hula hoop contests begin. The highlight of each reunion in recent years has been an intense and hilarious bocce tournament, where my cousins and uncles pair off and go at it for hours, jinxing each toss of the heavy plastic balls with catcalls and challenging every measurement. The winners are awarded the Carmelo Cup, a trophy of polished pine topped with a silver cup that my brother Alan made in his workshop a couple of years before he died.

As the first-generation hosts have aged (Aunt Elizabeth, the eldest, died in 1994; Aunt Bessie, the second eldest, died in 1988), we first cousins have kept the annual tradition going, usually at the campground, a couple of times elsewhere, but always in Cape May County.

That's what was so extraordinary about the morning of October 22, 2005. A Catanoso family reunion, a partial one at least, took place in St. Peter's Square. It was the day before the canonization, and Monsignor Jim McDonough, the priest in our family from Philadelphia, had arranged with friends at the Vatican to celebrate an early, private Mass for the Catanosos inside St. Peter's Basilica. When Laurelyn, our three daughters, and I arrived in the square at 6:45, it was chilly and still dark. We headed toward a group of people lined up on the right side of the basilica. As we got closer, I could hardly believe my eyes, even though I knew exactly who was going to be there.

"Justin! Laurelyn! Over here!"

It was my mom, waving and calling out. My dad was next to her, smiling. My brother Lenny was there, and so was my sister Marlene and her husband, Joe. My cousin Anthony came over and wrapped me in a hug. One by one, my eyes landed on familiar faces I usually see once a year back in South Jersey. I felt an adrenaline surge as I hugged some and waved to others. There was Aunt Leona, my dad's older sister, and their younger brother, my uncle Joe. My uncle Charlie was there, too, with an entourage—his wife, Louise; her cousin, Monsignor Jim; five of their six children—Cathy, Chuckie, Anthony, Billy, and Joseph—along with spouses; a bunch of grandchildren; and some family friends. I had other cousins there as well: Uncle Joe's son John Catanoso; Pat and Skipper LaRosa, whose mom was Bessie; David Catanoso, whose dad is Peter; their wives; and several cousins from the Foti family in Philadelphia.

In all, nearly sixty of us had been drawn together for the first time in the country of our origins for the most unique and remarkable of circumstances—the elevation to sainthood of someone with whom we shared a family name and bloodline. In all, four of Carmelo and Caterina Catanoso's seven living children were in St. Peter's Square that morning. They were in their eighties, or close to it, three brothers and a sister, the children of Italian immigrants together in Italy. If not for his arthritic legs, which he didn't trust would hold up during the long trip abroad, Uncle Tony would have been with us, too, along with Aunt Phyllis. They hated to miss it.

By seven o'clock, Monsignor Jim began shepherding us through a side door of the basilica on our way to the chapel of St. Joseph. With its multicolored marble columns and dramatic oil painting of St. Joseph himself, the chapel occupies a nave to the far left of Bernini's tall, spiraling bronze altar, which sits atop the bones of St. Peter, the founder of the Catholic Church. For a short while, we had the entire place to ourselves. This church, with its soaring interior, renaissance sculptures, and tombs holding the remains of past popes, is the holiest of holy spaces in the Catholic faith. As my parents, aunts, and uncles quietly filed into the wooden pews, they blessed themselves and kneeled to pray. My mother and father took their seats in the front row as Monsignor Jim prepared the altar with communion vessels and candles. Laurelyn and I and our girls filled a pew in the back. We were settling in when I saw my sister-in-law Anna and her two daughters over on the left, near the front. It was a stark reminder of what was missing from our family.

"I'm going to go sit with them," I whispered to Laurelyn, and she nodded. Anna and her girls were traveling for the first time without Alan, who had died ten months earlier. Anna never considered not making this trip. "Hey, girls," I said as I slid in next to my nieces, Marsiella and Lisa, and gave them a hug. Then Monsignor Jim, solemn and serene in his white vestments, stood before us with upturned hands and said softly, "Let us pray."

W hat is it like to have a saint in the family? We would hear that question again and again back home as we prepared for this trip. Being able to arrange a private Mass in St. Peter's is pretty special. So is the rush of incomparable family pride. At my aunt Leona's church in Wildwood Crest, her friends would greet her and ask, some joking, some not, "Can I touch you?" The local newspapers and television stations in South Jersey ate it up, calling my aunts and uncles together for interviews ("Saintly presence: Wildwood's family 'overwhelmed' at the recent canonization of their relative, Gaetano Catanoso," blared the *Press of Atlantic City*). Of them all, Uncle Joe, the one who witnessed the mushroom cloud rising over Hiroshima, was affected the most. The knowledge of this sacred relative came to him like a belated gift. It deepened his faith in God and especially in miracles. At the Home Depot, where he worked as a section manager in Cape May County, he gave out hundreds of St. Gaetano prayer cards, which he had printed for customers and co-workers. He compiled a list of seventy-five names—people in trouble, people with illnesses, people desperate to be in the healing presence of the Vatican—and carried the list with him in an envelope all weekend. And then there was Alan, my brother. Coming together like we were—in this place, for this reason and so soon after Alan's death—offered a tangible sense of healing. Even Lenny was inclined to agree with our mother: what a blessing.

There were lighter explanations as well. When you share the name of a saint during a canonization in Rome, you begin to feel like a special guest at a huge parish party. All the gift shops near St. Peter's Square were selling religious trinkets with the smiling face of our cousin—pins, rosary beads, medals, key chains, even posters. We bought our share. In one shop, I pulled out my driver's license to point to my name; the man behind the register hooted and shook my hand (no discount). And whenever we passed near the Vatican, we'd see the name Catanoso on huge, colorful, handmade placards. These signs were plastered on tiny cars and long buses that had come all the way from Reggio and Chorio. We were constantly laughing, pointing, and snapping photos of such sights.

After the private Mass, Monsignor Jim handed each of us bright yellow tickets he received from the Vatican, stamped with the pope's insignia, for *la canonizzazione* the next day. It was a historic event and not just for our family. The five Catholic heroes who would be sainted were the last ones approved by Pope John Paul II before he died, and they would be canonized in the very first such ceremony conducted by the new pope, Benedict XVI, who had become the Vicar of Christ just six months earlier. Naturally, we imagined special seating as we flashed these tickets the next morning. "Catanoso," we would say, and the Swiss guards would direct us to our honored places, we figured. Some of us surely imagined soon accepting the congratulations of Pope Benedict himself.

With such fanciful visions playing in our heads, we made our way out of the cavernous church, past Michelangelo's Pieta, to the front doors of the basilica.

"They're hanging the banners!" I heard someone yell. The banners?

We dashed outside just in time to see the *San Pietrini*, the so-called "Men of St. Peter's" who prepare the square for such events, hoisting with heavy ropes an enormous banner of Padre Gaetano Catanoso between the tall Corinthian columns that front the basilica. He was depicted with a gentle smile, dressed in his black cassock, holding a rosary in both hands. Looking up, I draped my arm over Anthony's shoulder and said, "Can you believe this?" He had a question for me: "Did your dad pose for that banner?"

Hundreds of people now crowded around us, staring at the banners as the *San Pietrini* went about turning the steps of the basilica into a huge stage and altar for what would be an internationally televised event. Tens of thousands of chairs were being lined up in sections in the heart of St. Peter's Square. All these images and emotions added up. This event was far bigger than a mere family celebration, which it somehow had felt like a few moments earlier at the St. Joseph's chapel. Just then, a gleeful group of Italians entered the basilica carrying white flags on long poles with Padre Gaetano's face on it. Over and over, they chanted merrily, "Ca-tuh-*no*-so! Ca-tuh-*no*-so!" They weren't relatives. They were Calabrians, devoted followers of our late cousin. They, too, had come a long way to revel in the sacred glory of this special man and it struck me that they no doubt knew far more about him than any of us did. Compared to them, we were interlopers, bandwagon riders.

C anonizations are a magnet for the faithful and have been for centuries. People are drawn from all over the world to witness and share in the uniquely Catholic spectacle of once-earthly, virtuous beings proclaimed by the pope, in an irrevocable and infallible decree, to actually, literally, reside with God in heaven. The word *saint* comes to us from the Latin *sanctus*, meaning "holy one." Once declared following the confirmation of a second miracle, the new saint becomes worthy of universal veneration. Pope John Paul II led fifty-one canonization ceremonies during his twenty-six-year pontificate. His own holiness combined with his innate flair for the dramatic packed people into St. Peter's Square for each event. There was a new pope now, one who had suggested strongly that canonizations would not be nearly so common during this reign. Pope Benedict XVI's first canonization was a great curiosity, coming at the end of a three-week synod with 250 bishops from around the world (where they reaffirmed the church's age-old position on celibacy for priests). People came by the tens of thousands, flooding the streets surrounding St. Peter's Square, which had been cordoned off with metal gates as the Vatican police created a half dozen entrances with metal detectors for people to pass through.

Our family had been advised to get to the square as early as possible. A lot of people were expected. A *lot*. So on the morning of October 23, a Sunday, Lenny and I agreed to meet at 6:30 A.M. at the foot of Ponte Sant'Angelo, a famous bridge over the Tiber River, which is lined with statues of angels carved by Bernini. We crossed and hustled down the wide boulevard leading to the Vatican in a gray, dense fog. Rain was predicted; it seemed imminent. The ceremony was scheduled for ten o'clock, but when we reached Piazza Pio XII at the mouth of the colonnade, we were stunned by the size of the crowd, which snaked in lines ten people deep in several directions. The scene immediately took on the distinctive air of an international sporting event. Five saints would be proclaimed later that morning—from the Ukraine, Chile, Poland, Sicily, and Reggio Calabria—and everyone, it seemed, had a favorite. People were waving flags and carrying hand-made placards. Cheers rang out as did chants and songs in many languages. Capuchin friars, in their long brown robes, were everywhere, along with countless priests in standard-issue black. There were plenty of nuns, too, in habits of black, gray, and blue. The largest single contingent came from Chile; most of them appeared to be working-class people in jeans and red shirts, hoisting their national flag and screaming wildly for their soon-to-be sainted working-class hero, the Jesuit priest Alberto Hurtado Cruchaga, who died in 1952.

Lenny and I had no trouble finding our group. As planned, they were directly back from the obelisk in the square. Monsignor Jim, dressed in a bright, magenta-colored priest robe with a red sash, stood out like a beacon, a head taller than my Catanoso relatives, who were laden with blankets, backpacks, and video cameras.

"We're outnumbered, Jus," Anthony told me in mock seriousness. "We've heard there are five thousand people here pulling for Gaetano, but that's nothing compared to the Chileans. Must be a national holiday; I think the whole country is here. We better start making some noise for our guy."

Every so often, a few people would wander by carrying a white flag with Gaetano's face on it, or wearing a pale blue scarf that was similarly decorated. I looked hard to see if they appeared familiar. They didn't. In my naïve thinking the day before, I assumed the yellow tickets Monsignor Jim had given us would send us to a section in the square reserved for Catanoso family, or at least for those with ties to Padre Gaetano. Given the language barrier, logistics, and our Italian relatives' penchant for not confirming plans, I had not tried to arrange anything in advance. I figured a huge gathering of American and Italian Catanosos would happen by itself, in the square, during the canonization. I was dreaming. Everyone had the same yellow ticket, which only afforded us the privilege of passing through the metal gates with the chance, if we ran fast enough, of grabbing enough folding chairs to keep our American group together. This was a special day, but we were not special guests.

Fortunately, I had a cell phone number for Daniela Catanoso of Reggio. She answered and told me where we could find their group. Anthony and I ran around the left side of the colonnade, past thousands and thousands of people, until we found them just off the left flank of the square. I spotted Pina Catanoso first, the older woman who had greeted me and my family so lovingly at the train station in Reggio nearly two years earlier. There was a small crowd of Italian Catanosos.

"Pina, *come sta?*" I asked excitedly with a kiss to both cheeks. I had been teaching myself Italian since our visit to Reggio. Pina was wearing a black raincoat with a pale blue Gaetano scarf around her neck and a white ball cap with the priest's face on it. *"In domino"* was printed beneath his face. In fact, all the relatives were wearing the same scarves and caps, which had been distributed back in Reggio by the Veronican sisters.

"Giustino, *parla italiano?*" Pina asked.

*"Sì sì, un po',"* I said: a little. She smiled and pinched my cheek before I was surrounded, a mini family reunion in a completely different language. Anthony and I stayed just long enough for a round of hugs, some quick photos, and promises to get together again.

*"A presto,"* I said as we headed back to our place in line. See you soon.

At eight o'clock the gates were opened, and it was as if a human dam had burst as we joined the deluge of pilgrims pushing and sprinting for seats. People of all ages, clergy and laity, rushed to the sections with plastic folding chairs, which filled up fast. We managed to stake out enough seats to keep our group intact in one section about midway in the square. For a moment, Laurelyn and our daughters were trapped in a different section; a stone-faced Swiss guard would not let them pass. We hadn't come this far to be separated for this event. Laurelyn kept moving until she found a cooperative guard. As we took our seats, with my parents to our right and Anna and her daughters to our left, I tried to clear my head to better absorb where we were and what was about to begin. There are few public gathering places on earth more grand and gorgeous than St. Peter's Square. The arching colonnade seemed to embrace us. Organ music filled the air. The five banners hanging from the sixteenth-century basilica, just beneath the tall statues of Jesus and his apostles, looked ethereal in the distance. The fog was beginning to lift. It was still cool and overcast, and the dome of St. Peter's was completely shrouded in mist. But the marble saints perched along the rim of the colonnade surrounding us, all 140 of them, were completely visible, seemingly a part of the crowd. Make room for Gaetano, I thought.

What played out over the next three hours—the centuries-old Catholic ritual and the weather itself—seemed stage-managed by a higher power.

The rich, flutelike voices of the Vatican boys' choir began singing as hundreds of bishops and cardinals from around the world, wearing tall, white mitres and gold robes, marched in solemnly from the right side of the square in single file, their hands clasped. The choir sang in Italian:

> Joyfully, heartily resounding
> Let every instrument and voice
> Peal out the praise of grace abounding
> Calling the whole world to rejoice.

The high clergy filled risers on both sides of the temporary stage as church and political leaders, along with special guests from the locales of each saint, marched in behind escorts of Swiss guards and filled the front rows.

Pope Benedict XVI, showing his German proclivity for precision and order, emerged at 9:30, right on schedule. Loud cheers rippled through the crowd as everyone stood. Stadium-size television screens were set up on the sides of the square to assist those of us who weren't closer to the front. Benedict wore a flowing white robe embroidered with gold bees signifying purity. His white mitre was stitched with gold, and he was carrying the long, silver shepherd's staff and crucifix. He smiled and waved in slow motion to his flock. Benedict did not exude the same charisma I remembered emanating from John Paul II more than twenty years earlier, but it hardly mattered. And even though the saints' banners weren't covered for a theatrical unveiling, as John Paul would have done, the moment still carried plenty of drama.

"Today, I have the joy of presiding for the first time over a canonization rite," the new pope said to us, in Italian, to more rolling waves of cheers. I looked all around at an ocean of faces squeezed together as far as I could see, filling the entire keyhole-shaped square and the streets beyond, more than one hundred thousand souls, I figured. Way behind us, I could see a clustered group wearing the white ball caps from the Veronican sisters and holding up two white Gaetano flags. Someone was also holding up a large, homemade poster with Gaetano's image and the words: Chorio di San Lorenzo, *luogo nati*; birthplace. It reminded me of someone else who was born in Chorio as well—my grandfather, Carmelo Catanoso.

Meanwhile, the fog had completely lifted. Defying predictions, the clouds were gone, too. Forget the rain. The sky had turned a deep blue and the dome of St. Peter's, which we couldn't see an hour earlier, sparkled like a renaissance gem in the bright sunlight. "Look at that dome; it's incredible," Lenny said over my shoulder as he snapped more photos. The saints were surely having their way.

As Benedict launched the canonization ceremony from his gold, high-backed chair at the top of the basilica steps, I saw my cousin Cathy, Anthony's older sister, holding up her cell phone, tears rolling down her face. Anthony was right behind me. "Is Cathy all right?" Anthony nodded. Cathy had LouAnn on the phone, their lone sibling who couldn't make the trip to Rome. It was four in the morning back in New Jersey, but she insisted that the entire family be together.

Cathy wasn't the only one misting up. My mother and my aunts constantly dabbed at their eyes. How could they not? The pope described the lives and virtues of the new saints solely in their native languages. The only word we clearly understood Benedict saying in his raspy voice was this: *Catanoso*, spoken again and again, floating over the vast crowd like a prayer. *Catanoso*. I looked at my mom; she had her hands over her heart.

In declaring our relative a saint, here's what Pope Benedict XVI did say:

"St. Gaetano Catanoso was a lover and apostle of the Holy Face of Jesus. 'The Holy Face,' he affirmed, 'is my life. He is my strength.' With joyful intuition he joined this devotion to Eucharistic piety.

"He would say: 'If we wish to adore the real Face of Christ, we can find it in the divine Eucharist, where the body and blood of Jesus Christ, the face of Our Lord, is hidden under the white veil of the Host.'

"Daily Mass and frequent adoration of the Sacrament of the Altar were the soul of his priesthood: with ardent and untiring pastoral charity he dedicated himself to preaching, catechesis, the ministry of confession, and to the poor, the sick and the care of priestly vocations. To the Congregation of the Sisters of St. Veronica, missionaries of the Holy Face, which he founded, he transmitted the spirit of charity, humility and sacrifice which enlivened his entire life."

Those words slipped past us in Italian, just out of reach, depriving all of us at that time of a deeper understanding of Padre Gaetano's worldly influence as described by the leader of the world's largest church. Unfortunately, in the Vatican-published canonization booklet placed on each seat in the square, the short biography on our relative was printed in three languages, but not English. So as we waited to hear the pope utter the one word we did understand, I struggled to make sense of my emotions. I thought about Alan a lot. I accepted, as my mother and Anna insisted, that he was right there with us. But I could not shake the notion that they had prayed for a miracle and it didn't come.

And yet . . . was it merely a coincidence that this saint became real to us in America at the very moment we needed him the most, during Alan's illness? I wrestled with that idea in the commentary I wrote for National Public Radio, which had been broadcast in America three days earlier. *"When my brother was diagnosed with inoperable cancer,"* I said on *Morning Edition, "my mother prayed relentlessly for a miracle."* I was hearing it again in my head. I thought about how much longer Alan lived than the doctors predicted and what that extra time with his wife and daughters enabled him to do. I thought about the heroic love he experienced each time Lenny lifted him from his bed to his wheelchair. I thought about our Italian relatives, somewhere in this crowded square, who had prayed for Alan as one of their own. I thought—were these the miracles Padre Gaetano gave us?

My faith had drifted for years, but now it felt like it was being tugged in a different direction. I almost laughed at the emotion, my natural skepticism in a race with something deeper. But I called off that internal contest. I let go just a little bit. I wanted to try to connect with whatever I felt stirring and this seemed an ideal moment to do it. So there, in the middle of St. Peter's Square, with the communion of saints gazing down on me, I realized it no longer felt acceptable to be an outsider looking in on this religious faith. With a new saint bearing the family name, it wasn't acceptable that I only possessed the slightest grasp of what his life and devotion had been all about, thus keeping alive the lingering suspicion that he was somehow less worthy of this honor than other saints in the canon. In so many ways, I always felt I knew who I was—a husband and father, a son and brother, a journalist and a teacher. But I was a Catholic, too, and I didn't know what that meant. Now, for the first time since Manoel Cardozo, my insistent Catholic mentor, knocked on the door to my soul more than twenty years prior, that wasn't acceptable, either.

When the canonization ceremony was completed, Pope Benedict XVI celebrated Mass, reciting the liturgy in Italian, swinging the canter of incense around the altar, consecrating the Eucharist. A veritable platoon of priests then descended from the stage and fanned out into the crowd with gleaming gold canisters to offer Holy Communion to tens of thousands. The lush voices of the Vatican boys' choir again filled the square as I lined up amid a smiling throng of Chileans, Ukrainians, and Sicilians. I was smiling, too, floating really, swept up in the mystical and historical elements of this incredible event. I was carrying, I realized, my own special piece of cultural baggage, and as the priest slipped the host onto my tongue, it didn't feel so light anymore. When I turned I saw Gaetano's banner hanging with the others between the columns of the basilica, over the temporary papal altar, beneath the statue of Jesus. His banner fluttered slightly in the breeze. Only his. I wasn't crazy. I wasn't seeing things. I wasn't in the throes of some kind of religious rebirth. I saw what I saw.

And if St. Gaetano Catanoso was trying to tell me something, I was ready to listen.

# 15

*Believe What You Can*

Sometimes when I can't fall asleep or wake up long before I should, I'll say a prayer. Raised Catholic as I was, prayer to me is proscribed and ritualistic. So I'll say a Hail Mary or an Our Father, just like my mother taught me as a little kid. Are there other prayers? Not in my repertoire. What about those freeform, ad-libbed conversation like prayers to God or a favorite saint? I am less skilled at those. Since the canonization, since the pope's declaration that a cousin was in heaven, I thought I would give that kind of customized praying a try. To get started, it helped to visualize the place such prayers were heading. Soon I had a mental image.

I imagined a gauzy, eternal telethon in the clouds with long tables banked several rows deep, a saint in each seat, an old rotary telephone within easy reach. Not all saints are patrons of specific causes, but a lot of them are. There was St. Jude taking calls for desperate causes and St. Lucy of Syracuse hearing another plea about sore eyes and detached retinas. St. Liborius had his hands full with kidney stones and St. George was hearing once again about the heartbreak of psoriasis. (I must make a note to call St. John of God, patron of booksellers.) Then there were the Sts. Anthony. Do their phones ever stop ringing?

"St. Anthony the Abbot here, may I help you? I see. You can't find your keys. You've looked everywhere. Yes, yes, I understand. Let me stop you right there, please. You need St. Anthony of Padua. He handles lost articles. But keep me in mind if your epilepsy acts up."

I must say, I worried a little about St. Ivo of Kermatin, the fourteenth-century cleric from Brittany. He would gladly take calls from judges, jurists, and lawyers, anyone in the legal profession, really. But who remembers him? He sat glumly in silence, doing the most amazing card tricks.

Then came the new guy, St. Gaetano Catanoso, way down at the end of the row with his black cassock, bald head, and round, horn-rimmed glasses. He was working a gorgeous set of wooden rosary beads in one hand and holding a telephone receiver in the other. His phone has been going like crazy ever since he was asked to join the eternal telethon. Local calls, usually, from his nuns and Italian relatives in Reggio and Chorio. But lately, there has been an entirely new set of calls from people whose names he recognized as his own, but in a language he was still mastering: New Jerseyese. That's Connie Catanoso again. And Mary Catanoso, such a sweet lady. And Joe Catanoso. And me.

"*Dear Gaetano.*"

Now what? What do I ask for? A favor? A blessing? A miracle? Do I speak of myself first? No. Selfish. Pray first for my family—my daughters, my wife. Pray for my late brother. Pray for my elderly parents. Let's start like that.

"*Dear Gaetano.*"

Or should it be *Padre* Gaetano? Or *St.* Gaetano? He's a relative, right? But, what should I call him? My Italian relatives call him "uncle." But he's not my uncle. Look, I'm getting off track. This happens all the time. Just get started, it's late. He has calls waiting.

"*Dear sainted and cousin Padre Catanoso.*"

Then I'm struck with this notion. Is he actually listening? Is anyone? And what power does this have to affect any change? I have to admit, it doesn't feel bad to pray in the darkness of my room, in the warm, comfort of my bed with Laurelyn sleeping (how does she do that?) beside me. I like it. But is it really any different than wearing a lucky pair of pants or wishing on a star? I can't help thinking like that. I'm skeptical; it's a professional hazard. But I don't go overboard with it. Like a lot of journalists, I have always been drawn to the big idea, to bold thinkers and risk takers who believe powerfully in themselves and their visions to make things happen. They make good stories. Like Jesus, right? Now *he* knew how to pray, and best I can tell, things happened, even if you don't believe he actually walked on water. What a story.

So let me think about that. Let me think that maybe it's not such a great leap to believe in the power of prayer, in its soothing, meditative qualities, in its influence on the heart and soul, and with any luck, on the everyday behavior of a common sinner like me. Okay, I can see that. Where's the phone?

*"Dear St. Gaetano. Help me find the remnants of my faith and believe that my prayers are more than a late-night sedative."*

A few Sundays after we returned from Italy, I found myself in the back pew of one of Greensboro's few Catholic churches, Our Lady of Grace. I had asked my teenage daughters at breakfast if they wanted to come along. None of them did.

"Don't look at me," Laurelyn said, wrapped in her blue fleece bathrobe, pouring another cup of coffee. "I'm not Catholic. You're going to have to do this one on your own."

I figured as much. And as music from the organ echoed through the vaulted interior of the church, I slipped a small notebook out of my coat pocket and wrote: What am I doing here? What am I searching for?

The experiences of the last couple of years had changed me in ways I was just beginning to understand. A new set of relatives had entered my life, making the world bigger for me and making my own history longer than I ever realized. One relative, my brother, had left my life, his death reminding me, as these things do with everyone, of our temporary place in this world and the brevity of our own history. Coming so close together as they did, I could not help but feel that those experiences—one joyful, one incomparably sad—were linked by the shining image of a humble priest and sainted relative, the faith he lived and the goodness he inspired.

So there in church I could answer my own questions, at least partially. I was searching for Gaetano, searching in the only place I could in my own hometown for a sense of the religious framework within which he built his life: the Mass and the Eucharist. As a kid, I instinctively tuned out the action at the altar and never really learned to tune it in as an adult. I vowed to do better now. I would read. I would listen. I would even take notes. If I could understand the elements of the Mass, I hoped, it would connect me more to Gaetano, which would surely connect me more to my Italian relatives. And in the process, I hoped it might also connect me to my own faith, which lay dormant even as Alan was dying.

Naturally, the priest's sermon that morning came off as if he knew I was there and why I had come. Faith, he said from the pulpit, is a gift from God given to us freely. What we choose to do with that gift is up to us. We will struggle in long nights of darkness, grasping for some light in the distance. We will rejoice in the knowledge that God is real and that His love is powerful. We will waver between the two. Faith is never easy; it requires active searching, the priest said. I found myself nodding. Okay, so far, so good. It had been convenient for me to look upon faith as a chore, a burden, but I was willing to accept the gift image. I stopped nodding though when the priest said that one day we will all be called to account, and that God, however merciful and forgiving, will want to know: What did you do with the gift of faith?

It was strongly implied that having the wrong answer meant a trapdoor would fall open and I would plunge, quite literally, into the depths of eternal punishment. I found that threat alienating and mean-spirited. If faith really is a gift, must it come in a box of fear? I wanted to picture a God who was more nuanced, more charitable, more patient. If He wasn't, I was doomed. The truth is, I couldn't picture Him at all. When I tried, He always appeared to me like Michelangelo's majestic silver-haired vision on the ceiling of the Sistine Chapel. I remembered a line by St. Augustine: "Since it is God we are speaking of, we do not understand it. If we could understand it, it would not be God." Fine. At the moment, it was easier for me to picture someone I had pictures of, God's servant, Padre Gaetano. I would not be sitting in this church pew wrestling with these questions if not for him, so I wondered if perhaps he were the one holding out the gift of faith, like a good saint, on God's behalf.

If I were more spiritually alive, I would have seen that clearly and embraced it like my very own relative. But I wasn't. And I wondered if I ever could be.

My doubts only increased a few weeks later, on Christmas morning. Same church, different priest. The place was packed with families. Most, it seemed, were toting crying babies dressed in red and green. A little boy in front of me coughed and wiped his nose nonstop. I found the sermon disappointing, its message barely connected to the sweet birth story of Jesus. The priest droned on. I looked around. I couldn't tell if anyone was actually listening. This time when I asked—*what am I doing here?*—I did not fall back on Gaetano. I felt like I was wasting time in a place I did not belong. I left dejected.

I stayed home for a month of Sundays. Then in late January 2006, I got a call at work from someone who had read the newspaper column I had written about the canonization. His name was Danny Murray and he worked as a project manager at a local engineering firm. He was Catholic and excited. He wanted to hear more about my experience in St. Peter's Square, so we agreed to get together for lunch. I brought with me some photos and mementos, and as I pulled them out, I noticed that Danny did not seem all that interested. I was confused. What did he want to know?

"Tell me about the miracles," Danny asked, bursting into an eager smile. "What miracles did your cousin perform?"

All right, I can do that. It's just another couple of stories. I started in on them as matter-of-factly as recounting the details of a ball game. Danny was looking at me funny again, like I was missing the point of what I was actually saying.

He leaned in over the table. "Do you *believe*, Justin?"

Believe in miracles? Me? Am I supposed to? I honestly had never thought of that and told him so.

"Well, *I* believe," Danny said with an urgency that struck me as entirely genuine. "Goodness, Justin. He's your cousin. You've *got* to believe!"

That Sunday, I met Danny at a different Catholic church, St. Pius X, that he attended with his family across town. In fact, I started going every Sunday, sometimes to Danny's church, sometimes to St. Benedict's, a smaller church near downtown. Each week I would concentrate, not just on the sermon, but for the first time in my life, really, on the entire arc of the Mass, the opening prayers of forgiveness, the gospel readings, the chants and the songs, the elaborate consecration of the host in preparation for Holy Communion. I began looking at each element as part of a long checklist—asking myself: What rings true, what can I accept, what lies beyond my ability to believe?

I liked the idea of the general request for the forgiveness of sin. It felt grounding and humbling: "Lord have mercy." That group prayer was not a substitute for a trip to the confessional—something I definitely wasn't ready for. But I learned that it was enough to wipe clean the meager sins staining the surface of my soul, like the week-to-week impatience with my daughters or my cursing out loud. It was a start. The benevolent Jesus of the New Testament made sense to me, too. Kind and generous, firm and just, he set an example during his short time on earth that was a powerful reminder to me that I could be, and should be, a better person. Those lessons, reiterated Sunday after Sunday, would pop into my head throughout the week. A good sign, I thought. Even the congregational chant—"Lord, hear our prayer," preceding a series of honest, tangible pleas such as asking God's support for a grieving family or ending the violence in the Middle East—felt like the kind of prayerful thinking I could actually embrace.

But the virgin birth? The resurrection? The thin wafer of bread literally becoming the body of Christ? These are the central tenants of Catholicism, and I had my doubts—to say nothing of papal infallibility and my problems with the church's politics regarding contraception, divorce, abortion, and celibacy for priests. I struggled with the difference between being Christian and being Catholic. There were not enough answers to be found in church. So I turned to the writing of historian Garry Wills, one of America's greatest contemporary Catholic thinkers, for help. Wills draws a sharp distinction between church politics—decrees handed down by the Vatican over time—and church doctrine—clear articles of faith embraced by true Catholics for centuries.

"Around those doctrines, firm and always believed in, there have been peripheral stances taken by church authorities, some of which are not only non-binding but scandalous and morally repulsive," Wills writes in *Why I Am a Catholic*, citing the medieval rule of being able to earn indulgences by killing infidels. "Some teachings are blatantly opposed to the New Testament—that priests may not marry. Others are merely silly—the ban on contraceptives."

Such thoughts struck me as practical and sensible. I could feel myself relaxing in the back pew. But Wills goes on to discuss the Catholic Church's core doctrine, the Apostles' Creed, and there, he writes, there is very little wiggle room. "Augustine taught the creed to those about to be baptized and said that it must be a thing pondered and lived henceforth," Wills wrote. "The creed is not all the church teaches, but it is its central message, against which the importance of other things is measured."

So I looked at this prayer. I studied it. I measured my own unformed beliefs against the certainty of the essential beliefs of Catholicism:

*I believe in God, the Father almighty, creator of heaven and earth.*

*And in Jesus Christ, his only Son, our Lord; who was conceived of the Holy Spirit, born of the Virgin Mary, suffered under Pontius Pilate, was crucified, died, and was buried. He descended into hell; the third day he rose again from the dead; he ascended into heaven, sits at the right hand of God, the Father almighty; from thence he shall come to judge the living and the dead.*

*I believe in the Holy Spirit, the holy Catholic Church, the communion of saints, the forgiveness of sins, the resurrection of the body and life everlasting.*

*Amen.*

This presented a problem. There wasn't much there I could actually say I *believed*, but I was not ready to declare that I would never come around. So while the congregation recited the Creed each week with the priest, I remained silent. Though not despairing. Beyond Wills and a host of theologians, I had also taken to rereading the letters sent to me years ago by Manoel Cardozo, the professor. And these words of his jumped out and kept me returning to Mass: "At your stage of the game, you're bound to proceed from doubt," he had written me. And if I could not believe everything the church taught? "Believe what you can," the professor had written.

So I kept testing the waters, approaching the shore's edge, slipping off my shoes, getting just a little bit wet. Some weeks literally. At St. Benedict's, the small downtown church, the priest there often followed the opening prayer of forgiveness by walking down the center aisle carrying a silver beach-pail–like bucket with holy water. He would dip in a knobbed wand and flick it, gleefully, to his left and right. I liked it when a few drops landed on me. What I found most surprising, though, was that after a while, I liked being in church, period. It had come to feel familiar and comfortable. That was, perhaps, my first realization.

After Laurelyn and I started having children, we had made a variety of attempts over the years to find a church that made sense to us, that felt genuine and reasonable, that didn't send us out shaking our heads with a sad sense of futility. We tried a Moravian church, a Methodist church, and, for a couple of years, a Congregational United Church of Christ. We liked the last one best mostly because the minister—a woman and converted Catholic—was a good friend of ours. But after a year of pretty regular attendance, we lost our staying power. Our lives were so busy. Weekends were so short. Not insignificantly, we were all happy and healthy. We rarely encountered crises we couldn't surmount. The rock in our lives was our love for one another. Without consciously deciding, we drifted away from church.

But for me, there was something else. Even when those Protestant services were good, and many of them were, I felt there was something missing. I expected something grander, more reverential. In returning to Mass, I realized that I actually liked the myriad rituals and symbols of Catholicism. I liked the colorfully robed priest's solemn procession into and out of the Mass, following altar boys and girls holding high a crucifix. I liked the mystical elements of incense and tabernacles and statues of saints. I liked the predictable formality of the Mass, which was similar from church to church. I know I did not pay much attention to those details as a kid, but they had apparently seeped inside and lay there, snoozing soundly for decades.

After a couple of months, I concluded that I really *was* a Catholic, and I could no sooner change that than I could become German or British, let alone Moravian or Methodist. But sitting in the stained-glass shadows of church and relishing the rich atmosphere with its echoes of ancient traditions, even finding some solace in the prayerful silence before Mass, does not make one a good Catholic, a believer. In that regard, I knew it would take a whole lot more than a few sprinkles of holy water on my face. It would also take more than a saint in the family.

Like a cardiologist with a stethoscope, I was listening closely for any stirrings in my soul. I could hear something, albeit faintly. Why else would I find myself on the verge of tears from time to time during Mass? Yet what had clearly grown more audible since Laurelyn and I had taken our daughters to Italy in late 2003 was the joyous sound of my ethnic heritage. Knowing my relatives in Reggio made me ever more proud to be an Italian American. I spent hours each week listening to and reciting *l'italiano* with my Pimsleur CDs, eager to learn the language my parents wanted to forget. I sought out native Italian business people in the Greensboro area to write about in my newspaper, relishing the familiar sound of their accents. I watched happily as my three daughters each gave up the practice of straightening their lovely curls after seeing so many ringletted beauties in Italy.

I daydreamed about launching another journey on a parallel track, seeking answers that were historical as well as spiritual. In an American family filled with entrepreneurs, I stand alone as the journalist, the communicator. The Catanoso family reunion in St. Peter's Square got all of us wondering what it truly meant to be related to a saint. Perhaps I could provide some answers. Going back to church in Greensboro, I realized, would only tell me so much about Padre Gaetano. I would need to go back to Reggio and stay longer. And if I wanted to understand why this remarkable priest and his Italian relatives had remained invisible to me and my American family for so long, I would also need to go back to New Jersey and talk with my father and his brothers and sisters, the children of Italian immigrants Carmelo and Caterina Catanoso.

As luck would have it, this tandem journey of faith and heritage became more than a daydream. My NPR commentary had drawn a good bit of attention. There was interest in a book. Despite my enthusiasm, I found the prospect overwhelming at first, even daunting—until I considered that I had been faithfully telling other people's stories for a quarter century; now, with the encouragement of family on both sides of the Atlantic, it was finally time to tell my own.

"It's not luck," my mother told me. "It's Gaetano. Don't you doubt that for a minute."

That spring, I sat down for a series of long conversations with my father, Leonard. I discovered how much my father resembled *his* father—quiet, reserved, hardworking, and determined. Like Carmelo, Leonard was an entrepreneur and his small, family businesses always succeeded. He even had heart problems like Carmelo, though modern medicine intervened for my father in ways that weren't possible for my grandfather. And just like his father, my dad was rarely effusive in his storytelling. I was always amazed as a kid at the few times he would share a tale from his youth when we worked side by side at the greenhouse or campground. But he was a good sport now, sitting there in my den, wearing khakis and a white, V-necked sweater with Penn State inscribed in small letters, considering all my questions. In his mideighties, he still retained the trim build and erect carriage of an athlete, a living testament to a life of regular exercise long before it was trendy. He called our sessions "interrogations," and I am sure they felt that way to him. He has always been private, circumspect, not one eager to answer prying queries from a journalist—even when the journalist happened to be his son. But at my house in Greensboro and later at his homes in Florida and South Jersey, he would tell me as much as he could remember, my mother sometimes filling in the gaps of his life as a young man, growing up a first-generation Italian American in the years between the world wars.

"He would talk to us in Italian and I would understand him, but I always answered in English," my dad said of his father, Carmelo. "To be frank with you, I was ashamed to talk in Italian. That's why I never learned. I was embarrassed."

With each conversation, a picture of a huge family creating a new life in America began to emerge. Chorio and Italy had no place in the picture; they were left out, erased, all family ties severed. They never knew Padre Gaetano existed.

At Aunt Leona's house in Wildwood Crest, we sat in her fifties-style kitchen where I had gone for countless dinners as a grade-school kid. In a comforting way, her home looked the same, crowded as it was with knickknacks, decorative plates, and potted plants. Aunt Mary was there, too, a St. Gaetano medal around her neck. Both silver-haired and widowed, they spend a lot of time together.

"We're the only two sisters left," Aunt Mary said; their two older sisters, Bessie and Elizabeth, are both long gone.

A cardboard box filled with black-and-white photos sat on the table. "Oh, here's one of your father; such a handsome young man—and he had hair then!" cooed Aunt Leona, who was always closest to my dad. From deep inside that box, she pulled out a tiny, curling snapshot, saying, "Will you look at this." It was of Uncle Tony, slim and smiling in his Army uniform, standing next to his aunt Maria in front of her home in Chorio.

"Wow. Can I have this?" I asked my aunt.

"Sure," she said, "I don't need it. Take whatever you want."

Uncle Joe showed up thirty minutes early for our discussion at my parents' house near the campground in Cape May County. He could not wait.

"Look, Justin, I want you to call this lady," he started right in. "She's a customer of mine at Home Depot. Her son has leukemia and I prayed for him like mad at the Vatican. She's been praying to Gaetano, too. Her son's getting better. She thinks it's a miracle. You need to talk to her."

I met Uncle Charlie a few miles away at Anthony's house. Uncle Pete I spoke to only sparingly—he was the youngest of the kids, and therefore had the fewest memories of the old Italian ways to recount—but Uncle Charlie, the most tenderhearted of Carmelo and Caterina's children, the one who brought the largest group of family and friends to the Vatican, cried softly when he recounted the awful night his father died of a heart attack in the living room above the grocery store.

And then there was Uncle Tony, the oldest living sibling, nearly ninety. For hours and hours over a long weekend at his condominium in Florida, and later at his canal-front home in North Wildwood, he regaled me with stories so rich with detail that I could have been watching a movie that he had produced. It's a "movie" he watches a lot. Because of his painful legs, he has a hard time sleeping, he explained. To occupy his mind in the middle of the night, he closes his eyes and wanders the streets of South Philly he knew so well as a kid, block by block.

"I remember going grocery shopping on Ninth Street with my mother," he told me as if he had just returned. "We'd go to Bonelli's to buy meats. There was a fruit market on Mole and Dickinson. We got staples from the Fotis, who had their warehouse on Thirteenth and Federal. That's where Pop worked. On the corner of our house on Dickinson was a drugstore, D'Sylvester's. There was a bar right across the street. And one block over on Tasker was Doll Fingers' Dairy, which later became Abbott's."

Uncle Tony, the first member of the family to have built a bridge to our relatives in Italy, had made a couple of trips to Reggio with Aunt Phyllis while traveling overseas on vacations, the last time in 1972. But he never again made it back to Chorio. He could tell me little about the relatives in Calabria and nothing about the saint. That part of the story I would have to get on my own.

I planned a month-long stay in Italy—first a couple of days in Rome at the Vatican, then the rest in Calabria, in June and early July 2006. I didn't trust e-mail this time to tell my Italian relatives of my plans; I called, first Giovanna, then Daniela. As we spoke, a little in Italian, mostly in English, I listened for any hint in their voices of hesitation or reluctance. There was none.

"Don't worry, Justin, we will help you," Giovanna assured me. Daniela told me the same, though with a heavy heart. Her mother, Pina, with whom she had lived and to whom she was extraordinarily close, the woman who hosted that magical lunch at their apartment in December 2003 and whom I had seen briefly at the Vatican, had died suddenly, three weeks after the canonization. "We are still sad, but we are getting better," Daniela told me. "It will be good to see you." Both cousins promised to arrange for translators.

The day before I left, Anthony called from New Jersey to wish me luck. He had been calling all week, actually. "We're all pulling for you, cuz," he said. "I wish I could go with you."

Lenny called a lot, too, and so did my sister, Marlene, far more than usual. I was so buried in the details of preparing for the trip that I rarely stepped back to consider what I was actually heading off to do. But they saw it. To them, I had become part emissary, part historian, going off in search of their story and mine. When my mother called, she reminded me that she had been praying for me, then said, "Your father wants to talk with you." Usually with such calls, he listens quietly on the extension, offering only a few words while my mom handles the conversation. "We just hope everything goes well for you over there," he said, "and we love you."

Whew. While I have never doubted that, I could only remember a few times ever hearing him say it. "Thanks, Dad," I stammered, too stunned to say "I love you" as well.

On June 8, Laurelyn and our daughters drove me to the airport in Greensboro. She was crying when she hugged me and I told her that this was the last time I would be going to Italy without her. "I hope you have a great time," she said. "Just do what you have to do."

Yes, I had to do this. I had to accept this gift—from Padre Gaetano Catanoso more than anyone. On the plane I said a prayer to the saint, imagining him sitting there at the end of a long row of saints at the eternal telethon, working his rosary beads, fielding all calls.

I hoped he was listening.

# 16

# *Making Saints*

The Vatican is no place for nonbelievers. That's what I thought the morning after my flight as I stood on the edge of St. Peter's Square, now nearly deserted of tourists and pilgrims. The air was cool and the sky held a few clouds in a sea of blue. The banners picturing Gaetano and others of his class of saints had long been removed from the front of the basilica. But the vast space still exudes holiness. Up near the steps stands a tall statue of St. Peter, the founder of the Catholic Church, his hair and beard deep swirls of marble ringlets. In his right hand, he holds the key to the pearly gates, through which all saints receive a free pass. Over Peter's left shoulder, perched directly above the imposing entrance to God's house, stands Jesus, easily managing a bronze cross in one hand as he points to the heavens with the other. He is joined across the top of the basilica by his apostles, and all along the edge of the circular colonnade by members of the communion of saints, massive in size, their flowing robes carved in travertine. Bernini, the post-Renaissance artist who designed the colonnade and arranged the statues, wanted no one to miss his message. This is the capital of the world's largest religion, a religion made real to the faithful by the lives of these saints. This is the place where saints are proclaimed and where the church's altar is built upon the bones of St. Peter himself. What I stood staring at was nothing less than an open-armed welcome to all believers—and one doubting journalist with a briefcase filled with pages of handwritten questions.

I had two appointments that morning, interviews with priests. They were Vatican saint-makers, long-time members of the Congregation for the Causes of Saints, the earthly sanctum where the merits of holy lives are scrupulously judged by mortals in black suits and white collars. I had been directed to these experts by perhaps America's leading authority on the entire process.

The previous fall, just a few days after returning from the canonization, I was driving from work to my home in Greensboro when I heard on the radio that Kenneth Woodward would be in town the next day as a guest of Guilford College. Woodward, *Newsweek* magazine's senior writer covering religion, a job he had held for forty years, is the author of *Making Saints*, a thorough, demystifying look at how the Catholic Church determines who becomes a saint and who does not. Before my NPR affiliate had shared the news of Woodward's imminent arrival, I had been sitting there behind the wheel thinking about the saint in my family and the canonization I had just attended. I had Woodward's book at home and for months had studied it more closely than I had ever studied the Bible. Now the author was coming to town. Tomorrow. The phrase "Divine Providence" marched right up to me and smiled, but I shooed it away. Instead, I called the college and arranged to meet with Woodward the next day.

In America, Roman Catholicism is by far the largest religious denomination. Even in the South, where I migrated from my Northeastern roots more than two decades ago, Catholic churches are mostly crowded on Sundays. And while Catholics across the country live in cities and attend churches named for saints, invoke the communion of saints during Mass, and pray for favors from their favorite saints, precious few have any idea how a once living being becomes officially recognized as a friend of God, a resident of heaven, a saint. You could count me among the ignorant. But Woodward knew. He had spent years, inside the Vatican and beyond, figuring it out.

Aside from going to church, I searched also for Padre Gaetano Catanoso in the pages of *Making Saints*, even though he is nowhere mentioned. Each page was a revelation. I was looking hard for the kind of proof a journalist requires to trust the story. It's not about faith. It's about facts. Was Gaetano worthy or not? It was fascinating to learn how John Paul pressed for the beatification of blesseds and the canonization of saints from growing Catholic countries in Eastern Europe, Africa, and South America. However worthy their causes, there's little denying the pope's political motivations in providing new, local heroes for Catholics to rally around in the face of oppressive governments or rising Protestant fervor. I took great comfort in those details, but not because I thought my cousin's case for sainthood was politically motivated. Just the opposite. What possible political gain could be had by elevating another holy man from Italy to sainthood? The church had plenty of those, from superstars like St. Francis of Assisi to lesser-knowns like St. Andrew Avellino of Naples. If the Vatican was honoring St. Gaetano of Reggio Calabria, it had to have been on the merits, I reasoned. I read on.

In 1983, with the approval of Pope John Paul II, the rules of saint-making changed dramatically for the first time since the late 1500s. To speed up the process, the office of the Devil's Advocate was abolished. That was the prosecutorial office in the Congregation for the Causes of Saints that challenged each case and slowed the ultimate naming of saints, sometimes for centuries. I found this example. Simon Rojas, a pious Spanish priest who died in 1624, wasn't beatified for 142 years, when Pope Clement XIII elevated him to blessed status in 1766. Another 222 years would pass before he was named a saint—by John Paul II in 1988. It was a pretty typical case.

The pope's changes also granted local bishops the sole authority to initiate causes of local heroes. And the number of miracles required for veneration was cut in half. To the skeptics, John Paul was cranking up the machine. Everyone, from the local diocese to the congregation officials at the Vatican, was now working on the same side of the cause, Woodward concluded. Once a cause was accepted in Rome, there seemed little to stop its steady march to sainthood. Good Lord, I shuddered. A conveyor belt.

Then near the end of the book, Woodward wrote: "The more conventional and innocuous the candidate—typically founders of religious orders—the better his or her chances of eventually being declared a saint."

Uh-oh. Woodward seemed to be describing Padre Gaetano, a simple parish priest, the founder of an order of nuns. Even having just attended the canonization, I didn't know much more about him. So it was hard not to wonder: Was that all it took to be inducted into the church's heavenly Hall of Fame? Try as I might, I could no more ignore that question than I could a huge elephant in a tiny room.

When I sat down with Woodward in early November 2005, he looked the part of the brainy, older journalist. In rumpled khakis and a cardigan sweater, his gray hair askew, he was friendly and talkative, a New Yorker, so I got right to the point: Should I think less of this family canonization because of what appeared to me, in his book, to be John Paul's greatly reduced barriers to sanctity?

"Probably not, probably not," Woodward offered. "I would just stand back and acknowledge that. And don't be so willing to judge. The questions you're asking me are ones you're going to have to answer yourself."

I handed him a St. Gaetano prayer card that bore the same portrait of the bald, smiling priest that was depicted on the banner in St. Peter's Square.

"Look at this guy's face," Woodward said brightly. "He just looks good. Go ask your questions and don't worry about what you find out. Okay, maybe you should worry a little bit. But you'll come to some kind of resolution."

The Congregation for the Causes of Saints, founded in 1588, occupies the third floor of the L-shaped, yellow-brick Palace of Congregations building on Piazza Pio XII. It sits just a few steps east of St. Peter's Square. The papal coat of arms tops a tall archway that leads to a marble staircase inside a portico. My first meeting that morning was with Monsignor Robert Sarno, a native of Brooklyn, the only American among the twenty-four staffers comprising the congregation of saint-makers. He had come to work in the Vatican in 1982. Woodward recommended I meet with Monsignor Sarno but warned, "He's a tricky guy, very sour. Don't use my name. It won't help you."

The monsignor seemed agreeable enough on the phone and we made an appointment a month in advance.

Going inside the walls of the Vatican is strange indeed. I have toured the Vatican museums several times. Its long, gilded corridors are filled with statues and covered with frescoes. I couldn't help but think that the work of God is done here. The art within, of course, commissioned by centuries of popes, only reinforces that impression as it hails the magnificence of God's creation and all the struggles between heaven and hell. So I figured the place where saints were made would look and feel just as rarefied. It didn't.

With the exception of a framed photograph of Pope Benedict XVI, the reception area was unadorned, decorated sparely with blocky, modern furniture and a potted palm. Forget the sacred feel inspired by the intricate brushwork of Michelangelo's ceiling in the nearby Sistine Chapel or Raphael's walls in Pope Julius II's chambers. This place was painted in one nondescript color, by hourly laborers using the Italian equivalent of Benjamin Moore and rollers. The slightest noises in the long, shadowy corridors echoed off the marble floors and bare plaster walls.

Monsignor Sarno's small office, at least, had some ornamentation: a silver crucifix hanging on the wall above his head, some postcards taped in place depicting tourist scenes of Rome. The wall facing his desk was lined with gray metal file cabinets and in the corner by the door lay a true relic, though hardly religious—an electric typewriter, illustrating that the great wealth of the Vatican had not trickled down to this office just a short distance from the pope's opulent apartment.

As I sat down in the straight-backed wooden chair beside his desk, I mentioned that I had been reading Woodward's *Making Saints*. Monsignor Sarno waved his hand in front of his face as if clearing a foul odor. "Worthless," he said abruptly, then sat down behind his desk, neatly stacked with files and papers, and folded his arms. Not a good start. Sarno was bald with a long, thin nose and a furrowed brow, dressed all in black save for his white collar. His eyes were hard behind wire-rim glasses and his face was impassive. A canon lawyer who has taught procedural law at the Vatican and the Catholic University in Washington, Sarno has too often had the unpleasant task of fielding brusque questions from ill-informed American journalists doing stories about the latest saint controversy. I tried to explain that that wasn't why I was here, but he seemed to have me pegged before we even got started. Perhaps it was the four pages of handwritten questions I laid out on the edge of his desk. Still, I smiled as warmly as I could and started with a softball.

"Monsignor Sarno, help me understand the importance of saints. Why do we need saints?"

A long time would pass before I would have an opportunity to ask another question.

"You hit the question on the head by asking: why do we need saints," he said, "because saints don't need canonization. By the process of canonization, it's not that someone who is in heaven gets a better place in heaven. It's not that the pope, as a successor for St. Peter, unlocks a door and sends a person from purgatory to heaven. If you want to understand what a saint is, let's start with the fact that we're all called to be saints. In other words, when we leave this world, we are called to live forever with God in heaven. He already knows who they are. That's what a saint is."

Yes, I thought. That's an important point. The Vatican doesn't actually "make" saints. Only God can do that, I remembered reading. The church, through the work of this office and the approval of the pope, seeks to identify and promote those it believes have already been tapped by God to sit within earshot and pass along the prayers of the faithful. I had wandered into the pope's marketing department.

He continued: "A saint is a person who, because of his or her life, is capable of seeing God face to face, and having that special relationship. So we are all called to be saints. It's a universal call to holiness. But when we talk about saints who are canonized, in the jargon, we're talking about canonized sanctity. In other words, there is something special and particular about these people who are eventually canonized. So to understand what a saint is, I like to say that a saint has two I's—an I for imitation and an I for intercession."

It dawned on me that Monsignor Sarno, ever the professor, was delivering a lecture he had given many times before. There was no joy in his delivery, no warmth. He was just plowing ahead, following a by now internalized script. He never looked at me as he spoke but instead gazed somewhere over my shoulder. That I was a relative of a saint was irrelevant to him.

"Imitation basically means that the individual has followed Christ so particularly closely that he or she is worthy of imitation on the part of the faithful. A saint is a signpost on the road that leads to heaven. And by following Christ more closely, they have made the grade, and they show us the safe road that we can follow to find Christ in heaven.

"With intercession, that's a human confirmation, a divine declaration. And that's the purpose of a miracle. It's divine confirmation that, first of all, the person is truly in heaven. And because the person is closer to God, at the throne of God, he or she has the power of intercession. God grants graces, favors, and even miracles through the person's intercession, as a confirmation that the person is really and truly in heaven."

In other words, the saint, no matter how popular or praised, is not the miracle worker. Only God has that power, according to the church. Just then, the phone rang and the monsignor spoke in Italian. I glanced at my questions. I would get around to the personal stuff, I figured. Monsignor Sarno wasn't exactly warming up to me. He seemed distant, uninterested. This aura of aloofness and arrogance dredged up for me so much of what I disliked about the Catholic Church. Woodward was right; this man was sour. But I was impressed with his clarity in laying out the theological precepts at the start of the canonical process, so I continued my questioning.

"Where does the process begin?"

"It can only begin, as of 1983, at the local level. The Holy Father, Pope John Paul II, in the new legislation for the causes of saints, gave to the local diocesan bishop the authority to initiate a cause. And the reason for that is: This reputation for holiness and intercessory power begins in the local church, where the person lived, worked, and died. Where the person lived and worked and died is where the proofs will be. But the bishop cannot start this cause until he can prove there is an authentic and widespread reputation for holiness and intercessory power on the servant of God."

That must have happened with Padre Gaetano Catanoso, I thought. But I was thrown off as Monsignor Sarno deigned to look at me. As if admonishing me for a sin he assumed I had already committed, he intoned, "Contrary to what we might see published in certain books and articles, the cause of canonization is not at all a pinning of a post-humous medal on somebody or making an ideological or political statement." He was preemptively defending Pope John Paul II, whose saint-making often seemed politically motivated.

"With a cause of canonization, the church is actually discerning what God is saying to the faithful. In other words, this reputation of holiness and intercessory power is the work of the Holy Spirit among the faithful, raising this opinion, this public opinion, among the hearts of the faithful. So the bishop, who is responsible for the liturgical and spiritual life of the dioceses, is the only one who can verify the exis-tence of this reputation and start the canonical process."

Monsignor Sarno certainly could make a point. And this is exactly what most Americans, Catholics or otherwise, don't realize or under-stand about how one becomes a saint. Canonizations don't happen when the clouds part for an archangel to deliver the name following a trumpet blast. They don't float down from above on the crinkled parchment of divine proclamations bearing the signature of God. If seeing how sau-sage is made will make you less inclined to eat it, it's possible that know-ing how saints are made might make you less inclined to believe.

The act of proclaiming saints is the earthly, meticulous, often mun-dane work of men and occasionally women. While the notion of saints retains a mystical aura, the actual process of getting there would give an insurance claims office a run for its money. When I first learned that Padre Gaetano Catanoso was in line to become a saint, years after the beatification, I assumed John Paul II had known his story, was moved by his life, and felt called to let the world know about him. That's not exactly what happened.

Monsignor Sarno explained that the late holy person's life and reputation must continue to resonate throughout the parish, as Pa-dre Gaetano's seemed to have done. At that point, the local bishop says, in so many words, let's promote this guy. A local tribunal is formed, headed by a high-ranking priest. A questionnaire is drawn up. Witnesses are interviewed, if there are people still alive who can offer firsthand testimony. Writings, sermons, and journal entries of the candidate are compiled. Closets are peered into in search of skeletons. All this information, which usually takes decades to gather, is put together in multiple volumes in preparation for it being sent to the Vatican, where it is scrutinized within the Congregation for the Causes of Saints for years, often decades, longer—and this is under John Paul II's accelerated program.

"The goal of the diocesan inquiry is not the canonization," Monsignor Sarno said. "It is to arrive at the truth, whether the person *should* be canonized. So you try to gather all proofs, for and against the person's cause. You want a clear and objective view of the person's life in this broad social, historical, and religious context."

He went on a bit longer, but I was ready to shift the discussion to the real purpose of my visit, the cause of Padre Gaetano Catanoso. As I glanced at my notes, I saw the monsignor pointedly pull back his sleeve and look at his watch.

"I have to wrap this up," he said flatly. "I have work to get done."

Already? It was as if we were walking along a footbridge, crossing a wide lake, barely halfway across, and he had just given me a shove. The water was freezing, and deep. He was finished with me. And I hadn't really gotten started.

"Can I have a few more minutes?" I asked, treading fast to keep my head above water.

"Just two more minutes. I have tons of things to do. I have to get ready for the Holy Father," he said in perhaps the most naked appeal to authority I had ever heard.

"From my research, I understand that my relative's cause for canonization began in 1981," I said gasping, flailing. "He was beatified in 1997 and canonized just a few months ago. Most of those cases take many decades, even centuries to complete. His was relatively fast. What is the significance of this case moving so swiftly?"

"You can't make a comparison and you can't draw any conclusion whatsoever," he said, offering no other context, stopping right there. Lecture over.

"If I wanted to get a sense of the total number of saints . . ."

"Impossible. That shows an anachronistic understanding of the canonizations," he said cutting me off. "To think that all saints in history were canonized in the same way they are today just shows a lack of knowledge of what reality is."

He had moved seamlessly from dismissive to insulting. I was really splashing now, trying to think of how I might have pissed off this priest while squeezing in a few more questions before he kicked me out of his office.

"How familiar are you with the cause of my relative, Gaetano Catanoso?"

"Not at all. I've got to go."

Gulp. He had told me on the phone he wasn't involved in that process, but I figured he would have at least familiarized himself with a few biographical facts. He had not. He got up from his desk to lead me to the door.

I had enough breath for one last sputtering question, a personal question, perhaps the most important question I had come to the Vatican to ask: "In terms of being related to a saint, having a saint in the family, how should we think about it?"

He didn't hesitate: "I'm not so sure that it means anything."

What? Nothing? *Thwip.* I slipped beneath the surface, my lungs filling quickly with water. I was sinking like a coin. So, too, it suddenly felt, was the premise for my entire project. If it means nothing, what the hell am I doing here? Who cares?

Perhaps Monsignor Sarno saw his harshness reflected in my face, because he went on to toss me a line, albeit a thin one, though the edge remained in his voice.

"We *all* belong to the community of saints. We are *all* a family and a member of the church of heaven, the church of purgatory, and the church on earth. So I'm not sure it gives any one earthly family a distinction or responsibility over any other member of the community of saints. Gaetano Catanoso has become a universal man because he is in heaven and he is a saint. He is a universal reality. In a sense, he is a family member of us all."

Maybe the priest in him offered those words generously. Maybe the lawyer in him meant them technically. And maybe it was my own spiritual failing that heard them in the way that soothed any guilt I was having lately about straying so far from the church: *Your relative might be special, but there's nothing special about you or your earthly family.*

That impression stayed with me in the weeks ahead as I learned more about the life of my cousin the saint and the lives of my Italian cousins in Rome and Calabria. Maybe Monsignor Sarno was right. Maybe being related to a saint didn't mean a damn thing. I needed to consider that. But as my steps echoed in the empty corridor of the Congregation for the Causes of Saints, another thought occurred to me. If saints are proclaimed to be emulated, who exactly had Monsignor Sarno been modeling? Maybe there's a patron saint of intolerant behavior in the face of lost souls searching for meaning. Maybe that was it.

I was early for my next meeting, but I decided to walk over to the Jesuit Curia just the same. It was two blocks away, off Via della Conciliazione, the wide Mussolini-designed boulevard that opened a clear, uphill view from Castel Sant'Angelo to St. Peter's Square. The sidewalks were beginning to fill with people in shorts toting backpacks and digital cameras. I wove through them in a blur, unsettled from my interview with the monsignor. I was meeting another saint-maker, Father Kurt Peter Gumpel, who had invited me to his private office. Father Gumpel was one of the longest-serving members of the Congregation for the Causes of Saints. A Jesuit priest from Germany who grew up under Nazi rule, he came to Rome to work in the congregation in 1960. He was a teacher then and longed for a parish of his own. But he had taken a vow of obedience and was sent instead to work in the congregation, and never left. As a Jesuit, he was well suited for the work. The Society of Jesus was founded in 1540 by St. Ignatius Loyola, and the order of priests has long been revered for its orthodoxy, its loyalty to the papacy, its scholarship, and its teaching. Father Gumpel, who greeted me in a small waiting room on the first floor of the Jesuit Curia, soon came to embody all those characteristics for me.

"Would you like to do this interview in Italian or English?" he said as he offered his hand. "I speak six languages."

"English is all I've got, Father, if that's okay."

"Fine, shall we go upstairs to my office?"

He led me to an elevator barely big enough for the two of us, which took us on a clanky ride to the second floor. Father Gumpel stood straight and thin, his white collar loose around his neck. His hair was silver and gray, but he appeared younger than someone in his early eighties. When he smiled, which he did easily, his mouth turned up impishly at the corners. We walked a short distance to his office, furnished with a small, rectangular conference table and a large, glass-topped desk. Wooden bookcases lined the walls and the only light in the room came from the tall windows near the desk that overlooked the Jesuits' garden and outdoor meditation space. I could see an orange tree loaded with fruit and hear birds chirping. I already felt better.

"Father Gumpel," I said, laying out my handwritten questions and intent on picking up where I had left off with Monsignor Sarno, "my hope here is to better understand what has happened to this relative, how I should think about his canonization, how my family should think about it, and really, to have a deeper understanding of the significance of saints."

Sitting back behind his desk, his elbows on the arms of his chair, his fingers loosely knitted beneath his chin, he looked right at me and started in. "That's what I was going to tell you," he said, taking the last part of my question first. "Why does the church proceed to beatifications and canonizations? Now, we are not interested in having more saints and blesseds simply to have them. The reason is simply and purely this, especially today: People can ascertain what the Catholic Church is teaching about faith and morals and behavior. We have the Holy Scripture, which is the foundation of Catholic and Christian doctrine in general. We have fathers of the church, doctors of the church, we have catechism. So if someone wants to understand what the Catholic Church is about, there are plenty of means.

"But—people do not read too much today. At times there is danger that it goes in one ear and out the other. Besides there are accusations these days, more than in the past, that the Catholic doctrine is utopian, spiritually unrealistic, and therefore it's not feasible to live according to the Catholic doctrine. So, the answer to this is to present to the faithful a large number of people who in their day-to-day lives have lived out the Catholic faith in a radical, consistent, and joyful manner. And for that reason, we propose a number of people, so that those who say it's not possible can actually see people who have done it."

There was a lilting quality to his voice and the soft presence of a German accent. If he wanted, he could have shifted into Dutch, French, Italian, or Spanish. His English was impeccable.

"You mention large numbers," I asked. "Does that help explain why Pope John Paul II made so many saints, and with beatification, so many blesseds?"

"Yes it does. The idea is to present the various categories of age and sex and culture and nations, and say, 'Here you are, here are people in more or less the same condition that you are living, and they succeeded in living the Christian ideals in a radical, consistent, and joyful way.' That's the idea."

"And Padre Gaetano Catanoso?" No sense in waiting this time. "How does such a humble mission priest, whose life may have been similar to so many others, rise to such a lofty level?"

"You must understand," Father Gumpel said, all but reaching out to lend a hand of insight. "The absolute beginning of any cause is the existence of the vitally spread renown of sanctity, which only happens through those who watched the life of this person, and are attracted to him. Causes are not ordered from above, or by the pope or the bishop or this office. Through the renown of sanctity, we have an example of God's grace to perpetuate his mission—in this case, the mission of your relative—to encourage people to follow his example."

This added an important layer of detail to what Monsignor Sarno had explained. Since 1983, the diocesan bishop retains the authority to initiate a cause for canonization, but only after the parishioners make clear—through the consistent direction of their prayers over time—that they believe they have a saint in their midst. Unless the pope changes the rules, as John Paul II did for Mother Teresa of Calcutta, the cause for beatification and canonization cannot start until at least five years after the death of the candidate. The Vatican seeks to avoid saint-making in the eruption of emotion following the death of a particular church hero. That's why Pope Benedict XVI first let the cries of *santo subito* (saint now) calm down following the death of John Paul II in April 2005, preferring at first to let the process follow its slow, mandated route.

Father Gumpel told me he agreed entirely. "I oppose very strongly this whole *santo subito* business. Let us take time and investigate the cause of Pope John Paul II." Benedict, of course, soon waived the five-year waiting period for John Paul and the investigative process quickly moved forward. With so many of the faithful worldwide still praying to the popular pope and seeking his intercession, his day in St. Peter's Square will surely come.

In the meantime, Father Gumpel explained, here's how it is done for everyone else: "When you get this movement of people who consider this person to be a good candidate for beatification and canonization, they invoke his intercession, they believe he is in heaven, they go to his tomb and pray."

This is the renown of sanctity a bishop must see. It connects the church on earth with the church in heaven through those dearly departed who followed the path of Jesus while they were alive, Father Gumpel said.

"We pray to them and ask them to help us with intercessory prayers to God for graces for ourselves and others. We do not believe that with our death here that everything is finished. We continue to live. This is essential to our faith, that we be admitted, God wishing, to eternal life with Christ. Therefore we are active. It is not just a matter of docility. I don't know if I make this clear, but you see, the Protestants do not understand this. They say we should only pray to God. They don't accept the communion of saints. They do not believe in any mediation. Well, this is nonsense, because they themselves pray together for good intentions. So why shouldn't we be able to do this in talking with those who preceded us?"

Little by little, this saint-making thing was starting to sink in, made up as it is of equal parts of continued earthly devotion followed by divine speculation. Father Gumpel hadn't exactly said so, but it seemed clear: Padre Gaetano Catanoso remained real and spiritually vital to enough people in the years after his death in 1963 that the bishop in Reggio saw a renown of sanctity. So I shifted my questions to the aspect of saints and saint-making that sets them apart from all other historical figures of great influence and renown: miracles.

I knew that Father Gumpel held strong opinions about the role of miracles in proclaiming saints, and he carefully took me through his thinking, insisting at the outset that it is the life of the individual that defines his or her sanctity—a life of heroic virtue, as the Vatican calls it—not merely miracles.

"I have been in this work for forty-six years," he began, "first as assistant postulator general and then as consultant to the Congregation for the Causes and later as an investigating judge and high-ranking official. I can say that from a human point of view, we do everything that is possible to see if a person is worthy of the beatification and canonization process. It is a most painstaking investigation. Numerous witnesses, collecting all the documents. We have no interest in submitting to the Holy Father a case unless we are morally certain we should do so. Nevertheless, in all human undertakings, omissions are possible. In every case, it's impossible to know if every document has been retrieved.

"Therefore, before the pope proceeds with the beatification of a nonmartyr, we require a miracle as a sign of God's presence. It is not the essence of the cause. It is simply a divine confirmation that the Holy Father can proceed tranquilly and securely with this matter."

It's more than just a matter of making the pope feel good about a cause. You could argue that the pope's credibility is at stake, and saint-makers like Father Gumpel know it. Each beatification and canonization is deemed a proclamation of papal infallibility—pure and perfect, final and irrevocable. Once a saint, always a saint. In high-profile canonizations such as that of Padre Pio, who had the bloody hands of the stigmata and an enormous worldwide following, and José María Escrivá de Balaguer, the Spanish priest who founded the controversial Catholic organization Opus Dei, critics have subsequently come forward to argue that aspects of their lives were far from saintly. Miracles, which the church holds out as evidence that the person in question is literally in heaven, serve as a kind of spiritual bulletproof vest, protecting both the candidate's cause and the pope's perfection.

"Some people seem to think the miracle is the essential element, it isn't," Father Gumpel told me. "The very essence is our investigation into the life of the person. But the miracle helps us overcome any omissions or mistakes that might be made in the fact-gathering process."

And by miracles, the Vatican means only physical miracles that can be seen and documented. And these physical miracles are virtually always medical miracles. Winning the lottery? Seeing the Red Sox finally take the World Series? Finding a parking space in midtown Manhattan? Not miracles, not in the eyes of the Catholic Church. Only medical miracles need apply. These were, after all, the kind of miracles Jesus mostly performed, curing the sick, raising the dead. And in that regard, when we are sick and dying, or we know someone who is sick and dying, we tend to turn to prayer. Sometimes these prayers are answered. But when it comes to proving it, the mystery of faith gets in line behind the cold precision of science. At the core of every miracle verified through the Congregation for the Causes of Saints lies a series of facts, scrutinized by medical experts and theologians. Both groups carefully sift the accumulated evidence like any jury would. Votes are taken. Decisions are made.

"In nine hundred and ninety-nine cases out of a thousand it's a medical case when it comes to miracles," Father Gumpel said. "These cases are very carefully examined. Here in this office, you can say that out of a hundred alleged miracles put before us, 90 percent are tossed out immediately. Many people think something is a miracle, but from a medical point of view, if you investigate these things, you find it's not the case. Let's say ten cases remain, and upon further investigation, five more cases get eliminated. Therefore, very few cases remain."

Who exactly is doing the eliminating? Doctors, Father Gumpel explained. The congregation has at its disposal about sixty physicians from Rome who make up what's called the *Consulta Medica*, a kind of medical review board. These doctors, all said to be highly accomplished and from a variety of specialties, sit on panels of five and review the medical records of improbable healings. From midfall to midsummer, these panels gather twice a month to look at diagnoses, prognoses, and whether the treatments given were adequate. They look to see whether a cure is complete and lasting in duration. Regardless of these doctors' spiritual beliefs—some aren't even Catholic—their role in this stage of the process is purely clinical. They assess whether there is any possible medical explanation for why a person once given up for dead has recovered and remained healthy for years.

Interestingly, because some illnesses and diseases are known to have high rates of natural remission, they aren't even considered as possible miracle healings. Even if prayer alone has delivered you from renal, breast, or skin cancer, a miraculous cure will not be considered. Same for lymphoma. And because a cure for mental illnesses often defies definition, those cases, too, are excluded from consideration. The congregation prefers a unanimous decision on the part of the five-doctor panel, but a three to two vote declaring that the cure is "medically inexplicable" is enough to send the case to the next level of scrutiny.

"After the doctors have done their work, it goes to a board of theologians," Father Gumpel said. "And they must determine: Is there a connection between this one candidate for sainthood—and only this one candidate—and this unexplained cure?"

Here's where the process parts with science, but still tries to retain the integrity of a thorough inquisition. Those people who said the prayers for intercession are actually questioned closely as to who exactly they prayed to. If you say you prayed to Padre Gaetano Catanoso as well as St. Jude, St. Teresa, and the Blessed Mother, the panel of nine theologians does not attempt to divine whose intercessory plea was taken up by God. If it appears certain that more than one heavenly being received the prayers, the cause runs the risk of being tossed. But if the theologians find a consensus of prayer to one departed person, and if the *Consulta Medica* finds that the cure is medically inexplicable, the entire cause is then sent for review to a group of thirty-four cardinals, archbishops, and bishops who are members of the Congregation for the Causes of Saints. They make the all-important assessments of whether the miraculous did indeed occur and whether the life of the candidate was actually virtuous and saintly. The final decision as to whether a blessed is declared through beatification, or a saint through canonization, is left to the pope.

To nonbelievers—Catholics, Protestants, whoever—the entire process must sound ludicrous, as far-fetched as a priest being able to transform bread and wine into the literal body and blood of Christ during Mass. I have to admit, such thoughts darted through my mind as I listened to the arcane array of rules and regulations involved in what I once figured was a thing of indescribable holiness. I wasn't about to poke fun at something Father Gumpel obviously believed in deeply and presented so matter of factly. But I couldn't help but tell him that it was amazing to learn that saint-making was so, well, clerical, so bureaucratic, not unlike a wholly different kind of white-collar work done at any office at any secular business in Rome or beyond.

Father Gumpel considered my comment for just a moment before asking: "How would *you* go about it? A subjective opinion is not enough. Some objective standards must be followed and met. If you don't believe any scientific investigation is needed, how would you proceed?"

I guess you could let God decide. But since there doesn't appear to be another Moses coming down from the mount with God's words burned in stone, a mostly scholarly process whereby as much empirical evidence as possible is gathered and evaluated is probably a good way to go.

As our conversation progressed, Father Gumpel made it clear that although he trusts the canonical process and admires its thoroughness, he is uncomfortable with what he considers an overreliance on medical miracles. Prayer can rescue marriages, it can reconcile estranged parents and children, it can relieve a whole host of human misery beyond disease intervention. He made these arguments, he told me, to Pope John Paul II.

"I was not persuasive," Father Gumpel said, "but I said, 'Look, the medical men want a diagnosis that is perfect and be able to document it in a very sophisticated way.' There are a number of poor countries where they don't have the technology to do this. No X-ray machines, for example. I said, 'Holy Father, we are in danger of discriminating between rich and poor countries.' And this we cannot tolerate. If a poor country cannot clearly document the medical history, it gets tossed out."

"So you really want this change in regard to miracles?"

"I said this should be considered," Father Gumpel stressed. "Medical science makes more and more progress. Doctors become more skeptical. A sickness you can't explain now you might explain a year from now. Doctors are becoming very cagey. Specialists on our *Consulta Medica* fear that if it gets known that they participated in something that later turned out to have a medical explanation, they could be labeled charlatans. It gets more and more difficult to prove a miracle."

Just as I began thinking Father Gumpel wanted to make it easier for more men and women of the church to be proclaimed saints, he veered off in another direction, saying he agreed with Pope Benedict XVI's decision, made implicitly not long after he succeeded John Paul, to slow down the number of saints being turned out by the congregation. Benedict, as Cardinal Joseph Ratzinger in 1989, stirred worldwide controversy when he suggested that perhaps too many holy men and women of too little spiritual renown were being honored as blesseds and saints. Father Gumpel seemed to remember those remarks as if they were just uttered, and I found his candor startling.

"Where is the justification of sanctity and the pastoral significance?" he said to me. "That's very, very important. You see, I have been in this work nearly fifty years and there are some candidates for sainthood of whom I've never heard. What is the possible relevance of that? We want to give credible examples for the purposes of emulation. If this person doesn't have a pastoral influence—take for example a person from the fifteenth century that hardly anyone remembers—what is the point?"

The journalist in me felt like I had the scoop. But given the reason I was here to begin with, I felt for a moment like I was back in Monsignor Sarno's office, struggling to stay afloat. Was Father Gumpel now implying that my sainted cousin, who was barely known a hundred miles outside of Reggio Calabria, had been given a halo that didn't quite fit? In the back of my head, I remembered Kenneth Woodward's advice: Ask your questions and don't worry about what you find out.

"Father Gumpel, you might not be comfortable answering this, but I'd like to know—do you think there were too many saints made under John Paul II?"

"I would have liked that we investigate some of these cases more carefully before we presented somebody as an example," he told me without flinching. "That's what I think, and in that regard, I am in full agreement with the new pope. I think they are all religious people [the blesseds and saints named under Pope John Paul II]. I don't challenge that. But my question is: Do these people really have a message, a pastoral message? Do they make an appeal? Do they solicit people to follow their example? In the future, we will ask, 'What can be the possible pastoral relevance?' And if there is none, we may say, 'This is a saintly person, there is no question about that. But we do not think there is any relevancy for beatification.' This will be a delicate judgment, because everyone will claim, of course, that this person deserves it. But we need the courage of the congregation to say we do not think there is this pastoral message. That, I think, has been neglected."

I was no longer thinking about making headlines. Suddenly, my heart felt like it had crept up into my mouth. Now *I* needed some courage. When I had asked Monsignor Sarno if he thought too many saints had been named under Pope John Paul II on the way to asking whether he believed Padre Gaetano Catanoso was a worthy saint, he told me, "Everyone is entitled to their opinion." He made it clear he wasn't about to share his. But Father Gumpel would. It was time to ask. What about my cousin?

"I have no problem with him," the priest said and then returned to his previous point. "The question is, if you have a good nun, someone who lives in an enclosed place and spends her days only praying, what is the pastoral message? What is the example? We have plenty of those. That is the question we have to ask."

"Can we go back to Gaetano Catanoso?" I asked, needing to be sure. "Is this the kind of person who should be recognized as a saint?"

Father Gumpel looked down at a small book in a red leatherette cover on his desk. It was open to a summary of Gaetano Catanoso's cause, in Italian. I waited nervously as his eyes moved over the lines on the page.

"Yes, I think so, given my knowledge of his life," he said, looking at me again. "Here is a person who lived out his specific faith radically, consistently, and joyfully amidst difficulties. His was an active life. This is good. It makes an appeal to people."

"You're sure."

"Yes, I think so."

I resisted the urge to reach across the table and give him a hug. Father Gumpel couldn't tell me much more. He was not a part of the team of colleagues at the congregation who reviewed the cause. But he knew enough to assure me that Padre Gaetano Catanoso had earned his place in the communion of saints.

I still had that lake to cross, the one that Monsignor Sarno had sent me sinking into. It was, after all, the fundamental premise of my journey back to Italy—what does it mean to have a saint in the family; does it mean anything? Sarno had been blunt. And Gumpel?

"You must remember that in the Catholic faith, your relative is not dead. He continues to live," Father Gumpel said. "And therefore, they usually protect people with whom they are closely related, members of their family, people in whom they have an interest. So that's a good idea to keep in mind when you talk about these things."

A few moments later, I was back out in St. Peter's Square, sitting in the shade of Bernini's colonnade, trying to process my first morning back in Italy. What a start. I was filled with information, and dizzy with elements of relief and dread. Father Gumpel had gracefully dispatched for me the nagging question of worthiness. To the elephant in the room, I said confidently, "Gaetano Catanoso deserved his place in the communion of saints. So kindly take your trunk and move along."

I could not so easily dismiss Monsignor Sarno's troubling remarks. Sure, I'm related to a saint. All of us Catanosos are. So what? Maybe it was just a beautifully wrapped gift box with nothing inside. Yes, I know, I tried to console myself, Father Gumpel did tell me that saints tend to look out for their relatives. But the fact is, I saw little evidence of that when my brother was dying. I hated to acknowledge that the sour Sarno might be right. Was he? I looked up at the saints crowning Bernini's colonnade. They stared off in stony silence.

There were no more answers for me in this beautiful square. But I knew exactly where else to look, and I was heading there next. Whether here in Rome or farther south in Calabria, I would seek my answers in the hearts and souls of my Italian relatives.

# 17

# Cousins

I have two cousins named Daniela, one in Reggio, the other in Rome. The latter Daniela I met purely by chance, the day after the canonization in the same Vatican auditorium where Laurelyn and I saw Pope John Paul II in 1984. She was there with her mother, Tosca, and her young daughter, Giulia, for the audience that Pope Benedict XVI held in honor of the newly named saints. The room was packed with more than eight thousand pilgrims from around the world. Somehow, the still-delirious Chileans managed to get a brass band inside. The raucous, celebratory throng went wild when the band played a lively version of the New Orleans classic, "When the Saints Come Marching In." As we awaited the pope's grand entrance, my mother noticed a woman standing near her with a blue Padre Gaetano scarf knotted around her neck. My mom touched her arm to get her attention, saying proudly, "We are Catanosos from America," pointing to my father, Lenny, and me. The rest of us were scattered throughout the hall. Then I heard: "Justin, you need to talk with this woman! She's a Catanoso, too!" That much was obvious. She looked just like Giovanna. She had no English, so we made do with my rough Italian. She was from Rome, a great-niece of the saint. She was an architect and had helped in the restoration of the Campidoglio, the famous Michelangelo-designed piazza near the

Roman Forum. She handed me her business card, *Daniela Catanoso, architetto*. As she and her mother left the auditorium, I learned later that she told Tosca, "Nothing happens by chance. Uncle Gaetano led us to those cousins." It was natural for them to think that, especially with their belief that Tosca never would have given birth to Daniela without the saint's intercession.

Several months later, when I wrote to Daniela in Italian, explaining that I would soon be spending a few days in Rome, she was practically expecting it. She called me on the phone. All I really understood was the bursting excitement, like fireworks, of her fast-flowing Italian. *"Lentamente, lentamente,"* I kept saying, slowly, slowly. Not a chance. The pure, unconditional love of family—the strongest of all Italian characteristics—rushed through the line. That much I could understand. And this, too: She would meet me at the airport, with a translator.

That is how it would go for those four weeks in Italy. Catanoso relatives would appear and grasp me by the hand, take me into their lives, and then get me where I needed to go. As we squeezed into Daniela's dented silver Fiat at Rome's Leonardo da Vinci Airport, she looked at me smiling, her hands over her heart. *"Sono molto contento,"* she sighed, I am very happy—as if we were dear old friends reuniting after many years.

The following evening, she and the translator, a young Roman woman named Marta, met me at my B&B in Old Rome. We walked to an appointment along cobblestone streets and winding, sixteenth-century alleys decorated with corner shrines to saints and the Virgin Mary. For months, I had tried to arrange a meeting with Monsignor Giuseppe D'Ascola, the postulator for the cause of Padre Gaetano Catanoso's canonization. He had recently retired from the Congregation for the Causes of Saints and was living near the Vatican. Through channels, his answer was always the same: not interested. When Daniela learned this, she called the monsignor herself. I know she didn't understand exactly why I needed to talk with the postulator, just that I did. That was enough. To her, "no" was unacceptable. My cousin is coming from America, she told the monsignor, and we will be coming to see you.

Monsignor D'Ascola was waiting for us in the loud, marble lobby of the Vatican residence for priests on Via della Transpontina. He was not an imposing figure at all, but rather short and avuncular looking with a round, jowly face and wispy gray hair that was matted around the edges with sweat. In his late seventies, he had a bald head speckled with age spots, and his eyes, which were troubling him, were red and rheumy. He was dressed in priestly black. We all got situated in the lobby's pale-green leather couches, and Monsignor D'Ascola sat back and prepared to hold court. On his lap lay a copy of an orange-and-brown covered book, the compilation of Padre Gaetano's canonization documents, which he had edited.

"Listen closely," he started, with Marta turning his Italian into English, "I want to tell you how this all began."

Then he explained how his friend Aurelio Sorrentino, the archbishop of Reggio Calabria-Bova, had invited him to a Vatican meeting in 1978 with Pope John Paul II and all the high clergy of Calabria. That's when the vibrant young pope, who was new to the papacy, encouraged Monsignor D'Ascola to bring forth for his consideration "saints of your land, your region."

"To us, Padre Gaetano was an exceptional priest—pious, humble, caring of the poor," the monsignor told me. "We found in him the gifts and virtues a saint must have. But without this audience with the pope—if it was not held, if it did not happen—it is possible that the process of canonization never would have started. That audience was fundamental. Very few people know this."

We spoke for nearly two hours, and Monsignor D'Ascola seemed happy to have the attention. He made it clear that he was a pivotal player throughout the process. "I was the one who pushed things along." He, indeed, was an advocate, a Calabrian, a seminary student of the saint's. He had a personal stake. But he also helped me see all this in the context of other saintly causes he promoted. He told me that in his thirty-seven years of work at the Vatican, he knew of very few that had gone as smoothly and swiftly as the one he had led for Padre Gaetano Catanoso.

"With many causes, there are doubts and obstacles. They get stalled," he said. "Not with this one. Everything was perfect."

As we said our good-byes, always a long and lingering ritual in Italy, Monsignor D'Ascola gave us each a copy of his book. And to me, he said, "You are very interested in this man. You should do something to help him be known and remembered."

The following afternoon at Daniela's apartment, which she shared with her husband, Domenico, and their two small children, she told me her miracle story about how Padre Gaetano had interceded to make her father temporarily fertile. To Daniela, her life had been a gift, perhaps one of the first gifts Padre Gaetano offered from his new perch in heaven. It was never documented, never vetted by Monsignor D'Ascola and the *Consulta Medica* of the Congregation for the Causes of Saints. It was not an official miracle. But to Daniela and her mother, it was no less real or authentic. She did not attend church regularly, Daniela explained, but her faith was strong. She believed in miracles and the intercessory powers of her great-uncle long before two popes confirmed such beliefs through beatification and canonization. I wondered if in the coming weeks I would hear more such unofficial miracle stories from relatives in Calabria.

In my own naïveté of such faith, I asked Daniela if she believed that her special relationship to a saint provided a kind of spiritual insurance on earth, protection from harm and personal tragedies, just like Father Gumpel had suggested. She shook her head as if to say, Don't be silly. Her father, whom she loved and revered, died of liver cancer when he was fifty-three; Daniela was a young woman at the time. She prayed then to Gaetano with the same intensity my mother had prayed for Alan. While I was inclined to conclude that in the absence of miracles there is only pain and loss, Daniela simply shook her head again. Listen. Learn.

"My father was very sick," she said. "It was God's will. I accept that, too."

I arrived at the airport in Reggio late in the morning on June 11 with far less drama than when I had pulled into the train station with my family two and half years earlier. After unloading my bags at a modest B&B on the edge of the city, my other cousin Daniela—shorter and a few years younger than the Daniela in Rome—drove me over to her apartment in the center of town. It was Sunday and her place was quiet, empty. This comfortable apartment, where Daniela's mother Pina had lived as well, was where we enjoyed that boisterous, loving family reunion of a meal. That rollicking afternoon in December 2003 had crystallized for me, Laurelyn, and our daughters into a cherished family experience, one that grew more elaborate and magical with each retelling. I had written about it in magazine articles and spoken about it on the radio; strangers got in touch to tell me that that story inspired them to seek out their own relatives overseas.

Now the same place was neat and empty. As Daniela searched for a map of Reggio to give me, I wandered around—to the foyer where we were embraced like prodigal sons, to the dining room where we feasted and laughed for hours. Daniela caught up with me, seemingly reading my mind. "For as long as I can remember, the family—many, many of us—would all gather here for Sunday lunch and my mother would cook. But since she died, we don't get together so much. And I don't cook. We'll go to the *lungomare* for lunch."

Reggio is a densely built city of more than two hundred thousand people. It rises up from its coastline on steadily ascending hills that eventually become the Aspromonte. The exterior construction of most buildings is drab and plain, made entirely of earthquake-resistant block and lacking the architectural charms found commonly in Rome and Tuscany. But down on the *lungomare*, beneath shady palms and towering magnolias, Reggio's gothic and Venetian-style buildings and promenade can compete with the finest of Italy's seaside resorts. Daniela and I sat outside with a clear view of the Strait of Messina and Sicily just beyond. It was warm and breezy with white caps on the water. As we awaited our lunch, a few relatives happened by. Adriana, the wife of Piero Catanoso, Daniela's uncle and law partner, was walking with her sister-in-law, Enza Catanoso Sartori. They joined us. Settling in, Enza, whom I had not met before, lowered her large sunglasses to eye me closely. With her throaty, accented English, she said, "It's true what they say; you look like a Catanoso."

Adriana insisted I come to her apartment for lunch in the next few days; Piero was eager to see me, she said. Perfect. He was the family patriarch, the man who had wanted his picture taken with me at that lunch at Pina's. I couldn't wait to see him again. As I would learn in the days ahead, Piero Catanoso, Enza's younger brother, had come to occupy the exalted stature of the saint among the living in Reggio. He wasn't a priest. He was a civil attorney, perhaps the best known and most revered in the city, newly elected as president of the bar association by a wide margin. He was in his midsixties and had provided pro bono legal services to the Veronican sisters for years. He was a nephew of Padre Gaetano and knew the saint well. Like so many relatives, Piero's financial support of the church and its far-reaching mission was unflinching and generous. He held the key, I believed, to unlocking so much family history. I was genuinely excited that I would now get the opportunity to know him better.

"Come on Thursday," Adriana suggested, with Enza adding, "You must come see me as well. I knew the saint. I have pictures of him. And there are others you must see, too."

Dinner that night was an impromptu affair. No months of planning this time around. Daniela made a few phones calls to see which cousins could meet us. Bruno, the George Clooney look-alike, was available. He arrived on the *lungomare* wearing bright red pants and a white tennis shirt, common Reggio attire by the looks of other men I had seen walking by. A cell phone hung on a strap around his neck. Bruno greeted me warmly by clutching my shoulders and pressing his cheeks to mine. Germaine Sciriha, a close friend of Daniela's, was with us as well. She would be my primary interpreter during my stay. Slim and fair with straight, light brown hair that fell past her shoulders, Germaine was a sweet-natured native of Malta, a tiny island country south of Sicily. She had married a Calabrian, had three children, and had lived in Reggio for nearly twenty years. "I am like a member of the family," she said.

Bruno led us a few blocks up from the waterfront to a restaurant owned by a friend of his, a spacious sports bar with long tables and huge flat-screen TVs all tuned loudly to the same station. The World Cup was just getting under way in Germany. The Italian team (a national obsession surpassed only by the Italians' love for cell phones) was a long-shot favorite to win. Bruno sat next to me and laid a cell phone on the table. He then placed a call with the one hanging around his neck. When he finished, I asked teasingly, "Bruno, *due telefoni, per che?*" He shrugged and pulled a third from his pocket: one for work, one for family, one for his girlfriend in Naples. Soon his sister Caterina Calarco arrived, as well as Caterina Catanoso and her husband, Vincenzo. More hugs and cheek kisses. Yes, we remember you, they said, how's your family? I had photos and passed them around. The table quickly came alive with easy laughter and ringing phones. Only mine stayed silent.

Vincenzo, the in-law I had befriended during my first visit to Reggio when we sat next to each other at dinner, seemed genuinely touched that I was learning to speak Italian. It hardly mattered that my vocabulary was scant and that my few verbs were limited to present tense. I was learning. With Germaine's assistance, I tried to explain to him, and everyone, just what I was doing in Reggio this time around. Vincenzo nodded thoughtfully, then said to Germaine: "Tell him that whatever he needs, we will help him. Wherever he needs to go, we will take him." Earlier in the day, another cousin, Paola Catanoso, Giovanna's sister, called to offer me the use of a car. Again, it was my turn to be touched.

"That's why I love this family," Germaine told me.

Beneath the surface of all this fun and frivolity lay an undercurrent of foreboding. Something was awry. I misread this initially. Because I remembered Vincenzo so fondly, I had asked Daniela before he arrived how he was doing. She shook her head with a look of concern and said, "Not good." I assumed he and his wife were having marital problems. That wasn't it. Vincenzo was my age, a solid, athletic guy with two teenage children. He had high cheekbones and a soul patch under his lip. He parted his straight brown hair in the middle. From across the table, I noticed that he only used his right arm and hand when eating. His left arm hung limp and loose at his side, useless. Before I could discreetly inquire, Vincenzo was talking again.

"You must see Anna Pangallo," he said. "In a couple of days, I will take you there."

I knew the name. She was the recipient of Padre Gaetano's second miracle, the one that made possible the canonization. I knew she lived in Roccaforte del Greco, a small village far off in the Aspromonte, at least a two-hour drive from Reggio. I knew I needed to see her. I just didn't know how or when. Now I did.

"We must go when Vincenzo can take us," Germaine leaned over to tell me, lowering her voice. "He is not well. He leaves later this week for more hospital treatments in Torino. It's been coming on for more than a year. First he lost the use of his left arm. Now his left leg is getting weak. We worry about him all the time."

I learned later that Vincenzo was afflicted with amyotrophic lateral sclerosis, or ALS, better known in the United States as Lou Gehrig's disease, an incurable degenerative muscular disorder. It is, almost without exception, an early death sentence. Naturally, every Catanoso in Calabria, not to mention every Veronican sister in Reggio, was praying to St. Gaetano for Vincenzo.

As we finished our pizza and the last of the red wine, I felt a little wobbly, though not from too much *vino*. One of the great luxuries of being a journalist is the distance you can keep from the pain of others, even as you ask personal, probing questions and tell stories that bring others to tears. If I didn't realize it before, I felt it now. I was delving into the heart of one of those stories—one brimming with elements of faith and doubt, life and death. But there would be no safe journalistic distance this time, no carefree Sunday lunches at Pina's mythologized as sweet perfection.

I realized, that evening in Reggio, that to truly become a part of these Catanosos meant sharing their pain as well as their joy. If there were tears to come, some would be mine. This was real. This was my family. I was one of them.

# 18

# The Real Gaetano

I started my first full day in Reggio in the place to me that made the most sense, the church of Padre Gaetano in Santo Spirito. I would make many visits there during my stay, attending Mass, staring into the glass cases that held Padre Gaetano's few possessions in the room where he had died, talking for hours with the nuns and some family members as I slowly came to understand the life of the saint. I would even say a few prayers in the sanctuary at the glass tomb that held his remains. That first morning, though, I was a stranger accompanied by a translator, Germaine. We rang the buzzer on the gated door to the Mother House, which was inside the courtyard where the statue of Padre Gaetano stood sentinel over the neighborhood. Sister Gemma answered. After a flurry of Italian from Germaine, the diminutive nun showed us in.

We were hoping to meet with Sister Dorotea Palamara, the mother general of the Veronican sisters. She was in charge of the forty nuns who lived in the Mother House in Reggio, as well as those nuns working at Padre Catanoso houses in the Philippines and Tanzania. Sister Gemma led us down a short hallway to a formal sitting room with a round, glass-topped table. A statue of the Virgin Mary stood in one corner near a full-length painting of Padre Gaetano on the far wall.

After several minutes, Sister Gemma returned carrying a silver tray with tiny cups of espresso. The nun, wearing a royal blue habit with a gray headdress, was in her seventies and stood no more than four foot eight. Her olive skin was perfectly wrinkled and her dark eyes were deeply set. I asked her to join us. I wanted to know how she became a Veronican sister and if she knew Padre Gaetano. She was reluctant at first, but Germaine, who once dreamed of becoming a nun and possessed great skill at putting people at ease, won her over.

"Padre Gaetano used to send his sisters to my village, San Giuseppe," Sister Gemma began. "There were so many children there, and everyone was poor. He would come visit the village to see if any of the girls there had the vocation to become nuns."

Gemma was the second of six children, the daughter of an illiterate dirt farmer. He wanted his children to get an education, so he had them gather oranges, tangerines, and bergamots to peddle in the village so they would have money for books. Gemma, though, had discovered the Veronican sisters and dreamed only of becoming one. She would have joined when she was twelve, in the early 1950s, so eager was she to escape the poverty of her village. But she was too young. She had to wait until she was sixteen and took her vows four years later in 1955.

"Padre Gaetano was always like a father and a mother to me," Sister Gemma said. "He was such a role model. His generosity, his spirit. I never saw him angry. He had us go to places no one else would go to. It was difficult, but he taught us how to serve. We opened orphanages. We took care of old people. We taught catechism. I cried the moment he became a saint. When the pope said his name, I just cried with joy. But to me, he was always a saint."

This story line of earthly perfection was soon picked up by the mother general, who entered the room in a fast-moving dash of gray. I remembered her from my first visit here a few years earlier, but she didn't appear to remember me. She was barely taller than Sister Gemma with large oval glasses and pale, smooth skin despite her age. She spoke in a high, authoritative voice and her mouth drooped a bit, as if from paralysis. It was hard to pin her down, to get her to sit still. She kept jumping up, running out, coming back. She was preoccupied, barking orders to Sister Gemma, who hustled out of the room and returned with a silver tray bearing glasses and a pitcher of fresh orange juice. Eventually, the mother general settled in with us at the round table.

Dorotea Palamara was from Roccaforte del Greco high up in the Aspromonte. When she was a young girl in the 1940s, she told us, the village had no electricity or running water. The first school, a kindergarten, didn't come until 1956. It was opened by the Veronican sisters, sent there by Padre Gaetano. Young Dorotea yearned to become a nun before she was ten. But her father, a miner, tried to discourage her. He needed the labor of his two daughters at home and on their little farm. Several years went by and she continued to plead with him. The Veronican sisters were a great inspiration to her. Her father would not give his blessing, but she wouldn't be deterred. One September when she was eighteen, she received permission to travel with the sisters to Reggio for the feast of the Madonna, an enormous annual celebration that lasts a week. Instead of participating, she made her way to Santo Spirito and the modest house of Padre Gaetano. It was as if she was defecting.

"It was the first time I was ever out of Roccaforte, and I didn't want to go back," the mother general told me, frequently waving a finger to make a point. "All the sisters from all the villages were there. I had never seen Padre Gaetano before. He was sitting there, smiling. To me, he seemed like Jesus with his apostles, sending them out to do miracles."

Young Dorotea listened as the nuns gathered around their spiritual father and described their accomplishments in the Aspromonte: adult men and women baptized, girls taught to sew and embroider, old people sheltered. "They were the only nuns who went to these scattered villages, always on foot," the mother general told me. "The nuns from the other orders refused to do it."

Eventually, the sisters introduced Dorotea to their mentor. They explained that she had run away from home and wanted to join the order. Padre Gaetano cautioned her that the congregation lived in poverty. She said she understood, that she, too, was poor. She wanted to serve. He nodded and told her that because of her age, he could not accept her without her father's permission.

"Now go to the chapel, child, and pray," she recalled Padre Gaetano telling her. "If your father comes here to bring you home, it will be as God wants. *In domino.* Whatever happens is God's doing, and we are to be grateful, in joy and sorrow."

Dorotea's father did come down to Reggio from Roccaforte to retrieve his daughter. But when he met Padre Gaetano and saw how loving he was, his anger began to melt. The father was persuaded that his daughter had been called to this spiritual vocation; he gave his approval for her to become a Veronican sister.

These were sweet stories, illuminating in many ways, but I really wanted more. I urged the mother general to describe for me the human side of Padre Gaetano—the side that surely got exasperated from time to time or overwhelmed by the magnitude of the pain all around him, that side that might have even doubted his faith, however fleetingly. Her answer made me think that Germaine hadn't handled the translation just right.

"When a person meets God," the mother general said, "he lives in happiness. Padre Gaetano never had the stigmata like Padre Pio or anything extraordinary. His characteristics were like that of a child embraced by his mother. He would say: I am but a poor donkey. When he saw people suffering, he suffered, too. Everything was God's will."

But what about the *real* Gaetano, I wondered, the one who certainly exhibited a few flaws. It was the imperfection of saints that made for such rich drama—the early hedonism of St. Augustine, the youthful intransigence of St. Francis. Even the late Mother Teresa of Calcutta was known to have black moments of doubt when she could not feel God's presence. I suppose it was unrealistic to expect such tales and insight from Padre Gaetano's nuns, particularly in such a patriarchal system. He had urged them to be like violets, hidden under the leaves, sending up only a pleasant scent. From them, I figured, he hid his doubts.

Maybe the priests who knew about him would tell me, man to man. I spoke with several over the next few weeks.

Among them was Monsignor Salvatore Nunnari, the archbishop of Cosenza, whom I met with at the cathedral in Reggio. He first met Padre Gaetano as a boy, recalling how the old priest handed out sweets and prayer cards to the children during World War II. When Nunnari became a seminarian in Reggio in the early 1950s, Padre Gaetano was both his confessor and his spiritual mentor. "He was the priest who most influenced my life," said the archbishop, whose silver hair matched the thick silver cross hanging at his chest. "He was a man of great strength, highly demanding and strict. But his temperament was that of a saint."

Monsignor Antonio Denisi, whose office was at the cathedral complex and who served the parish of Reggio, appeared to know Padre Gaetano best. That made sense. He had been appointed by Sorrentino, the archbishop, to manage each of the 120 interview sessions that took place in the 1980s over five years during the fact-finding phase of the canonization process in Reggio. He had also been in seminary under Padre Gaetano and had been greatly influenced. Tall and burly with dark, bushy eyebrows and wire-rim glasses, Monsignor Denisi assured me that his mentor was truly unique among priests of southern Italy during his time.

"What really touched me were his prayers, his patience, his interior serenity," he told me. "You could see it in the way he talked and acted, in his relationships. He managed to transmit those qualities to others, particularly those of us studying to become priests. Whoever was with him felt close to him. He could convey the presence of God."

It struck me, perhaps for the first time, that while saints are held high to serve as role models for the faithful, perhaps St. Gaetano, as an exemplary servant of God, could inspire a new generation of Catholic priests. I asked Monsignor Denisi this, mentioning the scandalous, deplorable behavior of too many American priests that had been brought to light in recent years. He nodded that he understood the question.

"Padre Catanoso was a priest second to none, in the heart of God," he told me. "He dedicated much of his life to the formation of the seminary and the training of priests. His pastoral activity was the central characteristic of his life. This was the shining example for all to see. And so many people and other priests did see it and experience it. This is why he is a model not only for us, the Italian clergy, but he is also an example for the whole world, for the church, and for priests everywhere."

For weeks I would try occasionally, gently, to scrape off a bit of the saintly patina gilding the life of Padre Gaetano. I had this notion that I would recognize him more fully, and relate to him more clearly, if I could somehow glimpse the man who walked the earth like the rest of us, foibles and all, before he ascended to the heavens to become, as the pope proclaimed, an intercessor of graces and miracles.

So much of what I was hearing, from the nuns and the priests, was the essence of what is known as hagiography, the glorified story of a saint: his aura of goodness, his rosary, his infinite patience, and his unshakable faith. Beautiful sentiments all. For me, though, Padre Gaetano continued to stand at a distance, solid as his statue in his church courtyard, but no more real. Yet who alive would know the real Gaetano? Who would be old enough now, forty-three years after the saint's death, to have known him as a peer, not as a child? Who would have seen him through clear eyes in the context of his time and in concert with other priests toiling in the same troubled fields?

A relative led me to just such a person. We arrived one morning at a cream-colored, two-story villa on Via Reggio Campi in the center of town, just up from the waterfront. "She lives here alone," Enza Catanoso Sartori said of her friend, Maria Mariotti. "She owns the house and is quite wealthy. But she keeps little for herself. She gives her money to charity."

Maria Mariotti pulled open the tall, oak front doors and was dwarfed in its frame. She stood less than five feet tall and was wearing a faded cotton peasant dress with a blue floral print. A mismatched silk shawl of gold and green paisley was draped over her shoulders. She welcomed us warmly and we followed her into a marble foyer and then to the first room on the right, her office. A crammed book-case filled the far wall and a wooden desk was cluttered with papers, magazines, and books, three of them, I noticed, about Padre Gaetano. A single bare lightbulb, switched off at the moment, hung on a long cord from the center of the sixteen-foot ceiling; a metal cot covered by a wool blanket sat in the corner by the open window, which lit the room. Enza and Maria chattered away until I urged Germaine to edge in and explain why we had come. Maria nodded and arranged three hard-back chairs in the tight space behind her desk.

Just before she left, Enza assured me that despite Maria Mariotti's age, ninety-one, her mind was still sharp. That was an understatement. She was brilliant, luminous, the most unusual of southern Italian specimens—a woman from an age defined by poverty and ignorance who was university-educated in history and philosophy. She had been a teacher and a writer. She never married, choosing instead to live a life of service as well as the mind. Maria Mariotti remembered what it was like to grow up in the rubble-filled aftermath of the 1908 earthquake. Her father survived World War I but drowned tragically in the Strait of Messina a few years later, leaving behind a wife and two young daughters. Her grieving mother was comforted by their parish priest, Padre Gaetano Catanoso, and they spent their lives in the embrace of his faith and charity. They often assisted him and his nuns in their outreach. But Maria's studies led her to become far more intellectual than mystical. Her faith was strong, but practical.

"I dedicated myself to scholarship and religious service," she explained. "I never wanted to be a nun, but I felt a vocation to give and work in an environment bigger than a family. The destination is the Lord."

This tiny old woman with thinning gray hair and thick glasses exuded a kind of intensity that was bracing and magnetic. As we talked, we huddled in close, our three heads just a few feet apart. Maria sat with her legs crossed at the knee like a young woman, leaning forward, waving her hands. Everything about her was vital and alive. One of her few apparent concessions to age seemed to be her missing teeth, top and bottom. Germaine and I were helpless in trying to direct the discussion. We let her ramble and harvested what we could, like diamonds on a vast sandy beach.

"I started following Padre Gaetano when I was very young, after my father died," she told us, long after regaling us with details about nineteenth-century Italy and its struggles for unification. "I helped him out whenever I could—at the parish or the orphanage. I did this for many years and knew him quite well."

What made him different, saintly? I asked. The question seemed to agitate her, insult her sense of practicality and her encompassing sense of history.

"He was not the only priest doing good; don't create these idols," she warned, her voice rising. "He was a good priest and he understood his mission. But don't think the other priests at that time weren't saints as well. They just haven't been named."

We tried to keep her focused. Did you see him as a saint in his lifetime, as so many others did?

"I don't like those kinds of descriptions," she said shaking her head. "He was extraordinary, but still a human being. Do you understand the difference? There were more than eighty parishes around here, and I got to know about twenty priests. I appreciated Padre Gaetano as a saint, but there were others I appreciated, too."

So, it seemed, Padre Gaetano was not a kind of religious Superman, after all. He was not fighting evil alone in the impoverished mountains of southern Calabria. It was easy to conclude that. Of *course* there were others joined in the battle, whose names and deeds have been largely lost to history. That was good to know; it rang true. So I went further. I asked her if she ever saw his faith waver in the face of the terrible circumstances she had lived herself. Without hesitation she said no. Maria Mariotti figured he wrestled with doubts as everyone did. How could he not amid so much misery and deprivation? But she believed he reserved such thoughts for himself and most likely for his prayers. Then she described an aspect of him I had not yet heard in such detail, which she came to learn and witness firsthand.

"Have you ever heard of the Mafia?" she asked. "These people wanted to exert their control over the community. It was terrible and very common. Padre Gaetano would not accept the Mafia. He would confront them directly, in Pentidattilo and here in Reggio. He was very courageous. One day he was talking with them, and a man took out a knife and cut his robe. It was an attempt to scare him, not injure him. The Mafia wanted total control, and they didn't like priests who interfered. Their message was: 'Don't disturb us, we don't disturb you.' Padre Gaetano knew they were dangerous. He knew they were killing people. And he responded with the word of God, preaching during Mass, going out and talking with families, even if they were Mafia families. He didn't care. He was not intimidated. He understood, as other priests did, too, that the people needed to be educated. It wasn't enough to just bring them food. That's when he realized he needed help, that he needed nuns to live in those places and open schools and try to educate the children early."

We spent more than two hours with Maria Mariotti until she exhausted us with her fevered and animated detours into history and philosophy, interspersed with a few Padre Gaetano stories. Germaine often had to lean forward, take Maria's hands in hers and beg her to stop talking long enough to listen to the next question. *"Cara signora, ascolta per favore,"* dear lady, listen please. Maria just laughed, paused momentarily, and darted off as she had before. "Let her go," I told Germaine, knowing Maria couldn't understand English, "just don't translate everything she's saying."

As we finally said our good-byes and were walking out, I found myself wondering about the confluence of faith and organized religion, how both shape one's behavior and beliefs. It was the kind of issue I tussled with from Sunday to Sunday back home in Greensboro. How much of this stuff did I really believe? So I asked Maria Mariotti one last question: Did she consider herself a devout Catholic?

"Yes," she said, "but not to the extent of all the mysticism, the processions and rituals, things like that." Then to illustrate her point, which I knew was coming, she reached into history.

"You've surely heard of Padre Pio," she said. "For me, if you look at Padre Pio and you look at Padre Gaetano, both priests of southern Italy living at the same time, they are identical. They lived their faith and served their people. Padre Pio had the stigmata, but what good are bloody hands? How either one of them became saints, only God knows. To me it makes no difference. They are the same."

To Maria Mariotti, it was the life that mattered, the courage, the service. That was the lesson of Christianity, I realized, that resonated with me the most in my reading and reflection, like Jesus without magic or miracles. Even if you set aside the multiplying of the loaves and fishes and His making the blind see again, you are still left with a powerful example of goodness, charity, and rectitude. Padre Gaetano's life offered a similar example.

Germaine and I walked quietly along Via Reggio Campi in the bright sunshine. The breeze blowing up off the Strait of Messina felt refreshing, restorative. After a few blocks, I saw a large, modern-looking church of angular design with steep front steps and a flat roof. I had seen it several times before and asked Germaine if she knew which one it was.

"Yes, that's Santa Maria della Candelora," she said. "That was Padre Gaetano's parish church here in Reggio."

I stared at the front doors for a few moments from across the street. Soon I was able to imagine an old priest, dressed in a black cassock, walking through those doors. He was bald and stoop shouldered and wore round, horn-rimmed glasses. He was carrying a cane and had a rosary in his hand. He looked familiar.

He also looked alive, real, flesh and blood, no longer a statue.

# 19

# Miracles and Medicine

Sister Paolina Ligato, the recipient of Padre Gaetano's first Vatican-sanctioned miracle, lived long enough to attend his beatification in Rome in 1997. She died three years later. The second official miracle occurred in 2003 and made possible the canonization in 2005. It was received by a middle-aged woman from a mountaintop village in Calabria. True to his word, Vincenzo Infortuna was taking me to meet her.

"Anna Pangallo will cook us macaroni for lunch. You will see," Vincenzo predicted as he steered his silver Honda SUV out of Reggio. I laughed. The statement seemed as funny as it did unlikely. I wondered: Does a modern-day Lazarus, a woman given up for dead and then rising on the wings of prayer, even need lunch? We would soon find out; we were off in search of the miracle lady. On a clear, sunny morning, escaping the heat and congestion of Reggio, we drove south along the Ionian coast and the very southern tip of Italy. Across the water, I could see the steaming peak of Mount Etna poking above the clouds on Sicily's eastern edge. Then we turned inland, climbing higher and higher into the Aspromonte. I was in the backseat with Germaine. Her husband, Nino, was riding shotgun with Vincenzo, whose steering wheel was adapted with a spinning handle he could grab so that he could drive solely with his right hand and arm, the only one that worked. In a few days, he told us, he and his wife,

Caterina Catanoso, would head north to a hospital in Torino where he would receive further treatment for his ALS. But Vincenzo had promised to take me wherever I needed to go before then. So now we were heading to Roccaforte del Greco.

As we ascended, the mountains, terraced in spots to allow for acres of vineyards, rose in humps and hills in summer-dry shades of brown and green. The roads narrowed and curved and were often lined with ancient stone walls. When we passed through villages, blocky cement houses with terra-cotta roofs came right to the curb. Old women dressed all in black sat outside in the sun. Every building was plain and modest; many were empty and abandoned, crumbling. We drove along a dry creek bed, and the vegetation all around was rugged and beautiful: gigantic fig trees and bougainvillea with blooms of purple and red; scrubby pines and bergamot trees heavy with lemon-yellow fruit; prickly pear and eucalyptus; and groves and groves of olive trees studded with tiny green nuggets. The harvest is in the fall, Vincenzo told me.

With each gut-churning turn and each meter of elevation, I thought to myself: These are the same roads my grandfather traveled as a teenager on his way out of here; they are also the same roads Padre Gaetano traveled on foot or on the back of a donkey, to offer hope to the poor people living in these remote villages. Two cousins, heading in opposite directions.

A road sign, giving the kilometers to an upcoming village, caught my eye and caused my heart to skip a beat: Chorio. We were going to pass right by it. I had no idea. I asked Germaine to tell Vincenzo to slow down when we got there so I could get a picture. Within a few minutes, we rounded a tight curve, and there in the shade of a wild olive tree was a sign in black and white with the name of my grandfather's hometown. I rolled down the window and snapped a shot.

"Go on, get out," Germaine told me. "I'll take your picture."

I put my feet on the ground and my knees nearly buckled. It was a strange sensation and I did not expect it. It suddenly felt like my dad was sitting on my shoulder, my aunts and uncles, too. Uncle Tony, with his vivid memory, was pulling me forward, saying something like, "I remember these old houses and this dusty road, but this sign, it's new." Only one Catanoso from America—only one direct descendant of Carmelo Catanoso—had ever before set foot on this very ground, the birthplace of our family as well as the saint, and that was more than sixty years ago. Until that very moment. I turned and stood by the sign, resting my left hand on its metal edge.

"Awww, look at him," Germaine said teasingly, pulling my camera away from her eye. "He's crying."

"We can't stop in the piazza now; he'll cry even more," Vincenzo said with a laugh. "Let's go. We'll come back later."

We approached Roccaforte around noon after more than two hours of driving, my stomach woozy from all the switchback curves. We slowed down as we entered the village. The farm smell of cow dung seeped into the SUV, and I could hear chickens in the distance. In typical Italian fashion, Vincenzo, who didn't know Anna Pangallo, had not told her we were coming, nor did he know where she lived. We stopped to ask a young man walking along the road; he just shrugged. I tried not to worry. A little farther along, Vincenzo stopped to ask an old woman sitting outside her home. *"Anna Pangallo di Santo Gaetano Catanoso?"* she clarified, then pointed up the hill. Vincenzo then reached for his cell phone. He had her number all along. Why didn't he call her earlier? Who knows. I listened closely for words I could understand. *"Sí, sí, bene, a presto,"* he said, and I understood perfectly.

There was one more steep climb to make past a jumble of stone and block houses and a baroque-style church on the edge of a cliff. We swung onto a street named Via Roma and followed it up, up, and around to the left to the top of the highest hill in Roccaforte. I could see a woman dressed in a black knit sweater and black skirt, standing at the curb on the left, looking our way, waving slowly. It was Anna Pangallo, the miracle woman.

"I am very happy you are here," she told Germaine, who greeted her first. "I was almost dead. But as you can see, I am very much alive."

I was amazed at how young she looked, in her late fifties, I figured. She bowed slightly when she shook my hand, saying, *"Piacere,"* pleased to meet you. Her short, wavy hair framed her head like a helmet and was mostly black, fringed with gray. She had small eyes, a long nose, and round, ruddy cheeks. Her skin was smooth. She was completely relaxed in welcoming a carload of strangers and we sauntered together up the steep driveway to her house, past an outdoor wash basin with slips and underwear hanging on a clothesline attached to a cherry tree heavy with fruit. We were followed lazily by two small mutts that didn't even bark. Like Anna Pangallo, they seemed happy for the company.

Her one-story house was more like a duplex; she and her husband lived on one side and her elderly mother lived on the other side. Her father, we learned, had died two months earlier. The house, which had just four rooms, was made of cinder block with a shed roof. A long cement porch stretched across the front hanging over a sheer drop-off of several hundred feet. A cord of split firewood was stacked neatly at the far end. The view across the valley of the craggy peaks and rolling ridges of the Aspromonte, dappled with the shadows of thick, puffy clouds, would have been quite valuable in a place not quite so impoverished. From this vantage point, though, it merely reminded the family of its isolation.

Anna invited us into her tidy living room, not more than twelve feet square, and we sat at a round table covered with a lovely needlepoint cloth. She had made it herself. The ceiling was low and the dimly lit room was big enough only for a love seat, a couple of china cabinets, and a small bookcase topped with baby dolls and plastic religious statues and pictures. A print of Padre Gaetano hung on the wall by the kitchen doorway. As Germaine explained why we were there, I handed her a card I made for the trip that bore my name and the word *scrittore*, writer. She turned it over and over as she listened to Germaine, her face perfectly serene. We had come to hear the story of a miracle, and she was happy to tell it.

"In my life I was fine, I was always in good health," she began. "Then on December 29, 2002, I got a fever. I went to bed with a very bad headache and a stiff neck. The village doctor said, 'Don't worry. It's nothing. I will give you an injection and it will go away.' But I only got more sick."

When she collapsed on her bedroom floor after vomiting in the bathroom, her husband, Domenico Spano, a forester, decided to drive her down the mountain to the hospital in Melito di Porto Salvo, more than an hour away. She had never felt so ill. The doctors could not adequately diagnose her, so they sent her by ambulance to a nearby hospital in Palmi. She spent three days there, where an initial diagnosis of meningococcal meningitis, or bacterial meningitis, was made. The fluids surrounding her spinal cord and brain had become dangerously infected. Rapid treatment with antibiotics is critical in such cases, but she did not receive any until she was finally transferred to the infectious diseases unit at Riuniti Hospital in Reggio.

"From that moment on, I can only repeat what I was told," she explained. "I don't remember anything."

By the time she reached Reggio, four days had passed without any significant therapy. A spinal tap confirmed the diagnosis. Her fever had spiked, indicating the infection was intensifying, and she lapsed into a coma, totally unresponsive to all stimuli. Doctors hooked her up to oxygen and a steady drip of antibiotics. It was a bad case, among the worst they had ever seen. Her heartbeat plummeted and she convulsed with seizures. After another twenty-four hours a doctor pulled Domenico Spano aside. The worried husband had driven down from Roccaforte with a host of others—their three grown daughters, siblings, cousins, nieces and nephews, neighbors. They all kept a vigil outside Anna's room, which had a glass window so they could see inside. The doctor had bad news for Domenico.

"There is nothing more we can do for your wife," the doctor said. "It is best that you prepare for her death; she won't live long."

Domenico instead placed a call to the Mother House of the Veronican sisters across town. He spoke with the mother general, Sister Dorotea Palamara, a native of Roccaforte who had known Anna Pangallo and her family for years. Anna had attended the Padre Gaetano elementary school in the village until the fifth grade; she was known for her kindness to other villagers and her caring devotion to the church. The mother general, who had always felt a special bond with Anna, took charge. Start everyone praying, praying to Padre Gaetano, she told Anna's husband. Do not stop. Tell the priest at the church in Roccaforte. Tell everyone in the village. They must pray only to Padre Gaetano. The church should be left open day and night. She said she would set the Veronican sisters to the same task, practically around the clock at the church of Padre Gaetano. They would pray novenas, long prayers with special intentions, along with the rosary. They often prayed at the kneelers beside Padre Gaetano's glass tomb in the sanctuary. This went on for days.

On the ninth day of Anna Pangallo's coma, as hope faded, a frenzied mother general gathered her nuns in the sanctuary and demanded aloud that God intervene on the suffering woman's behalf through Padre Gaetano's intercession. She then organized it so that the congregation in Roccaforte was praying the same prayers at the same time as the Veronican sisters in Reggio. Scores of people prayed in unison in two parts of Calabria.

At the moment they all finished, a phone rang in the Mother House. It was a delirious, stammering relative of Anna's calling with the most incredible news.

Anna Pangallo told us she had no memory of her nine days in a coma. She recalled no flashes of light or visions of Padre Gaetano or any other heavenly being for that matter. But she did remember opening her eyes and spotting a young nephew staring at her through the large, plate-glass viewing window of her room. The nephew's name was Gaetano. With some effort, she struggled to lift her hand and wiggle her fingers in a kind of wave. He saw her and about fell over. Seconds later, the window was crowded with faces of wide-eyed relatives who were soon screaming, hugging, and crying.

"A doctor came and took my daughter, Mariangela, by the hand and led her into the room," Anna told us. "She was the first one allowed to come in. The doctor could not believe I was awake. He assumed my brain was damaged. To see if I could think clearly, he told me, 'This is your daughter, her name is Bruna.' I said, 'No! Her name is Mariangela, not Bruna!' He was stunned. He couldn't believe it. I really *was* awake."

As Anna Pangallo related those details, I found myself rapt, transfixed. There was a steady, lilting quality to her voice that never wavered. The story just flowed. Germaine was locked in as well. Her translation was rich and precise, capturing all the nuance and drama that Anna was recounting. I figured it must have been a story she told often, but she said no, only a few times. Everyone in the village already knew. Who else was there to tell? She went on.

"They kept me in the hospital for a month and a few days," Anna told us. "They feared the meningitis would leave some lasting damage. After several days, I started to get up and move around. It hurt very much. I was given a walker. I was very weak. But little by little, I started getting stronger. When the doctors saw me in the hallways, they would joke that I was the walking dead come alive!"

By the time she returned to her hilltop home in Roccaforte, it was as if she had never been sick. She soon came to believe that her healing had literally been a miracle.

"That's when I learned that all the people in Roccaforte, every single one, prayed for me to Padre Gaetano," she said of the village and its population of about six hundred people. "They prayed from morning into the night. Continuously. I learned also that a neighbor had left a rosary and Padre Gaetano prayer card under my pillow when I was in a coma. After I awoke, I began praying right away to Padre Gaetano, too."

As Anna Pangallo brought her miracle story to a close, I had some questions. I found myself drifting back two years to a hospital room across the ocean, a room that also held prayer cards and reminders of Padre Gaetano Catanoso, a room that held my brother Alan, dying of cancer. My family had prayed the same prayers that Anna Pangallo's family and friends did. My mother prayed countless novenas. Yet our outcome was so different. I asked her about her faith.

"For me it is something great," she explained. "I am a believer. Look at my house; it is filled with saints and religious items. After an experience like I had, you believe even more. You have more faith. So I never miss Mass. I visit the sick. I help where I can. I feel an even greater responsibility than I did before."

"Do you ever try to understand why you would receive such a blessing?" I asked, leaving the rest of my question unspoken: "and my brother did not?"

She paused before saying, "Sometimes I try to understand. I ask, why me? But I have no answers. It's not for me to understand."

We lingered another half hour or so and chatted amiably like old friends. Anna Pangallo did not make us macaroni for lunch, as Vincenzo had predicted, but she did make us espresso. At one point, she went off in search of some photos, returning with enlarged color glossies of herself on the day of the canonization. Unlike us Catanosos from America, she really was an honored guest of the Vatican that morning, sitting in the second row with the mother general and the Veronican sisters. A Vatican photographer caught her at the moment she received Holy Communion from Pope Benedict XVI on the steps of St. Peter's Basilica. This elegant and modest woman from a poor mountain village described it as the most profound experience of her life. Her voice caught a bit, her emotions bubbling up for the first time since we arrived.

Out on her long front porch with its breathtaking views, we met her elderly mother, Angela Gulli, a perfect picture of a nineteenth-century Calabrian peasant woman. She was short and stooped and wore only black, including a black bonnet tied with a thick bow. It was her mourning outfit for her dead husband. Her tanned face was wrinkled and leathery and her pointy chin sprouted whiskers. She looked at her daughter as if she still could not believe she was alive. "Of course it was a miracle," the mother said, practically weeping. "The doctor told us she was dead and gone. I never thought she would wake up."

Before we left, Germaine, another true believer, asked me a favor. Vincenzo was nearby, chatting with Anna Pangallo, his left arm dangling at this side.

"Take Vincenzo back into the house for a moment," she whispered. "I want to ask Anna Pangallo to pray for him."

Early one morning the following week, I was standing at a busy corner on the *lungomare*, the waterfront in downtown Reggio, waiting for a ride. Edward Parker, a British expatriate who lived in Reggio and was married to a local woman, was on his way. He was a language teacher and helped out as my interpreter when Germaine wasn't available. He had arranged an interview at Riuniti Hospital with a microbiologist named Dr. Giuseppe Bolignano. The doctor had been Anna Pangallo's primary physician, the one who gave her up for dead while she lay in a coma. I had found Anna's story completely captivating, fascinating in every detail. I did not doubt her beliefs for a moment. Yet even as I was getting a better handle on the life of Padre Gaetano, this idea of answered prayers and of miracles orchestrated from heaven was still beyond my grasp. I was eager to talk with a man of science about this.

As I waited, I heard the beep-beep of a motor scooter. It was my cousin Bruno, stopped at the red light, on his way to work at the city's notary office. I went over and we exchanged small talk entirely in Italian. I told him about meeting Anna Pangallo and about my appointment with Dr. Bolignano. He reminded me that I must go see his mother, Antonia Catanoso Calarco, who was eager to talk with me. As the light changed, I felt like a local as we parted with a phrase Bruno taught me a few days earlier, *ci vediamo*, see you around.

By nine o'clock, Edward and I were standing outside the office of Dr. Bolignano. With its wide corridors, chattering intercom, and white-coated doctors and orderlies bustling in every direction, Riuniti Hospital had the chaotic look and feel of a sprawling, metropolitan medical center. Dr. Bolignano was running late. He stepped outside briefly to say he was in a staff meeting and would need a few more minutes. When he looked at me, he paused and broke into a wide grin. "You look like a Catanoso!" he said, shaking my hand. "I am a Catanoso, too. My grandmother was a sister of the saint's. I am his great-nephew." Then he ducked back inside.

What? Had I just heard him right?

Instinctively, my initial reaction was not, Good Lord, what a wonderful coincidence! It was, holy smoke, how do you say nepotism in Italian? This second miracle suddenly smelled of an inside job, with the relative pulling the strings not in heaven, but right here in the halls of Riuniti. How sick had Anna Pangallo really been? How truly unresponsive was she to therapy? How hard would it be for her primary physician, who just happened to be closely related to the holy being in need of a second miracle for canonization, to fudge a few facts and make it look like her amazing recovery was unrelated to the medicine she was receiving?

I hated that these questions were hitting me over the head. Hey, I was on the home team, wasn't I? But such skepticism was second nature, a professional article of faith. I knew I would have to raise these concerns with Dr. Bolignano, not at first, of course, but eventually.

Dr. Bolignano's office was narrow and uncluttered. His desk was stacked neatly with files and a few medical journals. Two large posters of bacteria cell slides hung on the wall over his desk and a Padre Pio calendar—similar to ones I saw all over Reggio—was on the opposite wall. There was no sign of Padre Gaetano. The doctor, who was in charge of the hospital's infectious diseases unit, came in from an adjacent meeting room and sat behind his desk. He was wearing a light-blue short-sleeved shirt open at the collar. He was a handsome man of fifty-nine with long strands of brown hair swept over his bald head, and his eyes were dark and pensive. He carefully led us through the case of Anna Pangallo, now more than three years after the fact, without referring to any notes.

"Meningitis patients usually respond to the treatment of antibiotics we offer, but Anna Pangallo did not," he told us. "I thought she would respond. But after four or five days, there was no viable medical alternative. She was in terrible condition and I told the family. I told them the gravity of the situation and that the patient would not survive."

Dr. Bolignano said he made a decision to continue her treatments even though he believed they were of no value and that her death was imminent. At one point early on, he was convinced she would die in a few hours. Instead, after nine days, she awoke from her coma. Like her family members and other doctors and nurses at the hospital, he was shocked.

"Yes, I was surprised, but I moved immediately to check for any type of damage that might have resulted from her very serious infection," he said. "The X-rays we took prior to her waking up showed damage in the area of her brain. We were all happy that she did in fact wake up, but we needed to confirm that she was okay. We did more X-rays and found no lingering problems. The damage we documented while she was still comatose was no longer evident."

He paused for a moment, allowing Edward time for the translation, then added, "As we worked through all the medical possibilities that might have led to her recovery and found none, we eventually gave in to the idea that there was another explanation, perhaps a religious explanation."

I let that notion sink in. Earlier in my career, I spent five years as a reporter covering medicine and health care. I interviewed doctors at the top medical centers in North Carolina about their research, about their patients, about the marvels of modern science, and the limitations as well. Never had I heard an American doctor say that some patient who enjoyed an unexpected recovery may have received the assistance of supernatural powers. There had to be some *medical* explanation, those doctors insisted, even if they couldn't explain it.

I pressed Dr. Bolignano on that point. But he just shook his head.

"When you look at the radiology—the brain scans and the X-rays—all this showed serious damage and the potential for more damage prior to her coming out of her coma," he said patiently. "Yet in one week, she moved from an extremely grave and life-threatening situation to one where she was essentially cured. Medical science cannot explain that because it happened so quickly. That's what is so astonishing."

He went on to say that even if Anna Pangallo had responded positively to the antibiotics, the onset of her meningitis should have left lasting damage to her hearing or brain in some way. But it didn't. She was healed. Completely, inexplicably. He was certain of that, which led me to wonder about his faith.

"Are you a devout Catholic?"

"Yes, of course," he said.

"Do you believe in miracles?"

With a deep sigh that surprised me, he said, *"Non lo so,"* I don't know. He shook his head slowly, thoughtfully. There was an earnestness to his voice that I found compelling. As he prepared to answer a question that was clearly charged with meaning for him, I found myself trusting him more.

"Miracles are simply incredible and the fact that they are incredible makes them impossible to rationalize," he said. "There is a line that is incredible and unexplainable, and when you cross it, there is nothing else left but faith. If we've never experienced a miracle, we believe it through faith. And if we have experienced a miracle, we don't try to explain it. We just accept it."

I wasn't quite sure who he meant by "we." Maybe he was including me, assuming we were of similar faith. We weren't. His faith was well beyond whatever I had managed to nurture in the past six months.

"In the end, it is not my decision to make," he went on. "The church defines this miracle, the Vatican. This huge commission, a part of the Vatican's *Consulta Medica*, came down here to check, to analyze, to thoroughly investigate the entire case of Anna Pangallo. When they were finished, they formally deemed her cure a miracle. That was their decision."

But as a man of science, I asked him, with his advanced education, his medical journals, and his posters of cell biology, how did he reconcile the miraculous with the scientific?

"The dividing line is not clear; it depends on your background," he said. "If your background and worldview is that of science primarily, you look at this case and say, 'It is medically unexplainable' and leave it at that. But if you look at it through the lens of your faith in God, then you don't have a difficult time accepting it as a miracle. Please understand, there is no distinction between my faith and my scientific understandings. It's a question of language and definition. To me, scientifically unexplainable matters can be understood through religious faith as miracles. That's how the church defines it as well."

Dr. Bolignano, without any prompting on my part, then turned the conversation to the man in the middle of all this, Padre Gaetano Catanoso.

"When I was a child, I went to church with the Veronican sisters. And yes, I knew Gaetano; he died when I was seventeen. I would go with my mother to see him almost every week. Uncle was so charismatic, so much fun, such a pleasure to be with." The pensive look Dr. Bolignano had been wearing changed to a sweet smile as the memories came to him. "When we knew we were going to see him the next day, we kids would be up at dawn, as if it were Christmas morning. That's the way it was."

Like so many of my relatives, the doctor had his own miracle story. It went like this: His father was a Communist and an atheist.

During the 1940s, the war years, his father's hatred for all institutions was intense, especially the church and what he perceived as pompous and hypocritical priests. Whenever he came across a priest, he would taunt him and provoke an argument. But with Padre Gaetano?

"He would kneel before him and cry, and open up to him as all of us nieces and nephews did," Dr. Bolignano said. "That was a real miracle!"

Did it change your father inside, I asked, did Padre Gaetano's goodness bring your father back to the church?

The doctor leaned back and laughed. "My father was only different when they were together. So in that sense, I suppose, it was a limited miracle! But my father's beliefs were so unbending that any change from that was amazing to me."

For a while, Dr. Bolignano got lost in the past. He shared one anecdote after another illustrating his great-uncle's sweetness and faith. He saw the impact Padre Gaetano had on those desperate for solace, especially in the Catanoso family. He experienced his great-uncle's spiritual generosity and even his sense of humor. (Once, when Padre Gaetano was finished with a doctor's appointment and asked for the bill, the doctor instead handed him an envelope with money as a charitable donation. "That's the first time a doctor ever paid a patient," Padre Gaetano chuckled.) He never saw his great-uncle angry. He never saw him doubt his faith.

"This is the charisma of a singular and special person," Dr. Bolignano told me. "This is not a person you will see again in your lifetime. As a child, I had a very short haircut. He would stroke my head and I would feel a shiver of excitement. We adored him."

I was beginning to adore Dr. Bolignano. The more he talked, the more I looked at his face and his eyes, the more he looked familiar, like family. His pride in being a Catanoso, like mine, was palpable, and his tender love for his great-uncle was warm and real. I thought how nice would it be to just stop there, thank this busy doctor for his precious time, and be on my way. But I couldn't. When it came to Anna Pangallo's miracle, I had to know what he knew and when he knew it. I felt nervous as I mentally phrased the next set of questions, perhaps even a bit unfaithful. But I edged in just the same, wanting to be more Larry King than Mike Wallace.

"Your love for Padre Gaetano is clear."

"He is an example. That's what sainthood is all about."

"Did you attend the beatification in 1997?"

"Yes, of course."

"Did you know one more miracle was needed for the canonization?"

"Yes, but it was immaterial. To me, he was already a saint."

"So the fact that Pope John Paul II beatified your uncle didn't elevate your view of him?"

"No, not at all. To be honest, Padre Gaetano would not have been interested in the beatification and canonization. All this show and pageantry would not have interested him."

I took a deep breath. I needed to be more direct, but wondered how far I could push. "Edward, please be careful with this translation," I said to my interpreter, then asked: "As you were treating Anna Pangallo, did you have it in the back of your head that Padre Gaetano, your uncle, needed another miracle for canonization?"

I was prepared for him to show me the door, but instead he simply showed me a bit more of his heart.

"No, no, no," he said softly, shaking his head. "I was unaware of the fact that there was this effort to pray to Padre Gaetano on her behalf. I only learned after she was released. When she was here, she was my patient, and I was taking care of her. I was happy she woke up and recovered, but I didn't need for it to be a miracle. You see, the canonization is only proof that the saint is real to those who didn't know him. Those who knew him, like me, knew already that he was a saint."

Padre Gaetano's advocates in Reggio seized quickly on Anna Pangallo's dramatic recovery. There was some sense of urgency. Year by year, Pope John Paul II's health deteriorated further from the accumulated ills of advanced Parkinson's disease. There was a genuine concern that should John Paul die, a new pope may not share his predecessor's heightened interest in saint-making.

Thus on May 15, 2003, just five months after Anna Pangallo awoke from her coma, three men whom I had met with during my time in Italy got straight to work. Monsignor Vittorio Mondello, the archbishop of Reggio Calabria-Bova, appointed a diocesan tribunal to examine the case. At question was whether her recovery could be a miracle attributed to the intercession of Padre Gaetano Catanoso; at stake was Vatican-sanctioned sainthood. Monsignor Antonio Denisi of Reggio conducted the research locally and forwarded the file, and all medical records, to the Vatican. There, Monsignor Giuseppe D'Ascola, the postulator for the canonization cause of Padre Gaetano, took over. There were more trips to Reggio, more interviews with doctors, Veronican sisters, and members of Anna Pangallo's family.

On April 1, 2004, a five-person panel of doctors of the *Consulta Medica* unanimously agreed that the recovery was medically inexplicable. Six months later, the cardinals and bishops of the Congregation for the Causes of Saints affirmed that "the healing of Anna Pangallo was a miracle worked by God through the intercession of the Blessed Gaetano Catanoso."

On February 24, 2005, a frail Pope John Paul II, less than two months before his death, approved the last five saints of his long papacy and set a date for the canonization, finally making official what the faithful in Calabria had long known.

During the second week of my stay in Reggio, I switched B&Bs, from one at the edge of the city to one in the center of downtown. My cousins helped me find a place near the National Archaelogical Museum (home of the extraordinary Riace bronzes) and just a few blocks up from the *lungomare*, which was teeming every evening with Calabrians of all ages relishing the cool night air after another steaming-hot June day. The outdoor dessert places were always filled with people eating gelato and drinking pink grapefruit juice. It was a noisy city after dark, with heavy traffic, rock bands performing on temporary stages, and on most nights, fireworks exploding over the shoreline. As the *Azzuri*, the Italian soccer team, advanced in the World Cup tournament, the waterfront never seemed to quiet down or empty out.

I often walked alone through the crowds, looking similar but standing apart. After so many busy days, it was good to just have some time to sort things out, or perhaps even piece things together. The saint and what he meant to this region was coming into focus. The faith he inspired was clear for me to see. And I was coming to understand how it inspired my relatives on this side of the Atlantic. I knew I would need more time to understand that connection better and I wanted to. But what it all meant to me felt like something standing farther back in line, something I would get to eventually.

I had gone to Mass a couple of times with Daniela at Padre Gaetano's church in Reggio and the emotions I felt there were hard to decipher. I couldn't really tell if encroaching faith was causing my spirit to soar, pushing me to the verge of tears, or if it was just the rich voices of the young Filipino Veronican sisters, who sang with acoustic guitar and tambourine, their songs—joyous and syncopated—bouncing off the hard surfaces of the sanctuary, making a glorious echo.

There was just so much mysticism around me that was fascinating but strange—and not just the visible, physical remains of a sainted relative laid out in a glass tomb for everyone to see. That was strange enough. There were also the gold-and-glass-encased relics around the church holding pieces of the saint's dried skin, locks of his hair, even a few teeth, roots and all. Now separated from the once-living being, those objects were thought to possess miraculous powers. My relatives certainly thought so. They seemed to look upon their Padre Gaetano medals and pins, which they faithfully carried on them, as more valuable than an insurance policy. When they stood or kneeled at Padre Gaetano's tomb, they would always finish a prayer by rapidly crossing themselves, kissing their fingertips, and touching an image of the Holy Face of Jesus affixed to the tomb. To me, it looked like they were making a wish, like tossing a pinch of salt over their shoulders. Try as I might, I could not distinguish the line between faith and superstition. Or maybe I just was wading in ankle-deep water at the shoreline of real religion while they were submerged in the depths.

As I walked along the *lungamare* lost in those thoughts, the cell phone on my belt jingled. It was my cousin Anthony, calling from New Jersey.

"Jus, I've got a surprise for you, hang on."

"Who do you think you are?" said a voice coming through the line in a strangely familiar singsong cadence. It took a moment for me to realize it was Father Hodge, my religion teacher from Wildwood Catholic High School. I was more than surprised. I was floored. Anthony had run into him back home, told him all about the canonization and my trip to Italy, and decided right then and there to get me on the phone. It had been nearly thirty years since I had last seen or spoken to him.

"Father Hodge! I can't believe it! How the heck are you?"

Then in a rush, I told him about the saint and his nuns, about the miracle lady and her doctor, about me going back to church and my new dance with Catholicism. I talked and talked, I know, because it felt good to go on in English with someone who could understand every word I was saying. But it also felt good—to talk with a priest. We really were speaking the same language.

"You sound happy, Justin," Father Hodge said.

"Yes," I said, leaning against a railing, looking out across the dark waters of the strait. "Yes, I am."

"I'm happy for you," he said. "You're growing up, just as I thought you would."

# 20

## Family Favors

As I got around to meeting more relatives, going into their homes, paging through their photo albums, hearing their memories of the saint, I realized that they all knew Padre Gaetano in the kind of intimate ways that we American Catanosos could not imagine. How could we? We knew nothing of this holy man until a few years ago. And all of us, from my grandfather Carmelo to my own daughters, grew up beyond the shadow of his influence. Except for the physical resemblance, he wasn't that much different to us than the ancient, stained-glass saints my aunts and uncles prayed to at St. Ann's back in Wildwood. Things were different here in Reggio. Padre Gaetano was no mere figurehead. He was the family's touchstone, or as Germaine kept repeating from her translations with relatives, its point of reference.

It was truly as if Padre Gaetano were still alive, still moving among them, still offering his wise counsel and loving blessing. For some, it was more than that. In a sense, they believed—always quietly, always privately—that Anna Pangallo had nothing on them, and that they, too, were the recipients of answered prayers and actual, though not official, miracles.

Like Daniela Catanoso in Rome, Daniela in Reggio explained to me that she is alive today only through the saving intercession of Padre Gaetano. Both her parents were extraordinarily devoted to the priest and visited him every Saturday. "My father was convinced that Padre Gaetano communicated with him through his thoughts, he was such a strong believer," Daniela said.

That faith was put to the test in 1964, a year after the priest had died. It was the year Daniela was born—two months prematurely. Her lungs were undeveloped and doctors at the hospital in Reggio struggled to treat her in an incubator. She couldn't breathe on her own, so tubes for oxygen were inserted in her nose. It seemed hopeless. After several days, Daniela's parents were told their newborn would not survive. But Pina, her mother, did not accept the diagnosis. She called the Mother House and spoke to the mother general, Anastasia, who had always been close to Padre Gaetano. The nun quickly came to the hospital's neonatal unit bearing a relic believed to have supernatural powers. It was a white handkerchief that Sister Anastasia had passed over the face of Padre Gaetano as he lay dying a year earlier. She handed it to Pina, who passed it over the frail body of her infant daughter. Then the two women dropped to their knees right there in the unit and prayed the rosary, invoking the name of Padre Gaetano throughout.

"My mother told me that later that same day, I seemed to be breathing better," Daniela said in her usual low-key, matter-of-fact manner. "She didn't believe it at first. Then she noticed the oxygen tubes had come away from my nose. She looked closely and saw I was breathing on my own. She called for the doctor and he couldn't believe what he saw. The doctor asked her what happened, and she showed him the handkerchief."

When I pressed Daniela for details, she told me, yes, the doctors were treating her all along, not just with oxygen but with the best medications they had on hand. It could have been science that saved her, she admitted, but that's not what she believed.

"I believe this was a miracle, my miracle," she told me, though it was never offered for investigation as an official, Vatican-declared healing. "My mother believed it, too. If Sister Anastasia had not come with the cloth, I believe I would have died. Maybe not that day, but soon. I would not be here. You must understand, this is very personal. I don't tell this story very much. Not even very many family members know it. This is mine. It's between me and my mother and Gaetano."

Other relatives, after our conversations got going, offered stories that seemed more like luck than divine intervention—a cousin feeling the sudden impulse to swerve at just the right moment to avoid an unseen car hurtling toward her at a high speed; the husband of an aunt rescued somehow from a crisis at work that threatened to land him in jail. Sometimes these relatives insisted Padre Gaetano had answered their prayers. Other times they believed he was dutifully watching out for them when there was no time to pray.

One cousin, Bruno's sister Caterina Calarco, showed me the faded cloth pin with the Holy Face of Jesus on it that her mother clutched throughout her troubled birth more than thirty years ago. Caterina now kept it in her purse. "I pray to Gaetano always," she told me, "but not for whimsical, frivolous things like good weather or a parking space. There are things that are important to me in my life. I am single. I want to meet someone who can be my partner. So when I meet someone and he seems important to me, I pray for Gaetano to tell me if this is the right person. I believe he will tell me."

Not all of my relatives were so patient. Enza Catanoso Sartori, the relative who took me to see the old-woman historian, told me she can get downright demanding. "I think about him every day," she said. "And I always pray to him and Padre Pio. But I don't yell at Padre Pio. When I feel my uncle is not listening to me, I let him know it! 'Uncle!' I say, 'I need you *now* and you are ignoring me. *Hey!* Help me out!'"

Remarkably, the family's faith in Padre Gaetano never diminished even when their prayers went unanswered, or when he easily could have been blamed for being elsewhere in times of crisis and tragedy. Catanosos suffered as everyone else did with financial plights, car accidents, broken hearts, terrible diseases, sudden death. I would have thought they would get angry with him from time to time. Impatient, accusatory. I know I would have. But to a person, my relatives' responses were consistently the same. In fact, they all referenced Padre Gaetano's own response to life's miseries: *in domino*—in God they trusted, and in their sainted relative, too.

O ne sweltering afternoon, when the scorching Calabrian sun pushed the temperature in the crowded city to 105 degrees, I was taken to see Domenica Catanoso Alfi, or Nimo, as she was called. She was in her midseventies. I was accompanied by her younger sister Luisa Catanoso, a university language teacher who was fluent in English. Their father had been Padre Gaetano's doctor for many years, they told me. Nimo was round and friendly with short, frizzy hair and a gravelly voice. Her fifth-floor apartment looked like a musty antique showroom and we sat down around her dining room table, where she offered me a piping hot espresso. It struck me as a funny choice for a drink. There was no fan in sight and her air conditioner was off. The apartment didn't just feel like an oven, it *was* an oven. I was basting in sweat. Nimo and Luisa, though sweating plenty, hardly seemed bothered. I prayed for a cold glass of water.

"Look at these silver rosary beads," Nimo croaked, pulling the strand from a clear plastic bag. "Padre Gaetano gave me these as a wedding gift. And these rose petals. I collected them from his tomb after his funeral."

Nimo had a long memory. She recalled the Allied bombs falling on Calabria in 1943 and the day that Archbishop Montalbetti was accidentally killed by British gunners near Melito di Porto Salvo. She remembered receiving letters from her father, who served in the Italian military as a doctor, and how she brought those letters to Padre Gaetano to read. She remembered standing in line at the cathedral to make her confessions to her dearest relative.

"I was always impressed with his faith, even in the face of so much death and devastation," she told me. "Whenever things would happen, he would say, 'Now I pray to God to help this bad moment pass.'"

Nimo had her own bad moment in the fall of 2001 when her husband lost control of their car on a rainy night and crashed. He was fine, but she broke five ribs, her collarbone, and her leg. She was rushed to the hospital and was in so much pain that she feared for her life. She began praying to Padre Gaetano, she told me, and never stopped. With the help of some painkillers, she drifted off to sleep. Then her story grew surreal, and, quite frankly, a little goofy.

"I opened my eyes after a while and I saw Padre Gaetano standing in my room. It wasn't a vision," she insisted earnestly, her voice a chorus of frogs. "He was in my room. He came close and put his hands on my ribs, and I heard each one crack, like the sound you hear when you crack your knuckles. I remained silent and just watched him. Then I fell asleep again."

In the morning, she told me, her ribs were fine, though her collarbone and leg were still broken. The doctors were astonished. It was a miracle, she told them.

The heat had made me a little punchy. I nearly burst out laughing. Why the ribs and not the collarbone and leg? I asked.

"He knew the ribs were the most painful injury."

Ohhhh, I said arching my eyebrows, so *that's* why. Then I turned to Luisa and asked, with a playful edge, if she believed her sister's story.

The university professor paused just a moment before saying carefully in a tone of utter respect and admiration for her older sister, "I believe that she believes it. You see, I believe in saints and their healing powers, but not like my sister does. I've told her, 'I don't get the kind of help that you do from Padre Gaetano!' But maybe, I think, we get some other help from him."

Nimo was waving to get her sister's attention. She wanted to make sure I understood where she was coming from: "It is because of his life and his example that I have this faith. I witnessed it. And I have never doubted him. In our family, he was always a saint."

It was moments and insights like those with relatives such as Daniela and Nimo where faith to me looked like letting go of all practicality, all common sense, all cynicism for hyperbole. These Catanosos were the living definition of the mystery of faith. And here in southern Italy, where religion for centuries has been far more mystical and magical than in the lands to the north, I stood witness to the kind of faith that Padre Gaetano sought for decades to carefully balance. A priest back in Greensboro once told me that "piety is nothing more than superstition with a faith element." And that appeared to be Gaetano's fundamental mission—transform pagan superstition into Christian faith. I could hardly tell the difference.

*Say your prayers to a statue of the Virgin Mary. Worship a sliver of bone chipped from a holy person before he is sealed in a see-through crypt. Believe in the supernatural power of saints and the miracles of Jesus himself.*

*But please, stop worrying about the "evil eye" and bad omens, and for goodness sake, take down those cow horns from over the door to your house. Don't you realize that it's unholy to be so superstitious?*

*Now, take this crucifix and hang it on the wall in your living room.*

My Italian relatives, many of them anyway, sorted through such messages and found their spiritual balance. But for someone like myself—practical and sensible, gingerly wandering back into the ancient realm of Catholicism—it was enough to make me stop and say, Whoa! This stuff is crazy!

My cousin Giovanna, who invited me into this Italian family with an e-mail from out of the blue just a few years earlier, always struck me as practical and sensible. She was a great-niece of the saint and was proud of his life and example. She had no miracle stories for me; she did, however, want me to meet her favorite aunt, who was also named Giovanna Catanoso. Germaine came along and we visited the aunt one evening when it was cooler. She had a pitcher of cold water set out for us in her living room. The elder Giovanna was in her seventies with large, brown eyes and a swirl of gray and silver hair. She started in by telling me about how she nearly died giving birth. She was a young woman and there were severe complications. She prayed to her late uncle Gaetano. Her daughter was born healthy, and she survived.

It sounded like a story I had heard before. But when I asked if she considered it a miracle, her answer sounded more like the feisty and pragmatic historian, old Maria Mariotti, than my Catanoso relatives.

"No, for God's sake! It's too easy to say it's a miracle. That's not it," she said. "I tell you this just to explain how much we believed in him, trusted him, and prayed to him. It's true that southern Italians have great devotion to their saints. But I don't get too carried away with that. When you do, you forget the real person and what his life was all about."

To the elder Giovanna, it was her uncle's life, not his miracles, that was so significant to her and should be significant to others. "He is an example to all priests," she said. "They should all follow in his footsteps. He lived in poverty and humility. He had nothing, but gave everything he could to others. He was a *real* priest."

I had long since given up on my desire to unearth evidence of Padre Gaetano's human weaknesses. The elder Giovanna knew of none either. But she knew this. She was a different person because of his example. She was a better person.

"He was a point of reference," she said. "He was a person we could go to with our concerns and our problems and he would give us the faith and the motivation to go on with life, especially in sad or difficult moments. He was a person who could give us serenity and nurture our faith in God."

The younger Giovanna, my cousin, picked up that thread. She never knew her great-uncle. He died before she was born. She was not such a devout Catholic either and only occasionally attended Mass. But she felt his influence in a very precise way and saw it in a much larger context.

"The character of this family is essentially good," my cousin said. "And this, I think, stems from Padre Gaetano. I know the members of this family, in all the branches. They are good people, not perfect mind you, but good. It is the character that has been passed down to all of us. My grandfather was Gaetano's brother. He did not see a bad example. He saw a good one. And so did my father and mother. All these relatives are generous and kind and always willing to help others. I don't know if I have told anyone this before, but I have always felt a bit different, a bit special to belong to this family."

It suddenly seemed as if I had been shown a fundamental truth in black and white with no shades of gray. As a saint, Padre Gaetano may or may not be able to orchestrate miracles from heaven, but he remains a model of goodness for all believers everywhere. And he had always been such a model to my Catanoso relatives. I had experienced that goodness for myself, beginning with the moment I arrived at the train station with my family more than two years earlier. Giovanna had just explained the wellspring of that goodness. That's what it meant to be a point of reference. That's what it meant to be related to a saint.

Later that evening, Giovanna and I strolled along the *lungomare* in the warm night air. I was ecstatic. I told her how incredibly insightful our conversation with her aunt had been. But she seemed concerned. She wanted to clarify the point she had made earlier. She feared she had been too boastful, a trait Padre Gaetano did not possess.

"I don't know, perhaps I am not so objective," she said. "Maybe every family feels it is special."

Maybe. But to me, I told her, her comments had spread light like a beacon. I gave her my perspective on these Italian relatives, what I had seen, what I had experienced, how it all made sense. There is an essential goodness in this family, just as she said. At the moment, I felt so fortunate to be a part of it all.

"You know, Giovanna, if you had never sent me that e-mail, I wouldn't know any of this," I told her. "I wouldn't even be here."

We walked a short distance in silence before Giovanna responded, "Sometimes I think I changed your life."

"You should always think that," I told her.

# 21

# One of Us

In February 1944, my uncle Tony, with Divine Providence and a happy professor named Alfredo Smorto leading the way, became the first American Catanoso to ever visit Chorio, the place where his father had been born. In June 2006, I became the second. I didn't see much when I drove past the village with Vincenzo en route to our meeting the miracle woman of Roccaforte del Greco. But one Sunday, Daniela and Germaine drove me up to Chorio for the afternoon, which was about forty-five minutes from Reggio. My cousin Patrizia Catanoso was already there with her husband, Orazio.

I found the village small and compact, bound on one side by a tall, barren hill of the lower Aspromonte and on the other side by the dry riverbed of the Tuccio. It had none of the Renaissance quaintness of some small, northern Italian villages in Tuscany, like San Gimignano or Lucca. It was poor, yes, but not without its charms. The village was mostly a tidy collection of two- and three-story block-and-stucco row houses with terra-cotta roofs. Flowering plants and vines overhung many balconies. These houses lined several winding streets that connected to two piazzas. Several of the streets were still strung with small yellow-and-white plastic pennants with Padre Gaetano's face on them in honor of the canonization. Such decorations had long been removed back in Reggio. There wasn't much commerce in the village—a couple of shops, a couple of cafés—and you could walk from one end to the other in ten minutes.

Like most villages in Italy, Chorio is dominated by a central piazza and a large church, St. Pasquale Baylon, which was rebuilt in the 1930s after the earthquake of 1908. I was struck by its grandness and beauty. The church's beige stucco exterior walls were trimmed in salmon-colored block, and its heavy plank doors were set in a tall arching frame. A bell tower adjoining the sanctuary rose five stories. And there in the courtyard to the side of the church, smiling sweetly in bronze and holding his ever-present rosary, was Chorio's favorite son, Padre Gaetano Catanoso. This life-size statue, paid for by the Catanoso family and set amid ficus trees and rose bushes, seemed to more closely capture the saint's gentle features as an old man than did the statue outside the Mother House in Reggio. Padre Gaetano last visited Chorio and spoke from the church's pulpit in 1959, on his eightieth birthday. I wandered inside. It was cool and airy with pink walls, marble floors, and rows of wooden pews. A large portrait of the saint was displayed in the back over a table holding a gold reliquary with a darkened, thumbnail-size piece of his skin.

Back outside, I looked around, down the side streets and above to the brown, grassy, nearly treeless mountains. I tried to imagine Uncle Tony dressed in his Army uniform and standing in this same spot, waiting to be led to his aunt Maria as a giddy crowd of villagers gathered. I wanted to find her as well, even though I knew she had died fifty years earlier. Her house was somewhere nearby, I figured, and I wanted to stand outside and at least see that much of what my uncle Tony saw. But I didn't know where it was and neither did my cousins. Instead, we walked to the Catanoso house we did know. It was two stories tall with a rooftop balcony and large windows covered by dark green wooden shutters. Fig, orange, and clementine trees grew in a side yard. The place was comfortably middle-class and had been in the family for many generations, right on the piazza, just a few steps from the church. Its size and prime location told me volumes about the Catanoso family and its relative stature and prosperity in this village through the years. Acres of farmland outside the village were still owned by the family.

Patrizia, who often spent weekends in Chorio, had arrived early with Orazio and had been preparing a large lunch all morning. She had actually started the tomato sauce the day before, cooking down a basket of homegrown plum tomatoes and straining the pulp before adding some parsley, basil, and fried garlic and letting it simmer for hours. She handed me a spoon to taste it. Delicious—pungent and strong. She was also making zucchini-flower fritters, fried eggs and wild asparagus, dark brown fava beans and baked chicken. I had been with Patrizia several times in Reggio (her sister is Caterina; her brother-in-law is Vincenzo) and felt a genuine kinship. She was in her midforties and worked as an administrative assistant at the hospital in Reggio. She and Orazio had two teenage children. Patrizia didn't speak English, but it was easy to tell that she was plainspoken and gregarious. Of all my Italian relatives, she was the only one who declared that she wished that her grandfather, like mine, had been an emigrant. Pressing her hands together in a mock prayer and casting her eyes upward, she told me one evening, "I always say, 'Why didn't *my* grandfather go to America? Why not? Why not?' I would be there now and my life would be better." Then she looked me in the eye, and with Germaine translating, said, "If I come to America, will you find me a job?"

"What about Orazio and your children?" I asked.

"They can stay here!" she said, laughing.

At lunch, I told everyone about my uncle Tony's visit to Chorio and what a big scene it had been. My grandfather Carmelo had left this place more than a century ago; no one here would remember him. But surely some old-timers would remember my great-aunt Maria Portzia Catanoso, and maybe someone might even recall when the American soldier came to town. A couple of locals dropped by during lunch and I tried my luck. Domenico Scordo was in his mideighties. He had been in Chorio ever since he walked home from northern Italy and the front of World War II in 1945. He knew plenty of Catanosos but couldn't remember Maria Portzia. Neither could Antonino Mangiola, who was twenty years younger than Scordo. He had the same last name as my great-grandmother—Carmelo's mother—and I wondered if we were related in some distant way. He told me that unlike Catanoso, Mangiola was a common name in the village.

I was desperate for a nap after lunch, having succumbed to the delightful Italian ritual of a midday rest, but Patrizia was eager to get busy as my research assistant. She served me a dark, syrupy espresso that felt like a donkey kick to the head, and off we went into the heart of tiny Chorio, with Daniela and Germaine in tow, intent on shaking the memories of everyone over seventy who came outside to see the American visitor, me. Word seemed to spread from house to house. It wasn't like the crowd I pictured Uncle Tony having attracted, but people came out, whispering to each other, waving their hands, gathering around us.

Patrizia took the hand of one ninety-three-year-old woman, Giuseppina Polimeni, who was standing at her front door on a narrow side street near the piazza. She was wearing a black house dress with small white dots and had only a little more hair than she did teeth. "Catanoso? Oh I remember Padre Catanoso," the old lady said. "I remember Maria Catanoso, too." My heart jumped. "No, no," she then said, her eyes clouding. "I don't remember her at all."

We soon followed a friendly and eager grandson to the home of his ninety-nine-year-old grandmother, Carmela Scaramazzino. She had lived in Chorio her entire life and he assured me his granny's memory was wonderfully intact. We waited in her tiny dining room with its six-foot ceiling and walls covered with pictures of Jesus, the Virgin Mary, and a variety of saints, including Padre Pio and Padre Gaetano. She hobbled in on a cane wearing slippers and a big smile. She spoke in a dialect so unique to Chorio that Germaine could not decipher it. Patrizia stepped in and turned the dialect into Italian, which Germaine then turned into English. What a production, but well worth it. "Once upon a time," she began, leaning sideways in a stuffed armchair, wearing a brown polyester dress and sagging support hose, "all the finest houses in Chorio belonged to the Catanoso family. They were well off. They had lots of land."

What about Maria Portzia Catanoso? She thought for a moment, her eyes closed behind thick glasses. "No. I don't remember her."

She did remember, though, how poor and difficult life was in Chorio, particularly when she was a child. Many, many villagers left for America, she told us, most of them never returning. Her late husband stayed a short time in America, arriving in the winter of 1917 as a young teenager. One evening an older friend told the boy to go through the neighborhood and beg for firewood from the American families. The boy couldn't speak English, so when a door opened, he merely said, "*Fuoco*," which means fire. But each time he spoke the word, the door was slammed in his face in disgust.

"*Fuoco, fuoco!*" old Carmela kept saying and started to laugh. Then Patrizia laughed. Then Germaine. By the time the translation made its way to me, I was confused. I looked at this ninety-nine-year-old woman who was giggling like a child who had farted in church. "Did she just tell us a dirty joke? I can't believe it!" I said to Germaine, who was now bent over laughing.

Back out on the street, a relative of the old lady's, Domenico Scaramazzino, was sitting with a friend, smoking a cigarette. He was in his late seventies and had a full head of thick white hair. He waved us over. Yes, *he* remembered Maria Portzia. She was a very dignified woman, always wore nice clothes. Her brothers sent them from America.

Bingo!

She had nephews who served in the U.S. military during World War II.

Jackpot! I held my breath awaiting Germaine's translation.

One nephew was a pilot and was in charge of dropping bombs, he said. Well, I thought, he could have meant my uncle Joe, who directed bombing raids as a flight engineer. Old Domenico went on. This American Catanoso nephew, he said, was ordered to drop bombs on Chorio, but the nephew courageously refused. He knew his Italian relatives lived here and would not harm them. His aunt Maria was very proud.

What a great story! Dramatic and touching, diminished only slightly by the fact that it was a complete and utter fantasy. I did not have the heart to tell him. He had no memory of the American nephew who had actually visited Chorio, but he was quite pleased to share the story he thought he knew. He assured me it had come from my great-aunt Maria herself. He then took my notebook and wrote his nickname: *Mico u funtaneri*, Mico the plumber.

I did find my great-aunt Maria a few hours later. She was in the cemetery on a hill high above Chorio that was set amid a dense grove of olive trees. We drove up there late in the afternoon. Daniela wanted to leave fresh flowers on her mother's grave. I was amazed at what I saw. The cemetery covered less than an acre and was surrounded by a block wall that was about chest high. Inside the walls were four long rows of marble-sided crypts, like catacombs, staggered and stacked three to five levels tall. The ground was rock. No one was buried. Everyone was bricked up aboveground in a concrete vault capped with a marble façade bearing his or her name and essential dates. Most also had photos under glass attached to the marble. After Daniela took me to the row where her mother Pina was placed ("Giuseppina Catanoso, November 25, 1931–November 19, 2005"), I wandered off on a search of my own.

*"I never knew we had so many relations,"* my uncle Tony had written his mother from Chorio in 1944. *"I could not count them all."* Nor could I. Soon I found Daniela's father, and Patrizia's father and mother, too. In fact, there were Catanosos on every row, staring out at me in black-and-white photos with gray hair pulled back or with tall collars and trim mustaches. I had no idea who they were or how they were all related. I kept looking. I wasn't certain I would actually find Maria Portzia Catanoso. I didn't know if she was buried here. But I knew it was possible to walk every row and scan every marble front. That's what I did. When I started to see the name Priolo, which was Maria's married name, I hoped I was getting warmer. I was. There over on the far right, on the front row and the bottom level, shaded by two tall cedars, were the remains of my closest relative in Italy, my grandfather Carmelo's younger sister. She had died on April 20, 1957, at age sixty-seven. Her husband, Bruno Priolo, with whom she was entombed, had died in 1944, roughly seven months after Uncle Tony's homecoming. Both of their unsmiling photos were on the white marble front on one vault. Maria, with short, wavy hair framing her face, resembled my aunt Leona in New Jersey. There was another photo on the tomb—that of a toddler, also named Bruno Priolo. He died when he was five. I stood there a while. I could hear only the breeze rustling the trees behind me and some birds chirping. It was a peaceful place.

Maria Portzia Catanoso, who embraced my uncle Tony here in Chorio with the instinctive love of family, died a few years before I was born, knowing little about her nieces and nephews in America.

However late I was in arriving, I was glad to be here now, making this connection and paying my respects on behalf of all my relatives back home. Daniela found me and was carrying some white daisies. I put them in the small, empty glass vase that was attached to the marble façade and got some water. Then we went back down to the village as the afternoon faded to evening.

It had been a long day. My notebook was full, as was my head. But Patrizia was eagerly awaiting us in the piazza. She had contacted the mayor of Chorio about my visit and he had just arrived. A doctor in general practice, Lilo Sapone was slim and handsome in a navy blazer and gray slacks. The mayor asked if I would be willing to return to Chorio and speak in the church after Mass the next Saturday night about the saint and his American relatives. He would make the introduction. Before I could respond, Patrizia and Germaine answered for me: Of course he will.

At 10:30 that night, I was alone in my room at the B&B in Reggio when my cell phone rang. It was Germaine. She was practically breathless as she relayed this news, a wonderful stroke of good fortune: Patrizia had just gotten her weekly call from her aunt Rina Catanoso from Messina in Sicily. When Patrizia related that she had spent the day in Chorio with an American cousin, her aunt Rina, who was born and raised in Chorio, got to thinking. When she was a teenager during World War II, she told Patrizia, a handsome American soldier showed up in the piazza one morning in search of his aunt. Rina remembered her father going out to speak to him. Patrizia nearly dropped the phone on the floor.

"I got the shivers when she told me this," Germaine said. "Patrizia is arranging for us to go to Messina to see her aunt Rina as soon as possible."

I had one question. "Can we leave tonight?"


Whenever I was driven through the streets of Reggio, I peered through the windshield as if it were the monitor of a large video game called Demolition Derby. Motorcycles would come right up behind us on tight two-lane streets and then whip around on the left, riding the center line as oncoming drivers honked and shook their fists. Scooters would pass on the right, sometimes cutting up onto the sidewalks as pedestrians jumped out of the way. Every intersection presented an opportunity to crash. Stop signs? Red lights? They were obeyed only by suckers. If you chose to drive defensively, you would be roadkill. Everyone drove like Mario Andretti. Which is exactly what Salvatore, Patrizia's teenage son, was doing at the moment, skillfully weaving his father's Lancia sedan through the chaotic center of Reggio to the port, while his mother screamed at him to slow down, be careful. He yelled back, presumably urging her to be quiet. I just watched the monitor, clutching the sides of my seat, waiting for the game to be over.

We were on our way to Messina, and I was excited for this unexpected adventure and thirty-minute jetfoil ride across the strait with Patrizia and Germaine. I was eager to get another perspective on that magical day in Chorio in 1944. No one could top the details that Uncle Tony had shared. Still, I felt like an archaeologist preparing to dig in an elder's memory, brushing aside the dust and cobwebs for whatever new sliver of family history might be revealed. Rina Catanoso's son-in-law met us at the port in Messina and drove us across town. And Rina, who was in her late seventies, was waiting outside the door of her third-story apartment, bursting with anticipation. She looked like the quintessential Italian grandmother—short and plump with silver wavy hair and sparkling eyes running with tears. She hugged me and pinched my cheeks. *"Piacere, piacere!"* she kept saying. It's nice to meet you!

We followed Rina inside and met her husband, Antonino Palduto, a World War II veteran, and three of their grown daughters, whom Rina had called and invited over. "Come meet our American cousin!" she had squealed. It was an impromptu family reunion. I shook hands with all of them and then Rina led Germaine and me to the living room, where we sat around a small table. I began with the part of the story she didn't know, about my uncle Tony going AWOL from Palermo and wandering around Reggio until, by some stroke of amazing luck, he met a man from Chorio who knew his aunt and took him to the village.

"Yes, I remember him," Rina jumped in, eager to pick up the story from there. She was a teenager at the time. "I could see this gentleman had come to the piazza. He had a handsome American soldier with him, in uniform, and the soldier had a slip of paper in his hand that said Marietta Catanoso Priolo. That's what we called your aunt Maria—Marietta. She was lovely. So my father—I remember clearly—he heard the commotion out in the piazza and went from our house to see what was happening. I followed him out. When my father saw the soldier and the slip of paper, he embraced him. 'I am your cousin,' he told the soldier. 'I will take you to this lady. She is my cousin, too.' There was a big celebration. All of Chorio came out."

Just like my uncle Tony did when he told the story, Rina was brushing tears from her eyes as well. She had drifted back to a time and place she never thought she would have cause to revisit and she offered a delightful detail that had somehow escaped my uncle's own remarkable memory—the slip of paper he carried into the piazza bearing his aunt's name. I made note of it as if it were an unearthed treasure. Rina didn't follow the procession to Maria's house, she told me. She was too shy for that. But she remembered Maria from living in the village.

"My father respected your aunt very much," she told me. "When she came to Mass, she was so distinguished, always dressed so well. Some people called her Donna Marietta. She was so beautiful."

Before we left, Rina drew a little map in my notebook, doing her best to recall where Maria's house was located in the village. Mostly, though, she just gazed at me and smiled, squeezed my arm and slowly shook her head as if in disbelief. Just like my uncle Tony, I was a brand-new relative, a stranger who had arrived out of nowhere. But I felt as if she had loved me forever.

The afternoon we returned to Chorio, a Saturday, was brutally hot, again. I had been in Calabria for weeks and there hadn't been a drop of rain. Every day was in the nineties or hotter. I drove up with Patrizia and Orazio, and as we approached the village, I could see wild fires burning in patches in the brown hills of the Aspromonte above Chorio. Yellow tanker planes, like small flying boats, swooped over the fires and dumped water.

I knew I would be speaking after Mass in a few hours, but there were a couple of places I was eager to see—birthplaces, actually. When we arrived in the piazza by the church, Germaine was already there with Daniela. They were talking with Antonio Mafrici, a native of Chorio. He was in his midfifties and was a longtime friend of the family. He told me my great-aunt Maria had babysat him a few times and he knew where she lived.

The four of us—Germaine, Daniela, me, and our tour guide—headed for a shady, narrow alley named Via Garibaldi and started a slow march into the past. The alley was lined with old one- and two-story brick buildings in various states of disrepair. The alley curved and dipped. I tried to absorb every detail of the route. I was walking in the footsteps of my uncle Tony with the same exact surroundings, though with far fewer people trailing behind me. After several blocks, we came out into an opening, a small piazza that was strung with the plastic yellow-and-white Gaetano pennants. Four children in bathing suits were chasing around in circles, tossing water at one another from a nearby tap. Antonio Mafrici stopped walking and pointed across the square to a building on the far corner. It was three stories, made of stone and brick. The wooden shutters on the upper floors were weather-beaten and rotted. The terra-cotta roof had caved in over the center. It was the only abandoned building on the piazza.

"That's it," he said.

As we drew closer, looking through the glassless, first-floor windows, Antonio pointed out the room where he believed my great-grandfather tended his barber and tailor shop. It was empty, with a dirt floor. He also showed me where the animals would have been kept. There was no telling how old the house was; a couple of centuries, possibly. Even in its dilapidated state, it was easy to see—again from the size and prime location—that a family of some means had once lived here. My grandfather Carmelo, in fact, had been born here, maybe even my great-grandfather Antonino. I had never before glimpsed so far into my past—certainly further than my father ever had. In a general way, I had learned why Carmelo chose to leave this place, but

I also came to realize that he would have been fine, like so many of his cousins in this village, had he chosen to return from America.

I took a few steps back and looked at the upper floors. I decided that there—on the second floor facing the piazza where there were double wooden doors and a small balcony with a plain, metal railing—that that's where Maria Portzia Catanoso heard that a young, American soldier was waiting downstairs to meet her. I could picture the crowd of villagers nearly filling this small square and I could see my uncle Tony standing there anxiously, awaiting his aunt.

"Can you imagine your uncle in this place?" Germaine asked. Easily, I told her.

Across the village—back down Via Garibaldi, through the main piazza and then up a few blocks toward the hillside part of the town—was another Catanoso home. Patrizia led us there. It was in similarly miserable condition. There was some debate over whether Padre Gaetano was actually born in this large, freestanding, tumbledown house of block and stone. But there was no question that his family once lived here and cultivated some of the land surrounding the house. Patrizia said there was talk of trying to restore the property as a kind of shrine or museum, but it hadn't gotten very far.

I was thrilled to have seen both home places, no matter how decayed they had become. My final week in Calabria was fast approaching and my checklist of things to see and people to meet with was still fairly long. At the top of my list was making time to meet formally with Piero Catanoso, the family patriarch, a native of Chorio, just like my grandfather and the saint. I had enjoyed long lunches with him and his family twice during my stay. When he first saw me a couple of weeks earlier standing in his kitchen, he greeted me like a son, smiling broadly and holding his arms open wide. No cheek pecks, just a big American bear hug. During those lavish lunches, we made small talk in Italian, we toasted each other with raised glasses of wine, and we perused family photos. But we still had not arranged for a sit-down discussion with Germaine translating. There was so much I wanted to talk with him about.

I was reminded of this when Patrizia and I walked back down to the main piazza by the church. Piero had just arrived with his wife,

Adriana. Several other relatives also made the drive from Reggio that evening. They had come to hear me speak after Mass. The piazza was busy and bustling with locals as I greeted my relatives. Everyone was heading to Mass. The mayor of Chorio, Lilo Sapone, came by and introduced me to his wife. I noticed he was wearing a small lapel pin with Padre Gaetano's face on it, which I hadn't seen anywhere before. With Germaine's help, the mayor and I spoke for a few moments. Then he leaned close with his hand on my shoulder and said almost confidentially, *"Tu sei uno dei nostri."*

I looked to Germaine. "He said, 'You're one of us,'" she told me.


After Mass was completed, Father Aldo Carridi invited everyone to stay for a special presentation. I tried to keep from hyperventilating as Mayor Sapone called me to stand with him in front of the altar. I could feel my heart banging around in my chest. I hadn't prepared a speech. I had a pretty good idea what I wanted to say and hoped it would come to me. Germaine, meanwhile, stood by my side. I could not do this without her. The scene inside this beautiful church, with all these eyes on me, was surreal, one I wouldn't have even dared dream about when planning this trip. But there I was, an honored guest in a tiny Italian village, the birthplace of both my grandfather and the saint. The confluence of bloodlines, good fortune, and more than a little bit of faith, I suppose, had brought me here to this place at this moment. I thought about Alan, and I wished my parents could have been here, Lenny and Marlene, too, even Anthony and Uncle Tony and all my aunts and uncles and cousins back in America. In a way, this was their moment, as well. Then I looked into the audience and saw so many Catanoso faces, and I realized I had plenty of family here already.

"There is a person here tonight. He does not live here, he is not from here," Mayor Sapone began, speaking into a cordless microphone. "But I can guarantee—he is one of us. In the name of everyone here, and on behalf of all of Chorio, I want to greet him and welcome him. His grandfather was born here in Chorio. And that's why I can say, he is one of us. I am honored to introduce him this evening. What

I know about him is this—he loves this country, and he loves our saint, Saint Gaetano Catanoso. He came from so far away to see where Saint Gaetano lived. His relative, our saint, is from this wonderful village. He came here to see the sights and breathe the air and to know how the saint lived."

Turning to me, the mayor continued as Germaine kept translating in my ear: "The saint means so much to this village. He taught us so much. He left us an example to follow that is so rich and important. We must put it into practice. And when I see you here and understand what you are trying to do, it makes me very pleased. That's why I say you are one of us. We hope you will help us get out the message about this extraordinary person. We hope you are going to send a message about Saint Gaetano to all America and all the world. We want to thank you infinitely for your visit, and we thank God for giving us this saint. He really is a saint. He protects us from up there in paradise. He protects our community. Now to you I say, thank you, *Giustino*. Thank you for being here. You are one of us."

My hands were shaking a bit as I held the microphone. I took a deep breath. Looking out on the audience, I greeted everyone, the priest, the mayor, the villagers, and *mia bella Catanoso famiglia*, a phrase Germaine did not have to translate. I told them about how my grandfather had been born here but left with so many others to start a family in America. I told them how he had never returned and lost contact with nearly all of his relatives here. I told them how one of my uncles came back here during the war and how warmly he was received. They clapped at that. I told them it was a great privilege to return to Chorio to learn about my Italian family and the saint we share in common.

"*Sono molto contento essero con voi,*" I closed in Italian, reading the phrase Germaine had written out for me—I am very happy to be here with you. They clapped again, Piero being the first to stand.

Before we finished for the evening, there were gifts. Mayor Sapone pinned to my shirt a Padre Gaetano pin like the one he wore on his lapel. He also gave me a book about the history of San Lorenzo, the region that included Chorio. The author of the book was in the audience. Then three Veronican sisters, who had driven over from a nearby village, came forward carrying a huge portrait of Padre Gaetano Catanoso in a carved, wooden frame made for me that week by a local craftsman. It was lovely. Piero's wife, Adriana, gathered all the relatives with me and the nuns for a photo together on the altar steps, a group picture of family pride.

Outside in the piazza, I loaded the portrait into the back of Piero's car, reminding him, "I only have one more week before I return home. We have to set a time to get together."

He pulled out a small pocket calendar and flipped through the pages. Monday would not work, he said. He was being installed as the president of the bar association in Reggio. There was a big ceremony planned. But Tuesday looked good. We could spend the afternoon together, he promised. Perfect. Germaine and I both made a note of it. Then he suggested I call him tomorrow, Sunday. Perhaps I could come by for lunch, he said.

Everything was falling together. If ever there was a time when I was willing to accept and believe that my sainted cousin was pulling strings on my behalf from heaven, it was this incomparably sweet, memorable evening.

But by the following afternoon—sadly and shockingly—I would be thinking just the opposite.

# 22

# *Piero*

I got the news in Pentidattilo. My cell phone vibrated with a message. It was Germaine. "Don't go to Piero's house when you return," the text said. "He's had a heart attack."

Until that moment, it had been a perfect morning after a perfect evening. My cousin Giovanna had picked me up around ten o'clock to take me to the medieval hillside village where Padre Gaetano had begun his life as a parish priest in 1904. I had eyed Pentidattilo each time I had gone up into the Aspromonte in recent weeks, seeing it far in the distance below a massive, five-finger rock outcropping. Now I would get a chance to walk the same streets that the saint had walked as a young man. It was about a thirty-minute drive from Reggio.

The road from Melito di Porto Salvo on the coast up to Pentidat-tilo, which Padre Gaetano covered either on foot or on the back of a donkey, was winding and steep. The hillside was blanketed with shaggy brown grasses and patches of prickly pear and olive trees. Heavy boulders were strewn everywhere. We could only drive so far. The village was abandoned in the 1950s as a result of minor earthquakes and flooding. Like our late relative, Giovanna and I, breathing hard, ascended the last half mile into Pentidattilo by walking. The setting was starkly beautiful. Round humps of the Aspromonte rose all around us and the Ionian Sea spread out down below. Following a narrow and rutted dirt path, we came up into the empty village beside a large brick building on our right. It was the Church of St. Peter and Paul, Padre Gaetano's first church, built in the 1500s. Its tall oak doors, carved, paneled, and locked up tight, looked out on the only open space in the village, a small piazza bound on the left by a rock retaining wall at the edge of a cliff. This is where it first happened, I thought. For seventeen difficult years, through massive emigration, a devastating earthquake, and all of World War I, this is where Padre Gaetano spoke to the children and urged them to attend Mass and catechism classes. This is where he entered the homes and persuaded the peasants to set aside their pagan beliefs. This is also where he hurled himself into the fistfights and Mafia mayhem in hopes of bringing some peace and hope to this hopeless place. A bronze plaque with Padre Gaetano's face in bas-relief was affixed to a wall across from the church.

For nearly an hour, Giovanna and I climbed the dusty streets and alleys of the village, peering into clusters of vacant stone houses, listening for echoes, watching for ghosts. Pentidattilo, the needs of its people and the response of its priest, had put Padre Gaetano Catanoso on a trajectory toward sainthood. I had started this journey in Rome several weeks earlier with serious doubts about whether my relative was actually worthy of such official, infallible, and universal religious veneration. Standing now in the shadows of his legacy with a cousin—whose life, like so many of my Italian relatives, had been shaped by his example—I realized my doubts about Padre Gaetano had long since dissipated. I felt incredibly happy. If the Church of St. Peter and Paul had been open for Mass, I would have gladly gone in and taken a seat down front. I would have even offered to do the Gospel reading. Everything seemed to make perfect sense. Then I got Germaine's text message.

"A heart attack? This morning?" Giovanna asked. She was as incredulous as me.

I called Germaine as we were driving back to Reggio. Her voice was flat and unsteady.

"Piero had a heart attack this morning. Around eleven," she said. "I thought he would pull through. But he is not with us anymore."

I heard what she had said. I understood it clearly; she was speaking English. But I couldn't believe it. Piero dead? Gone? This morning?

How is that possible? We were together last night. He was perfectly alive. He was even expecting me for lunch. Germaine, please, tell me this isn't true. She couldn't.

"Call me later," she said. "I'll take you over to the house."

I stayed in my room at the B&B for hours. I didn't know what else to do. Piero's sudden death was stunning. It felt like the cheery carousel I had been riding for weeks had been struck by lightning on a cloudless day. Piero was the family's rock, its beneficent leader. I could only imagine how news of his passing was reverberating from brother to sister, from nieces to nephews to cousins, across Reggio and throughout Calabria. I called Laurelyn. I had plane reservations to leave in eight days, but I wondered if I should leave sooner. Several relatives had already invited me to dinner in the coming week. Several others had agreed to meet with me, like Piero had, to talk about the family and the saint. None of that seemed important now, or even appropriate. Worse still, I felt defenseless to the change coming over me—creeping doubts, like I had been deluding myself for weeks, like I didn't belong here after all, not at this moment of such personal and profound loss and grief. I flashed back to my first night in Reggio earlier in the month when I learned about Vincenzo's illness. Being a part of this family, I realized then, meant sharing the bad as well as the good. But had I been here long enough to truly be a part of this family in this time of tragedy? Sitting there in my room, I just didn't know. Besides, I couldn't help but wonder if this was all more than I had somehow bargained for. I understood too well how much it hurt. I had just gone through this with my own family, and my own brother, not eighteen months earlier. I felt helpless then, beyond the reach of any spiritual comfort. I felt superfluous now, and hardly any more spiritual.

Maybe I should just come home, I told Laurelyn.

"No, listen to me," she said calmly, her voice an ocean away. She remembered Piero as fondly as I always had. She knew, day by day from my phone calls, what I had been experiencing in Calabria. "I wish I could be with you right now. I wish I was there. But *you're* there. And that's a good thing. This is your family, Justin. You know that. You really do. You need to be a part of whatever happens. You need to stay."

G ermaine came by to pick me up late that afternoon and we drove several blocks over to Via Possidonea where Piero lived. I was nervous and tentative. I had no idea what the funeral customs were in Calabria. I learned quickly that they bore little resemblance to my experiences back in the states. Piero, who was sixty-five, had suffered a heart attack on the sidewalk outside his apartment building at eleven o'clock that morning. He had been talking with his brother Enzo. He was rushed to Riuniti Hospital across town, where doctors tried unsuccessfully to revive him. A couple hours later, his body was taken not to a funeral home, but rather back to Via Possidonea where the viewing began immediately in his niece Daniela's second-floor apartment. As I hung out in the quiet of my B&B early that afternoon staring at the ceiling, Daniela rushed to turn her place into a funeral home. Meanwhile, funeral service workers went about plastering Reggio with paper handbills about three-feet square announcing the death, naming the survivors, and giving details about the viewing and the funeral Mass the next day. Just a few hours after Piero had died, scores of these obituary notices had gone up all over the city, usually covering the notice of someone who had died a week earlier.

When Germaine and I arrived, Via Possidonea was lined with cars. We walked past Piero's death notice, still wet from having been recently pasted up. It was posted on the wall outside the entrance to his apartment building (*"Ne danno il triste annunzio . . ."* We are sad to announce . . .). People came in waves. A crowd was gathered outside the door to Daniela's apartment.

On a Sunday just after Christmas in 2003, I had passed through that very threshold for the first time with my wife and daughters for a joyous, memorable lunch prepared by Daniela's late mother Pina. Now the foyer was filled with mourners red-eyed and whispering. A crowd was smoking in the dining room and out on the balcony. Barbara Catanoso, a younger cousin I had seen several times during my stay, introduced me to her father, who was also an attorney, also named Piero Catanoso. I didn't ask for Germaine's help with translations. There was nothing to say. I waded in deeper, back to a small sitting room. Patrizia was there on a couch, a tissue balled up in her hands. For weeks, I had known her only as a strong, collected force of a personality. She got up quickly and threw her arms around me, her body racked with sobs, briefly falling apart. Enza Catanoso Sartori was there, too, sobbing in fractured English, "I can't believe this. We had such a good time in Chorio last night and Piero was talking about seeing you again today. Now this. I've lost my best friend, my best brother, my best everything."

I stood there quietly between these relatives, holding their hands, realizing that whatever Italian I possessed could not be recalled. I did manage to learn one new word, *triste*, sad. Then I saw a familiar face in the doorway, someone I had not seen since that lunch here in December 2003. It was Sergio, the relative who had been the delightful, blue-eyed clown that afternoon, the one who brought in the guitar and presented it to Laurelyn so that she could play and sing for the family. He looked at me a moment, then leaned over to slowly press his cheeks against mine. *"Mi ricordo di te,"* he said softly, I remember you.

A line of people filled the hallway outside the room I was in. Adriana was standing there at the far end, next to her daughter Claudia. She was leaning back against the bathroom door, holding her glasses in her hand, a look of pain and utter disbelief on her face. When I reached her, Adriana immediately held out her arms. "Justin," she said and then cried on my shoulder. What could I say to her in words she would understand? Only *mi dispiace* came to me, I'm sorry. But the genuine warmth of her embrace resounded clearly. I was not an interloper, as I had feared earlier. I belonged here, offering my own silent condolences as well as those on behalf of every Catanoso in America.

Adriana squeezed my hand and nodded to her left. Piero was there in the adjacent bedroom, lying on top of the bed, as if merely asleep. It was the same bed, I knew, that held his older sister Pina's body after she had died suddenly just eight months earlier. Now he was there, his eyes closed, a rosary in his hands. He was dressed in a gray suit. A black cloth was knotted around his ankles to keep his feet together.

Five Veronican sisters, including the mother general, sat in folding chairs at the foot of the bed, busy at work, praying the rosary in unison. My only thought at the moment was this: *Wake up, Piero, please just wake up.*

There was a sudden commotion in the hallway. Several men came in carrying a plain narrow casket of polished wood. It was of a size that would slip into an aboveground vault up in Chorio. The men had difficulty managing the tight corners in the apartment. Once in the back bedroom, they transferred Piero's body to the casket, placed it atop the bed, and covered it with a sheer, yellow veil. Adriana then went in and sat down next to her husband, clutching a rosary, joining the nuns in their murmuring prayers.

Germaine and I stayed a while longer, leaving just before dark. She kept saying, "Piero would have wanted to go like this—fast, without any suffering." She knew him well and loved him like a father. She believed that. I could not.

As I walked alone through the noisy crowds on the *lungomare* that evening, I doubted Piero would have wanted to go at age sixty-five, before he could see his son or daughters married, before he could revel in the delight of grandchildren, before he could take his beloved Adriana to the rooftop balcony of their apartment and watch the sun set behind the mountains of Sicily one more time.

The speed with which he departed was staggering. Last night we had agreed to get together; now I was listening to the plans for his funeral, which would be tomorrow. With my brother Alan, at least, we had months to come to grips with the severity of his condition, and for my mother and his wife, months to pray for a miracle. For Piero, there had not even been time to pray. And wouldn't he, of all people, have been entitled to special protection from a saint who was his uncle, whom he actually knew personally and had always loved and supported? I felt my spirit spiraling downward, much like it did after Alan's death.

This journey to Calabria, I had hoped, would bring me, among other things, some spiritual clarity. For weeks, I watched closely for how St. Gaetano Catanoso lived in real and practical ways in so many of my relatives. I listened to their miracle stories and was touched by their unflappable faith. I went to Mass with them and followed them in line to receive Communion. Later, I thought again and again about the healed peasant woman and her doctor when they told me that the saint surely had supernatural powers. These were extraordinary stories and extraordinary people. I was inspired by them. In turn, I felt my own faith eager to stand on its own two feet. But with Piero's death reminding me now of Alan's death, I was finding the ground too unstable to bear me up. There was so much I still didn't know, couldn't sense, didn't believe.

"Believe what you can," the professor had urged me so many years ago. But I felt as if I didn't know anything anymore.

The love of God is shown in different ways than we would want," Monsignor Antonio Denisi explained to me the day after Piero's death. Germaine had taken me to see him at his office at the cathedral. She knew I was looking for some answers; she thought the kindly priest might be helpful. Monsignor Denisi had known Padre Gaetano as a seminary student in Reggio and was deeply involved in the canonization process. He had also known and admired Piero for many years. Now he was patiently enduring my naïve inquiry—where was our saint when we needed him most?

"The love of God only considers the moral and spiritual goodness of a person. Sickness and death are not punishments from God," the monsignor went on. "There is a life that continues even after death. And Piero, he is in front of God, in the company of Padre Gaetano. He is much happier in this condition, even though he has left behind a bereaved and suffering family. In front of God, you've lost nothing."

That core element of faith remained a soothing and consoling sentiment—for others, not me. It certainly hadn't helped me when Alan died. I wondered if Adriana and her children were now finding solace in such a belief.

What I could see and what remained constant in the wake of Piero's death was the family's unshakable faith in Padre Gaetano. It seems that I may have been the only one, in my simpleminded notion of the practical value of sanctified relatives, who deigned to think that *our* saint, the one bearing *our* name, could have been a little more diligent when it came to Piero, the best among us.

Bruno's mother, Antonia Catanoso Calarco, was, in a pious way, nothing if not practical and sensible when I sat with her at her apartment. "God made miracles through Jesus, it's true," she said. "He gave the blind man sight. He raised Lazarus. But he didn't save everyone, even if they believed in Him and prayed to Him with all their hearts. It's the same with Padre Gaetano. If that happened, if every prayer was answered, we would never get to the end."

"I agree with my grandmother. I really do," said Simona Calarco, Bruno's wise and beautiful seventeen-year-old daughter, who had joined us. "Padre Gaetano is our relative, but that doesn't mean he is going to protect us in everything that happens. He is our point of reference. He has given us a rich model to follow. And that is quite a lot."

Even Daniela agreed. And she had every reason, I thought, to be shouting at the heavens, demanding some accountability. "I have never felt that Padre Gaetano has failed me or my family, even when my father died young and my mother died suddenly. And now Piero. I am sad at these losses. And sometimes it is difficult to go on. But I have never doubted Padre Gaetano and I have never been angry with him. He is my constant. He is always there for me. And I believe that now, he is there for my father and mother and Piero."

Around 4:30 on the afternoon following Piero's death, the hottest time of the day, I rode with Germaine and Patrizia across town to the Cathedral of St. Agostino, a large, old church near the train station. A silver hearse drove into the piazza and backed up to the church steps. Huge, round sprays of roses, daises, and lilies hung on their metal stands on both sides of the vehicle. A half dozen men sprang into action. They detached the flowers and hustled them inside. Another eight men pulled the casket from the back, including Orazio, Patrizia's husband. As soon as the door swung up, the men urgently crossed themselves, as if warding off evil spirits, then hoisted the casket awkwardly onto their shoulders and carried it inside. The casket was covered with a blanket of white roses and had no handles. The men's faces, some hidden by dark glasses, were stricken. The term "pallbearer" had never seemed so literal. Germaine, Patrizia, and I followed them into the Gothic-style sanctuary with its soaring stone arches, side chapels, and a sparkling gold mosaic of Jesus and the Virgin Mary on the ceiling over the altar. Piero's family was already seated in front.

By five o'clock, as the Mass began with solemn organ music, the church was half empty. Germaine looked around with disappointment. "The game, you know. That's why more people aren't here," she said. The Italian soccer team was playing Australia in the fourth round of the World Cup tournament at the exact same time. The choices Italians must make, I thought. But Germaine's judgment was premature. Within thirty minutes, the sanctuary was packed to overflowing with hundreds of people, sitting and standing in the thick, hot air, in every available space. Most women waved paper fold-out fans in front of their faces. I was surprised to see how many people I recognized, how many relatives I had already met. I caught Bruno's eye. He was standing on the left side. He made a face and shrugged his shoulders as if to say, "What are you going to do? This is life."

"We are here to thank God that we had Piero for as long as we did," intoned a smiling, older priest dressed in a purple robe during the eulogy. He had known Piero for more than forty years. "It is important to remember that this is not the end of a life. There is more. For the person who dies, there is happiness in meeting God. For those of us who remain, death is so much suffering. We shed many tears. But St. Paul reminds us that these tears are part of our humanity. And in these tears, there is hope. This lovely family is in such pain and grief, but in faith there is hope. I pray that the family of Piero be consoled. It's hard not to think that we've lost Piero, but we haven't. We pray for him and he prays for us. Still, it is especially sad that he leaves his lovely children. They still need their father. But we pray that Adriana has the strength to carry on without her beloved Piero. We ask God this favor."

I was a puddle next to Germaine, of sweat and tears, as was everyone else. I got in line behind Orazio for Communion, then allowed several older relatives to get in front of me as we inched toward the front. They pressed their wet cheeks against mine, their eyes dark pools of sadness. A choir was singing and my emotions were raw. I could smell the dusky aroma of incense as I neared the altar. Adriana and her children were over on the left, heads bowed and sobbing. Piero's younger brother and two older sisters were on the right with Daniela, holding up no better. I passed Piero's casket before I reached the altar and set my hand on top for just a moment. Piero had been so warm and welcoming of me, from the very first time we met. I knew he was proud of our physical resemblance and prouder still that I had returned to Calabria to pursue a story about the saint and our family. That his death was now a part of that story just about broke my heart. I wished for life in a parallel universe, in which we had had lunch together yesterday and would have talked for hours together tomorrow, finally getting to know each other, just as we had planned. Then I took communion, feeling as much a part of this grief and as deeply a part of this family as I did at my own brother's funeral.

There were more tears still. Piero's casket spent the night at the church of Padre Gaetano over in Santo Spirito, the remains of both Catanosos, uncle and nephew, resting together in the sanctuary. There was another Mass that morning, attended mostly by family members and the Veronican sisters. I was sitting in the back when my cousin Caterina arrived with her husband, Vincenzo. They had just returned from Torino and Vincenzo's ALS treatments and had missed the viewing and the Mass at the cathedral. They were extraordinarily close to Piero and his family. I watched Caterina stride down the center aisle toward the altar. I thought she looked remarkably composed—until she reached Piero's casket. She practically fell on top of it, stretching her arms out to grab the sides, resting her face on the top. She stayed there, her sobs filling the church, until Adriana took her hand and led Caterina to sit close beside her in the front row with her and her children. I went up and sat just behind Vincenzo, putting my hand on his shoulder so he knew I was there. *"Come stai,"* I whispered, meaning far more than a simple greeting. He turned and nodded sadly.

About a dozen cars followed the hearse up to Chorio. When we reached the village, and before we climbed up to the cemetery, the hearse pulled over on the side of the road in the main part of town. We all stopped as well, though I didn't know why. The hearse driver got out and raised the back door. I watched as villagers materialized from the nearby houses and from down side streets. Scores of them. Soon there was a crowd around the hearse. They reached in to touch Piero's casket and bless themselves. Adriana and her three children stood in the middle of the street, in the bright, unforgiving sun, and accepted the tearful embraces of the sons and daughters of Chorio.

Later, up in the hilltop cemetery I had visited a few weeks earlier in search of my great-aunt Maria, I stood nearby as the pallbearers slid Piero's casket into a shoulder-high, empty cement vault. Everyone gathered loosely in a semicircle and watched as a couple of young masons, in dirty T-shirts and jeans, sealed the opening with bricks and mortar. It was the equivalent of watching a grave filling with dirt, shovel by shovel. Americans, of course, leave before the final act of the burial is completed; Italians stay until the very end. They may be superstitious. They may believe in the wispy, dreamy notion of saints and miracles and the supernatural. But over the last several days I had never witnessed so much sweet, loving, hands-on grappling with the eternal reality of death, from the body itself, to the last brick in the vault. It was extraordinary.

I waited in a patch of shade as the brick masons finished their work. Enzo Catanoso, Piero's younger brother, came over. He was in his midfifties and heavyset, wearing wrinkled blue slacks and an untucked, blue tennis shirt. He was a bear of a man, smoking a cigarette, as rumpled as his brother was elegant. Enzo worked in the Calabrian regional government and had offices in Reggio and Rome. He was there the night I had spoken at the church here in Chorio.

"Come with me," he said, and I followed him down the long, front row of stacked tombs, past my great-aunt Maria, to the very end. He pointed out two marble façades—Natale Catanoso, 1893–1963, and Carmela Mafrici Catanoso, 1903–1972. "My mother and father," he said.

In English, Enzo then told me about his brother, his hero, his closest friend. They had shared everything and rarely quarreled. Piero was fair and just and decent, loved by everyone, everyone in Reggio and Chorio, he told me. Now a piece of Enzo's heart was gone. His eyes were wet and bloodshot. He had been crying for three days. He started to apologize that I should be here in Calabria at this terrible time. But I stopped him and tried to explain, as best I could, that it had been, in every way imaginable, an honor.

Enzo thought for a moment. "Yes, you have seen a lot. You have seen how we live and how we die."

# 23

## Gaetano's Love

My last day in Reggio, now into July, was a Sunday. I was ready to go home. I had learned so much. More than I ever imagined. And while I was never far from relatives during my stay, a month was a long time to be away from my own family, from Laurelyn and my daughters. That morning, Enzo Catanoso arrived early on the street outside my B&B to take me to Mass one last time at the church of Padre Gaetano. I got into the front seat of his white hatchback Fiat.

"I have some things for you," he said, reaching back for an envelope. He slid out a large photograph of Padre Gaetano kneeling in prayer. I recognized it as a copy of the first picture I had ever seen of him years earlier. Then Enzo handed me a Vatican-published booklet from the 1997 beatification, the one led by Pope John Paul II, the one we in America had missed. These are for me? I asked.

"Yes, and these, too," he said, pulling out two small items that were vacuum-sealed in heavy plastic. One was a swatch of hemmed, white cloth, fraying and yellowed with age. The other was a smooth, rounded, inch-long piece of varnished wood. "This was a part of Padre Gaetano's priest collar. And this—this is from his original casket from when he died in 1963. Take them. Treat them well. They are very important."

They were more than that. They were sacred keepsakes, holy relics, the kind of objects the Catholic Church urges the faithful to gaze upon, caress, and pray to. Such relics are seen as conduits for the supernatural. I had seen them encased in elaborate containers of gold or silver and displayed prominently in church sanctuaries and church museums. The Vatican even classifies them. A first-class relic was a part of the saint's body, like a tooth or a piece of bone. A second-class relic, like the cloth collar in my hand, was worn by the saint. A third-class relic, like the casket fragment, had been in contact with a first-class item. The veneration of relics stems from what the church calls "beneficent contagion," meaning that a person's virtue, holiness, and protective healing powers do not die with him. Rather, they continue to reside in the things he left behind and can be called upon in prayer by believers who come close to such remains or objects.

Enzo's gifts were beyond kind, beyond generous. They were spiritually profound.

At Mass, as if to remind me that he was really an irreverent, playful guy at heart, Enzo nudged me in the ribs during the priest's long-winded sermon. "Can you understand what he's saying?" he asked. I shook my head. "Don't worry. He doesn't make sense even in Italian. He starts in one direction, then flies off in another. Crazy. I try to follow, but it is impossible."

Sister Dorotea Palamara, the mother general of the Veronican sisters, had invited me to stay for lunch at the Mother House shortly after Mass. I was tickled by the idea of eating with a large group of Italian and Filipino nuns in the dining hall, something I had never done before, or ever thought I would want to do. But the mother general explained through Daniela, who had arrived after Enzo left to help with translations, that men were not permitted in the dining hall. The mother general and her closest assistant, Sister Comia, guided us to a small, adjacent room with place settings for four over a white table cloth. Two young Filipino sisters came in and out like waitresses, serving us our wine, veal cutlets, and salads.

I was comfortable with all these nuns. I had been here many times during my stay and they had grown accustomed to my visits. Whenever I was in the front receiving room reading or talking with someone who knew Padre Gaetano, I loved the way tiny Sister Gemma would come scooting in, all smiles, toting a silver tray of drinks, sometimes ice water, sometimes espresso, or fresh orange juice. One afternoon, I left the mother general photographs of my family back home in America so she could see me in a broader context of my life away from Reggio.

"I showed the other sisters the pictures you left here," the mother general said at lunch. "We all agreed that your father looks like Padre Gaetano; he looks identical to the saint. And you look like Piero. You have his eyes and the form of his face."

Piero's passing was hard on the Veronican sisters. They accepted it as God's will, of course. But it left a hole in their hearts as it did with his family and friends.

"Aside from his legal assistance, he was just a wonderful human being with great character," the mother general said. She could have been describing Padre Gaetano. "Always with a smile, always showing his affection. When he resolved problems, he was able to establish a kind of peace between both parties. That is rare. The Bible says when you find a friend, you have found true riches and treasure. Piero was our friend, first and foremost. And now it feels like our treasury is empty."

As we finished lunch, I heard nuns out in the hallway talking and laughing. Then they paraded past the door in their gray habits. I asked Daniela what was going on. "They want a photograph with you," she said. So up into the sanctuary we went, nearly twenty of us, squeezed together in front of the altar beneath the mosaic of St. Veronica and the Holy Face of Jesus. I towered over these tiny women, an unusual feeling for someone not quite five foot eight. Then they led me to the back of the sanctuary where we all actually posed around the glass tomb and remains of Padre Gaetano Catanoso.

"This is hilarious," I told Daniela, and the nuns must have thought so, too. They were giggling as they lined up, and all smiles when the photo was taken.

There were just a couple more people I wanted to talk with before I called it a night and went back to pack for my early morning flight. Germaine was available and we rode together to the apartment of my cousin Caterina and her husband, Vincenzo, whose ALS treatments in Torino seemed to be making little difference. For Vincenzo, the central concern in his life remained constant. He was still scared, still afflicted with an incurable degenerative disorder, still praying for a miracle.

We sat together at their kitchen table. Caterina could not stay still at first. She would nervously jump up to make coffee, or dart off to talk with her children. She looked weary and exhausted with dark circles under her eyes. She had spent most of every day since her return at Adriana's apartment, helping to cater to the steady stream of friends and relatives coming to keep Adriana company.

"My condition has changed a lot of things for me," Vincenzo was explaining, his limp left arm resting on his lap. "It started eighteen months ago with a pain in my arm. I didn't worry too much. I stayed active, playing sports, riding my bike. Then I lost the use of my arm, then my hand. Now I can feel it in my leg. I have to be careful because I can lose my balance and fall."

He was still working as a regional sales representative for Monsanto, selling farm supplies throughout Calabria, but he was doing so less and less. He spoke of how now, in his midforties, almost exactly my age, he took nothing for granted. He appreciated everything around him—a beautiful day, Caterina's constant care and delicious cooking, his kids' teasing pranks and youthful energy. And he appreciated, too, being in a family with an unflagging Christian faith that was also in close proximity to a saint recognized for his healing powers.

"My faith in God, it has gotten stronger, and especially my faith in Padre Catanoso," Vincenzo told me. "My faith gives me strength— that and my family and friends. The sisters of Padre Catanoso always pray for me. When I see them at church, they come and hug me and tell me about their prayers. Caterina has even more faith than me. This gives me hope. We never stop believing that Padre Catanoso will give me this gift of healing."

I asked if he thought he stood a better chance of gaining such grace because of his family connection and he said, "No, not because I am a relative, but because I am a human being. I am honest and I am good. The saint can see this and judge whether or not I should be favored, whether or not I should be cured."

Vincenzo spoke those words carefully, with a sense of humility and not a trace of entitlement. In many ways he was confused by his condition, where it had come from and why it couldn't be treated. There was only one approved drug on the worldwide market for ALS. He had just come from a series of treatments with an experimental drug at a hospital in Torino. He couldn't say whether it had helped at all. He would return in a few months for more infusions. Like my brother Alan and his incurable brain tumor, Vincenzo faced an immediate future with few medical alternatives. Prayer often seemed like his best option.

"I am always praying now," said Caterina, who had finally settled in with us at the table. "Before, when I was cooking, for example, my mind would go to other things. Now I talk only to Padre Gaetano. He was my great-uncle and I explain things to him. It is not that I expect a miracle. It is never that easy. They know what they are doing up there. It could be that they are testing us, testing our faith. Look at Vincenzo's illness and Piero's death. These are big tests."

And still they believed, resolutely, unshakably. These relatives of mine were the personification of the southern Italian culture in its relationship to religion. With their St. Gaetano pins and medals and their belief that such things could bring them tangible protection, they were not that far removed from the peasants of rural Calabria a century before who put cow horns over the door to their homes to ward off the evil eye. Their superstition, though, was infused with Christian faith. And it was that kind of intense and magical faith—in people as simple as Anna Pangallo and as educated as Dr. Antonio Bolignano—that led Vatican officials, I had been told, to know that they would always have an easier time collecting the evidence necessary for sainthood in southern climes like Calabria than they ever would in northern Italy or northern Europe. But these beliefs were not a crutch. They were an ever-present comfort.

I saw this day after day in recent weeks. I saw, too, in my Italian family, exactly what it meant to be related to a saint.

"There is something that is important for you to understand," Vincenzo told me. "Padre Catanoso is the whole pillar of the Catanoso family. They are attached to him. They do nothing without him. There is no gathering when they don't think of him. There is no morning when they don't pray to him. Always Padre Catanoso, in good times and bad. Caterina and I have been married more than twenty years and there isn't a day that we don't mention Padre Catanoso. That is a sign that he is in each and every one of us, even in our generation, and we never knew him personally. We have listened to what our elders have told us. We know his example. And so he is constantly in our thoughts and in our lives. Not because he is now a saint, but because of the life he led as a priest."

The life, always the life. The point of reference. The spiritual road map. The Vatican called it heroic virtue. Call it what you will, but it coursed through the lives of my relatives like the blood moving through their veins. This realization made me think of Monsignor Sarno back at the Vatican. When he had told me a few weeks earlier in his office that it may mean nothing to be related to a saint, I worried that he might be right. I knew better now.

It was hard to pull away from Vincenzo and Caterina. But they were eager to get back to Adriana's home, and I was eager to see Caterina's sister, Patrizia. We had spent much time together in the previous weeks and had grown close, but we had never made time to talk, just her and me, with Germaine translating. Now was my last chance.

Patrizia was waiting for us at her nearby apartment, sitting in a blue vinyl armchair in her living room, the family's floppy-eared mutt barking and sliding on the smooth, marble floor. *"Basta! Basta!"* she yelled at the dog. That's enough! Orazio, her husband, was rushing about gathering fruit and vegetables he had grown on Catanoso land outside Chorio to bring over to Adriana's. His voice echoed through the apartment. Their teenage children kept coming in and out, interrupting with questions or cell phone calls. Patrizia would shoo them off, and then turn and look at me as if to say—continue, please—her legs crossed at the ankle, her hands folded on her lap.

But there were too many distractions. It had been a long, draining week. It was late in the day. Try as we might, Germaine and I could not get the conversation on track. It wasn't all our fault. Patrizia was not particularly reflective. She was sensible and practical—a transparent, no-nonsense, problem-solving kind of woman. I liked that about her. She didn't even go to church very often. That's why the story she finally settled in to tell—one last miracle story, both personal and unofficial—resonated with me so strongly that I knew it would be the first miracle story I would retell.

It happened, she told me, a few years ago when the teenage son of a close friend was nearly killed in a motorcycle accident on the narrow roads outside of Chorio.

*The collision was head on, and the boy, just seventeen, landed in the road like a box of dishes. He now lay in intensive care in a hospital in the city of Reggio, cracked and broken, on life support.*

Patrizia's faith in her great-uncle was as strong as her sister Caterina's. And when Padre Gaetano appeared to Patrizia in a dream and explained what she must do to rescue the dying boy, she never hesitated, never doubted.

*"Don't worry,"* the image spoke to her. *"He won't die. Ask the sisters for a handkerchief and tell them to pray."*

She faithfully went to the Mother House, got the handkerchief, a sacred relic that had been Padre Gaetano's, and did as she was told. The boy, on life support and given up for dead by the doctors at Riuniti Hospital, revived later that day.

*I know what happened, she whispered to her friend, pulling him close, tears running down her own face.* "E stato miracolo." *It was a miracle.*

However tired and distracted Patrizia may have been, she was focused now, riveted, recalling every detail. Her brown eyes glowed at the memory, yet she told the story without flair or excessive drama. Just the facts, what actually happened, as she experienced it.

"Did you feel strange doing this," I asked, "waving a white hanky over a dying boy's body?" I was surprised at my own amazement of her story, but as always, I was ready to run down the check list of my typical, skeptical questions.

"Yes, I was trembling," she said.

"What do you believe about this?"

"To me it was a miracle, I am sure."

"Are you superstitious?"

"No."

"Do you believe in magic?"

"No."

"Are you, by any chance, a little goofy about stuff like this?"

"No, I never even read my horoscope."

"But you believe in the supernatural power of saints."

"Of *course*. We have one in the family!"

"Did you bring this miracle to the attention of the Vatican?"

"No, this is mine. I tell very few people."

"If someone else told you this story, would you believe it?"

"I don't think so. I am a skeptic. But with this, I have no doubt."

I was out of questions. I just stared at Patrizia. She stared back. Slowly, I broke into a smile. I had been listening to the miracle stories of relatives for weeks, some glorious and moving, some that made me want to laugh. But sitting here now with Patrizia, a cousin as uncomplicated as she is unmystical, I had an altogether different reaction. That's why I was smiling. I believed her. I truly believed her.

The next moments went by in a rush. Orazio was bellowing to hurry up. He was eager to leave; there was a crowd at Adriana's. Germaine had to get home to her family. I said my good-byes to my new friend, my patient and talented interpreter. Then the rest of us piled into Orazio's Lancia and we headed a few miles over to Via Possidonea. On the sidewalk across from Adriana's apartment building, Patrizia saw a young man walking past whom she recognized. She yelled out for him. He came back. She started talking so fast, so excitedly that I could only catch a few words.

"Show him, show him!" I gathered. The young man, in his late twenties I guessed, reached into his wallet and pulled out a swatch of white cloth maybe three inches square. It appeared to be a remnant of a handkerchief. The young man was battling cancer and Patrizia had given it to him some months ago. Then it dawned on me. It was *the* handkerchief, the relic that once belonged to Padre Gaetano and had saved the boy in the motorcycle accident. Patrizia took the swatch from her friend and carefully tore off a corner.

"For you," she said.

That final night, one week after Piero's death, I walked into the same kitchen where he had twice hosted me for lunch with his family weeks earlier. I had just been in the living room of the fourth-floor apartment, greeting Adriana, who smiled when she saw me. I spoke with other relatives. People had been there all day, every day that week, in fact, leaving Adriana alone only between midnight and seven in the morning. Now it was after nine o'clock at night and the television on the counter above the kitchen table was tuned to the World Cup. The Italians were playing Ukraine in the quarterfinals. Ordinarily, all eyes would have been on the set, as if time itself had stopped, as if nothing else mattered. But this had been an extraordinary week; soccer slipped off its lofty pedestal. Orazio waved me over to sit next to him, my back to the open windows looking out over the rooftops of Reggio and the twinkling shoreline of Sicily. Enzo was at the stove cooking fish, conducting the gas burners and iron frying pans like a maestro before an orchestra. He sautéed a bony white fish and laid it out in a glass pan under a drizzle of olive oil and lemon to bake in the oven. Then he began to brown swordfish steaks in a skillet of sizzling olive oil.

"I love to cook," he told me with a wave of his spatula, "but only when I can use the most fresh ingredients. When you come here in winter, I will take you hunting for mushrooms in the mountains. *Funghi*, mushrooms. I love them."

Claudia, Piero's eldest daughter, was on Enzo's right and laughed at her uncle's accented English. She was slicing a large round loaf of crusty bread and set out two heaping baskets. Claudia had already prepared the calamari, which had been chopped and cooked, and was sitting in a ceramic serving bowl in front of me. Her boyfriend, Salvatore, sat quietly nearby. They had just started dating and he had met Piero only once, but Salvatore, tall and handsome with an easy smile, was seldom far from Claudia's side throughout this difficult week.

Slowly, the small kitchen began filling up with relatives, drawn by the aroma emanating from Enzo's frying pans and the sweet Italian ritual of family mealtime. Daniela came in, saw me, and joked as if she were tired of running into me, "You're still here?" Adriana followed with Vincenzo just behind her. They settled in together on the love seat wedged into a nook on the far wall just beyond the edge of the table until it was time to eat. Piero's quiet, older sister, Francesca, was there, with her curly-haired daughter Gabriela and son-in-law Andrea; they had been down from Rome all week. Allesandra, Piero's middle child, who also lived in Rome, took a seat across from me, next to Patrizia. When Caterina came into the kitchen, there was a sudden cheer in the room, led by her teenage son, Domenico, who had arrived at the apartment still dressed in his soccer practice clothes. The Italians had just scored. Domenico had two silver studs in his left ear. With his stylized haircut and dreamy eyes, he looked far too cool to wrap his mother in a huge hug, right in front of the family, and plant a warm kiss on her cheek. But that's what he did. And his mother, whose broken heart was practically visible, smiled for the first time all day, maybe all week. I saw Caterina catch the eye of her husband Vincenzo across the room with a look that seemed to say, "We're going to be okay." He smiled back.

The Italian team was in full control of the game, up 2–0 and a step closer to the World Cup title it would claim a week later, when the fish came out of the oven. Enzo set the steaming glass pan on the table as the son-in-law from Rome blurted out, "Luuuuuke! Dee feeeesh!" to gales of laughter. Suddenly, everyone who knew a bit of English began tossing out words like birds chirping, to even more shouts and laughing. Enzo came around and squeezed in next to me, then in exaggerated English, offered his version of a basic language lesson. "The bread is on the table," he articulated with great drama. "Would you like a piece of bread?"

There were now more than twenty of us in this kitchen, standing and sitting, in a space that would have been overcrowded with less than half as many. No one cared. Through the fish, the bread, the calamari, the bottles of red and white wine, and the baskets of fresh peaches, pears, and nectarines all picked on Catanoso land outside Chorio, the hand-waving and chattering din around the table, now completely in Italian, escalated to a pleasant roar. The words flowed over and around me in a comforting rush and I felt on the very edge of understanding everything being said, like I was just a half step away from fluency. But I wasn't. So I sat back and relaxed and listened one last time as if it were opera, the most beautiful opera imaginable on a stage filled with the liveliest characters.

When Natale, Piero's son, made a late entrance into the kitchen, Enzo jumped up to bone and plate a piece of fish for him. Claudia offered her seat. And his mother, Adriana? She sat amid this noisy crowd, joining in the teasing and the conversation, in the seat Piero would have occupied. Enzo had told me that the last thing Adriana wanted, especially now, was to be left alone. And the family had every intention of accommodating her as long as they could, bearing her up with all their hearts.

As I drank in this scene with this lovely Italian family, I couldn't help but wonder if this is what God's love felt like to this roomful of true believers. I knew this for sure, though. It *was* what Padre Gaetano's love felt like—the holy, unconditional love of family. I had been immersed in it for the better part of a month, and I realized then that I had experienced it long before, I just didn't recognize it then. It first happened during that magical lunch with my own family and many of these very same relatives more than two years earlier in Pina's apartment downstairs. I never thought it would happen again, certainly not after Piero's death, like hitting the lottery twice. But it had tonight, as this family, doing what it does so naturally, wrapped Adriana and her children in a warm embrace of love, Padre Gaetano's love. The saint would have been proud.

For someone so eager to go home, and I was, I did not want to say good-bye. Relatives took my pocket address book and filled it with their phone numbers and e-mail addresses. Slowly, gradually, I got around to each one of them, hugging them and pressing my cheeks to theirs. Daniela and her niece Giorgia, Allesandra and her sister Claudia, Caterina and her husband, Vincenzo. For Adriana, I mentally composed a simple phrase in Italian. *"Mi piace la tua famiglia,"* I told her, I like your family. It was not enough; my heart was overflowing. But it was the best I could do without Germaine's assistance. She thanked me, then thinking of Piero, she lowered her eyes and said in Italian, "But unfortunately . . ." and left it at that.

Patrizia and Orazio followed me downstairs and outside to the sidewalk. They had one last gift. Not a sacred relic. Something far more practical and sensible. Orazio handed me a one-liter soda bottle filled with clear green olive oil from olives he had grown, harvested, and pressed himself up in Chorio. It might as well have been emeralds.

*"Arriverderci, cugino,"* they said. Good-bye, cousin.

# EPILOGUE

✠

I walked into the house on a cold afternoon in February, and Laurelyn was giving me a funny look.

"What is on your forehead?" she asked. "And all over your face?"

"What? Oh, ashes," I told her, suddenly remembering the dark, thumb-size splotch over the bridge of my nose. "Father Louie must've loaded me up."

"How long do you have to leave them on?"

Good question, I thought. The night before, I had talked on the phone with my mother. She reminded me that the next day was Ash Wednesday and that I wasn't supposed to eat any meat all day. Why? I asked her.

"Why?" she stammered, stunned once again that I would ask such a question. "Why? Because, because—*we're Catholics.* That's why."

So I answered Laurelyn's question as truthfully as I could: "I have no idea."

In the months following my return from Calabria, I continued my regular pilgrimage to Mass almost every Sunday, usually at 7:30 in the morning when the sanctuary was far less crowded and there was no folk band performing. It was quieter, more serene. I preferred it that way. But lately, I had been going to Mass on Wednesdays as well. There is a Franciscan Center in downtown Greensboro where Father Louie Canino holds midweek services at noon in a small, windowless chapel behind the gift shop, where about forty of us, a few my age, but mostly elderly, retired folks, gather on folding chairs.

For me, I was merely intensifying my search for my own spirituality, my own Catholicism. I had surely found Padre Gaetano in the hearts of my relatives in Calabria, yet my search was far from over. Having not gone to Mass with any regularity since high school thirty years ago, I felt like I was simply making up for lost time. But to someone else, someone who had known me for decades as an unreligious man, someone who had watched me make the kids giggle during the dinner blessing, someone now seeing me going to Mass not once a week but twice, I was starting to look like a person far more devout, far more certain than I am. And it was unsettling—to my wife. I didn't realize it at first.

Laurelyn and I were sitting in our kitchen eating sandwiches after one of those Wednesday afternoon services and she was saying, "It scares the hell out of me what you're doing, if you want to know the truth. You could be headed in a direction that I can't follow."

She had mentioned something like that months earlier when my mother raised the ante on her regular urgings for us to get our daughters baptized by requesting—what with me going to church now—that Laurelyn consider becoming a Catholic. That wasn't going to happen. I knew that and I assured Laurelyn that she had nothing to worry about. Obviously she wasn't reassured. So one Wednesday I asked if she wanted to come with me to hear Father Louie and see for herself that what I was doing just wasn't that threatening. She surprised me by saying yes.

We drove downtown and sat in the back of the chapel. I did what I normally do at Mass—listen intently, but say none of the prayers out loud except for the Our Father. I still couldn't recite the Apostles' Creed and won't until I figure out what I truly believe. I'm still working on that. Father Louie's sermon that afternoon was a reminder of how to get there: Take time to be quiet and listen to your soul to develop your relationship with God. That's what I'm doing here, I thought, nothing more, nothing less. But Laurelyn heard something different and to her, it was the opposite of the soothing effect I had intended.

"Father Louie said people need to remove the obstacles to their faith," Laurelyn told me as we drove home. "And as you go further into this Catholic thing you may come to see me as that obstacle. And that scares me because I can't go there with you. And I don't want you to leave me because of that."

"Leave you. You're kidding, right?"

"We've seen it happen before. You know it's true."

Laurelyn's voice was steady, calm, almost resigned. Devout religious belief had been the source of the greatest pain in her life. It helped drive her parents apart after thirty-five years of marriage, one of the finest marriages I had ever seen. No one would have predicted it. And nothing, it seemed, could have prevented it. Not her parents' once-bottomless love for each other. Not their enduring love for their children. Not their children's fevered attempts at intervention. Nothing. Laurelyn's mother had gone in deep, far deeper than her father felt comfortable following. She kept going; he wouldn't go any further. God, you could argue, who had brought them together and intensified their bond, had also torn them asunder. Of course, it took several years and other complicating factors to get to that point, but the marriage played out to its sad conclusion when our daughters were small. In a terribly significant way, the divorce of Laurelyn's parents made religion feel like a dangerous place to us as a couple and as a family. That cloud followed us as we tried off and on over the years to find a church of our own. We were never that disappointed when it didn't work out.

Things were different now, for me at least. Laurelyn had long resolved her own beliefs and spirituality and was comfortable with her conclusions. I was just getting started. But how could I truly assure her that my own conclusions, when and if I ever reached them, didn't carry the same threat of division, of pulling apart?

I did what I could. I reminded her of one of the most painful moments of my own life. It came the day after I stood in a hospital room with my parents and Lenny and Marlene and listened as an oncologist carefully handed Alan his death sentence. It fell to me to deliver the tragic news to Alan's wife, Anna, the next day. We all gathered in Marlene's living room. Laurelyn held Anna's hand as I explained what the doctor had told us, how there was so little hope for recovery. Anna pressed her lips together tightly and closed her eyes. Tears rolled down her face as she said sadly, "We had so many dreams."

Alan's death put so much of my life in perspective. I had, I could see, the continued good fortune to be happily in love. We had three healthy daughters who still liked, more often than not, being around us. And I had the simple joy of being able to wake up to greet another day, to pursue my dreams. And if I spent part of the day reaching for some spiritual significance, and if I called on my sainted cousin to offer a hand, that was all well and good. My goals, after all, were modest. I wanted to become more patient, more compassionate, more spiritually aware and reflective. And I did not want religion to become a wedge between me and the ones I love. I didn't think God would want that, either.

I tried to tell Laurelyn these things. I tried to explain that sometimes at Mass, when the priest clears the smoke away from the Gospel readings and offers a sermon of pure Christian clarity, that I feel myself getting it, falling in, making sense of everything. Other times, I told her, I sit there and think—this is silly, a huge charade. And I feel like a phony going through the motions.

"I'm just trying to figure this out," I told her.

After attending Mass regularly for a couple of years, I finally realized I wasn't alone in these seesawing emotions, and that's why virtually each sermon sounds like a riff on the same theme: Everyone doubts, everyone struggles, everyone is at risk of drifting away from faith. The rituals of the Mass, each one of them, provide a steady reminder that finding and maintaining one's faith is a constant process, a persistent push and pull, a never-ending journey. But to me, some things are constant.

"I don't quite know what I believe, Laurelyn," I told her. "But I believe in you. And that's not going to change."


Friends had kept telling me about Father Louie and how I needed to meet him. More than a year passed before I finally did so. After the first Wednesday afternoon Mass I attended at the Franciscan Center, I watched as he stood at the door of the gift shop, filled as it is with rosaries, prayer cards, and plastic statues of saints. His voice carried an upstate New York accent as he addressed by name everyone who was leaving, remembering some small detail. "How's your sister doing, Marie?" "Jack, when do you get your test results?" I wanted to arrange a time to meet with him and figured I would have only a few seconds to do so. The line was long. As I started to introduce myself, he cut in with a big smile, "Justin, I've been waiting for you. I'm so eager to hear about your saint. You have time for lunch, right? My treat."

One of my friends, it turns out, had told Father Louie to expect me that day. As the priest and I sat down to lunch at a nearby restaurant, he told me, "This is the miracle, you coming back to faith as a result of your cousin. I get chills just thinking about it. Related to a saint. I can't imagine. So tell me, what's it like?"

That started a conversation that Father Louie and I would pick up periodically, whenever I felt the need to talk, whenever he could squeeze me into a schedule overburdened by the reality of too many parishioners and too few priests. I told him my story, about growing up Catholic and falling away from the church. About the either/or challenge the professor presented me with as a young adult and my decision to go with Laurelyn and follow our own churchless path. I told him about Alan and Piero and the prayers I have seen go unanswered. And I told him everything I could about my canonized cousin.

"It's remarkable to hear about a man who loved the Lord so completely," said Father Louie, whose immigrant grandparents were also from Calabria. "And look what he accomplished. This is the kind of priest I can identify with. He's so inspiring to me."

To me as well. For the first time ever, I knew what it meant to look upon someone as a pure example of the kindness and generosity of Jesus's own life. My cousin's message of faith and service, a message that would carry him all the way to canonization, resonated with me: Feed the hungry. Shelter the orphans. Educate the ignorant. Believe in the beneficent powers of a being far greater than yourself. I still had trouble, though, with those ancient Catholic beliefs rooted in the mystical. These are the kind of mysteries Gaetano never questioned or doubted as absolutely true, but I still did. A virgin birth. A dead man rising. A thin cracker and watery red wine becoming actual flesh and blood.

Father Louie listened patiently. He never responded quickly, almost as if he were saying a prayer before he spoke. "I think you're basically a good person," he told me. "But you're going to have to work at this. Life usually doles out a lot of blows and you haven't gotten many. The first one was your brother, and so now you're trying to make sense of this, anticipating that there are more blows to come your way. There will be. And you want something to hold you up when these struggles come. What you're doing has the potential to strengthen your faith life. But there are no guarantees. You might just continue to be a mediocre Catholic."

Father Louie was so genuinely nice, his voice so warm and avuncular, that the bluntness of his assessment caught me off guard, like a sharp thorn on a lovely rose. Still, I couldn't argue. I had been honest with him. I told him I had far more doubts, far more questions than I ever imagined having answers to. Having listened closely, he had been honest with me. Saint or no saint, I *was* a mediocre Catholic, surely better than I was prior to the canonization in the fall of 2005, but in reality, only a few steps down a very long road.

"For many people, there comes a time when you just start asking fewer questions because you accept that there are no answers to be had; you have to trust," Father Louie explained. "You search and you search until ultimately, you have to say: 'I believe.' I don't know if that's going to happen to you. You're a pragmatist. You're a rationalist. You're very American. That doesn't mean you're doomed. You have to be true to yourself. You have to be honest. But basically, it all comes down to one thing: Faith is a gift. Are you accepting the gift?"

It was July 2005, a few months before the canonization. I was still trudging along in leaden boots of grief in the months immediately following Alan's death. I found myself thinking about him every day, all the time, wondering where he went. I was morose. When Mark Hall, a friend of mine, invited me to spend a week with him at Wake Forest University's academic houses in Vienna and Venice where he was teaching, I leapt at the opportunity to change the scenery. I cashed in all my miles. I flew Austrian Air, first class. For days I wandered through manicured gardens and art museums. Sometimes I would step into a dark, musty church and light a candle for Alan. It was a good week, but trouble arose early on the morning I was to return home. I had a 6:15 flight from Venice's Marco Polo International Airport, followed by three tight connections on jammed flights between Germany and Greensboro. Any delays and I would be stranded. I bought a bus ticket in advance and was assured that the 4:30 bus would get me to the Venice airport in plenty of time. When a double-length bus pulled into slot number 5 at 4:20, I breathed a sigh of relief. But it didn't last. I was the only one there. The parking lot was dark and deserted. The bus driver didn't get out or open the door. So I knocked. The driver looked at me.

"Airport?" I said loudly.

He shook his head.

What? "Does this bus go to the airport? I have a plane to catch."

He rolled his eyes, obviously annoyed. He opened the door and came out. He was gruff and grumpy, not happy at all. *"No parla Inglesi,"* he muttered, then showed me the bus schedule for that Sunday morning. I saw what he meant. My ticket was worthless. The first airport shuttle didn't arrive until nearly 6. I would miss my flight. I would not get home that day. I was exhausted and anxious, edging toward panicked. I tried to explain my situation. But he waved me off as if he could not hear me. He then climbed back into the driver's seat and started talking on his cell phone. He motioned for me to come in and sit down. I did, lugging my heavy backpack and a canvas bag. He talked for what seemed like a half hour. I could not understand anything he said. Time was wasting. I needed another plan. Maybe I could hitchhike. The longer he talked, the more agitated I became. Then he closed his phone, turned to me, and said flatly, *"No aeroporto."*

Great, I'm stuck, I thought. I got up, grabbed my bags, and headed to the door, which swung shut as soon as I reached them. I turned to the driver just as he started the engine.

*"Dove va?"* I asked, where are you going?

*"Aeroporto,"* he said, without changing his dour expression.

I did not say another word. I just sat down in the first seat in the first row and hoped that I wasn't dreaming. Italy is famous for random acts of kindness. But a Venetian bus driver, so accustomed to enduring the rude antics and boorish behavior of a never-ending glut of stupid tourists? He owed me nothing. He could not even understand what I had said. Or could he?

The enormous bus with its accordionlike hinge in the middle could have easily carried two hundred people as it sped across the *Ponte della Liberta*, the bridge over the lagoon that connects Venice to the mainland. There was just the two of us. When we arrived at the airport entrance, I thanked the driver profusely and handed him nearly all the euros I had left in my wallet. He put his hands up and waved them off. I insisted. He refused. I got off the bus holding my bags and the euros, and he drove off, giving me a little wave and a hint of a smile.

I watched the bus make a wide U-turn and disappear into the darkness. At that moment, I got to thinking about my brother Alan again. His fiftieth birthday was in a few days, his first birthday since his death. Now I was in Italy, the country he had planned to visit before cancer caught up with him, and this strange thing had happened. It seemed inexplicable, except for this: Alan would have expected his little brother to buy the wrong bus ticket, he never would have done that. He would have little sympathy for my desperate plight, he would have been prepared. He wouldn't listen to my excuses, he couldn't hear. He wouldn't take my money, he didn't need any. He wouldn't be happy about it, but he would do it. He would help me get home to my family.

The more I mulled those thoughts while waiting in a long customs line inside the terminal, the more I realized that I needed something at that moment, something far beyond a timely ride to the airport. I needed to know my brother was okay, that his spirit, at least, was still out there somewhere. I got lucky. I got both.

More than a year passed before I could overcome my own uneasiness with such mystical thinking to even tell Laurelyn that story. Like the Apostles' Creed, I could not get myself to say it out loud. I didn't really understand my reluctance, or the meaning of what I had experienced, until I sat later with so many of my Italian relatives and listened to their remarkable tales of special graces and supernatural healings. In their lives, such things were never viewed as coincidences. Rather, they carried the weight and beauty of far greater meaning, intensified by their blood connection to a holy being who was always there for them. Their stories were so powerful and so personal that they kept them mostly in their hearts. That is, until a long-lost relative from another country came to visit and sat with them for hours, asking question after question, trying as hard as he could to understand what it means to be related to a saint. I believe I know now. I also believe that what happened to me in Venice wasn't really a miracle. But in that moment of unexpected good fortune, I had felt my brother's presence. It wasn't a coincidence. The saint had given me a special grace I could call my own.

The church tells us we are all called to be saints. It seems an impossible request. But Padre Gaetano Catanoso heard that call clearly. He lived a life in service to the ideals of Jesus Christ that spanned eighty-four years and the worst of times in southern Italy. That life means everything to my Italian relatives. And it has come to mean so much to me—enough to lead me to fill in the long-blank pages of a family history going back more than two centuries; enough to lure me and my family to return to Italy to reclaim scores of relatives with whom we have so much in common; enough to make me rethink my own faith and begin to see life in a larger dimension. The saint, now, is always with me, reminding me of his virtuous life, causing me to consider more carefully the decisions I make. I continue to slip up, to fall short of even the modest goals I have set for myself. I suspect I always will. Yet I have accepted the gift he has offered—a new prism through which to view life, a model of goodness to strive for, a rock to stand upon in times of sorrow.

Father Louie was right. I have been very fortunate. But Alan's death was a harbinger of things to come as I move into middle age, as my parents grow older, as my daughters leave the safety of the home in which Laurelyn and I have always sheltered them. There's no escaping it. So I have gotten a little better at saying my prayers. Unlike my Italian relatives, I don't pray for miracles, those rare and inexplicable acts of random mercy. I pray instead for the strength to endure what surely lies ahead with a faith that continues to deepen. I can't do this alone. I won't need to. I will call on my wife and my daughters, my relatives in America and Italy. And I will call on my cousin, my cousin the saint.

# SELECTED SOURCES

✠

Alvaro, Corrado. *Revolt in Aspromonte*. New York: New Directions, 1962.

Bagnato, Carmelo. *San Lorenzo*. Reggio Calabria: Kaleidon, 2003.

Bove, Cristoforo. *San Gaetano Catanoso*. Torino, Italy: San Paolo, 2005.

Brinkley, Douglas, and Julie M. Fenster. *Parish Priest*. New York: William Morrow, 2006.

Cunningham, Lawrence S. *A Brief History of Saints*. Malden, Massachusetts: Blackwell Publishing, 2005.

Dal Lago, Enrico, and Rick Halpern. *The American South and the Italian Mezzogiorno*. New York: Palgrave, 2002.

Dal Toso, Paola. *Bruciato dall'amore di Dio*. Torino, Italy: Editrice Elle Di Ci, 1997.

Doyle, Don H. *Nations Divided: America, Italy and the Southern Question*. Athens, Georgia: University of Georgia Press, 2002.

Dubner, Stephen. *Turbulent Souls*. New York: William Morrow, 1998.

Ellsberg, Robert. *The Saints' Guide to Happiness*. New York: Doubleday, 2003.

Gallagher, Nora. *Things Seen and Unseen*. New York: Alfred A. Knopf, 1998.

Garland, Albert N., and Howard McGraw Smyth. *U.S. Army in World War II: Sicily and the Surrender of Italy*. Vol. 26. Washington, D.C.: Office of the Chief of Military History, U.S. Army, 1965.

Levi, Carlo. *Christ Stopped at Eboli*. New York: Farrar, Straus & Giroux, 1947.

Mangione, Jerre, and Ben Morreale. *La Storia: Five Centuries of the Italian American Experience*. New York: HarperCollins, 1992.

Manseau, Peter. *Vows*. New York: Free Press, 2005.

Martin, James. *My Life with the Saints*. Chicago: Loyola Press, 2006.

Noonan, James-Charles Jr. *The Church Visible*. New York: Viking, 1996.

Paolicelli, Paul. *Under the Southern Sun*. New York: Thomas Dunne Books, 2003.

Rotella, Mark. *Stolen Figs and Other Adventures in Calabria*. New York: North Point Press, 2003.

Ruffin, Bernard, C. *Padre Pio: The True Story*. Huntington, Indiana: Our Sunday Visitor, 1992.

Schachter, Gustav. *The Italian South: Economic Development in Mediterranean Europe.* New York: Random House, 1965.

Schoener, Allon. *The Italian Americans.* New York: Macmillan, 1987.

Silone, Ignazio. *Bread and Wine.* New York: Harper & Brothers, 1937.

Sorrentino, Aurelio. *Il Volto Santo e la Mia Vita.* Milan, Italy: San Paolo, 2005.

Talese, Gay. *Unto the Sons.* New York: Alfred A. Knopf, 1992.

Wills, Garry. *Why I Am a Catholic.* New York: Houghton Mifflin, 2002.

Wills, Garry. *What Jesus Meant.* New York: Houghton Mifflin, 2006.

Woodward, Kenneth L. *The Book of Miracles.* New York: Touchstone, 2000.

Woodward, Kenneth L. *Making Saints.* New York: Touchstone, 1996.

# ACKNOWLEDGMENTS

✠

In a book almost entirely about family, my gratitude starts there. I thank my parents, Leonard and Connie Catanoso, and my brother and sister, Lenny Catanoso and Marlene Catanoso Testa, for their unyielding support and cooperation. They were always patient and candid, especially when discussing the most difficult thing, losing Alan. I thank my sister-in-law Anna and my nieces Marsiella and Lisa Catanoso. I thank my aunts and uncles, the children of Carmelo and Caterina Catanoso, for being so generous with their memories, especially my uncle Tony Catanoso, whose tales from Sicily could fill a book of their own. I also thank my cousin Anthony Catanoso for his endless support and for being my best pal since birth, the guy who set me straight on the Easter Bunny and Santa Claus.

I thank all of my extended family in Italy, especially Giovanna Catanoso, Daniela Catanoso, Patrizia Catanoso, Enzo Catanoso, Paola Catanoso, Barbara Catanoso, Vincenzo Infortuna, and Orazio Velardi, all in Reggio Calabria; Pasquale Catanoso of Vibo Valentia; and Maria Priolo Nucera in Marina di San Lorenzo. Each one shared his or her thoughts, arranged appointments, carted me around, and fed me the most amazing food. In Rome, I thank Daniela Catanoso, who was equally helpful and supportive.

Also in Reggio, I thank my interpreters who made it possible for me to understand what everyone was saying: Edward Parker, Luisa Catanoso, and especially Germaine Sciriha, who felt like a cousin by the time I left. I thank Sister Dorotea Palamara, the mother general of the Sisters of St. Veronica of the Holy Face, and all the nuns in Santo Spirito, who always made me feel welcomed when I visited the church and the Mother House. And in Rome, I thank Marta Piermarini, who was my interpreter there.

There is very little written in English about the life of Padre Gaetano Catanoso and I depended on the diligence and enthusiasm of these translators in Greensboro, North Carolina, to help me bring the saint to life: Carlo Costa, Lucia Besozzi DeRatmiroff, Bill Ledford, Anna Pani McLin, Maurice Schwartz, and especially, Serena Isavolpini Colquhoun, who served also as a committed research assistant.

I thank these priests for their wisdom, insight, and patience with my myriad questions: Father Kurt Peter Gumpel, Monsignor Robert Sarno, and Monsignor Giuseppe D'Ascola of Rome; Monsignor Antonio Denisi of Reggio Calabria; Father Ladislas Orsy of Washington, D.C.; Monsignor James McDonough of Philadelphia; Monsignor William Hodge and Father Ed Namiotka of South Jersey; Monsignor Anthony Marcaccio of Greensboro; and Father Louis Canino of Stoneville, North Carolina.

I thank these professional writers for their expert advice as I prepared for my research: Anthony DePalma, Father James Martin, and Kenneth Woodward, all in New York. And I thank these friends, and a few relatives, for their many contributions: Bobby Amoroso, James Barron, David Catanoso, Annette Condello, Darlene Dossett, Mary Cabell Eubanks, Frank Foti, Mark Friguglietti, Dan Margoles, Katherine McPherson, Eric Merrill, Danny Murray, Stephanie Nickell, Luciano Pascucci, Abigail Seymour, David Talbot, Lee Thompson, Myles Thompson, Jeffrey Ward, Jay Weiner, Frank Wilkinson, and especially Lisa Chase, whose early input got me going in the right direction.

My two employers were enormously supportive. At Wake Forest University, I thank President Nathan Hatch, Eric Wilson, and Wanda Balzano, a native Neapolitan who was reassuringly calm in helping me prepare for my month in Italy. At *The Business Journal*, I thank Doug Copeland, Pat Froman, and Kevin Bumgarner, who all made it possible for me to take two extended newsroom leaves to complete this project.

During my writing leave, two neighbors and film professors were also on sabbatical and immersed in projects of their own. I met weekly with Michael Frierson and Eric Patrick to critique each other's progress. Their feedback was invaluable.

This book seems to have been blessed with good fortune from its moment of conception, a moment that didn't even belong to me. I thank my agent Randi Murray for having the radio on and hearing the makings of a book in a five-hundred-word NPR commentary. She coached me through a book proposal and has been a trusted friend and advisor ever since. I thank Cassie Jones, my editor at William Morrow, who, with careful input, patient explanations, and steadfast enthusiasm, led me through the long process to publication. I thank her assistant, Johnathan Wilber. And I thank Maureen O'Neal and Judith Regan, whose initial belief in this project made it possible to get started.

And finally, I thank my travel partners in this great journey we are on, my daughters Emilia, Rosalie, and Sophia Catanoso. And above all, I thank my wife, Laurelyn Dossett, whose love and encouragement and faith in me and our entire family is never in doubt.

## DATE DUE RETURNED

| | | | |
|---|---|---|---|
| 7-31-09 | | | |
| 9/1/09 | | | |
| | | | |
| | | | |
| | | | |
| | | | |
| | | | |
| | | | |
| | | | |
| | | | |
| | | | |
| | | | |
| | | | |
| | | | |
| | | | |
| | | | |
| | | | |
| | | | |
| | | | |

Demco, Inc. 38-293